Uplift

Uplift
The Bra in America

JANE FARRELL-BECK AND COLLEEN GAU

PENN

University of Pennsylvania Press
Philadelphia

Printed in the United States of America on acid-free paper

10 9 8 7 6 5 4 3 2 1

Published by
University of Pennsylvania Press
Philadelphia, Pennsylvania 19104-4011

Library of Congress Cataloging-in-Publication Data
Farrell-Beck, Jane.
Uplift : the bra in America / Jane Farrell-Beck and Colleen Gau.
p. cm.
Includes bibliographical references and index.
ISBN 0-8122-3643-2 (cloth : alk. paper)
1. Brassieres—United States—History. I. Gau, Colleen. II. Title.
TT677 .F37 2002
391.4/2 21 2001027974

To

MARVIN S. BECK, PH.D. *and*

GERALD T. GAU, M.D.

whose support throughout this project

has been truly uplifting

Contents

Some Developments in Bra History

1863	Luman L. Chapman: Patent for breast supporter
1888	Emma Goodman: First maternity bra patent
1889	Rayon (artificial silk) invented
1892	Introduction of term cups as description
1893	Marie Tucek: First push-up bra
1902	Penney's (Golden Rule) first retail of bra
1904/5	Introduction of "brassiere" as name
1904	Laura B. Lyon: First sports bra patent
1909	Madeleine Gabeau: First underwire support
1917	DeBevoise: First strapless bras
1920s	Training bras for teens
1930	Adjustable strap patent
1930	Carothers and Staudinger make synthetic rubber
1930	First seamless knitted bras
1931	Letter sizing introduced for cups
1939	Nylon introduced by Du Pont
1944	Maidenform: Self service for brassiere sales
1950s	Foam rubber (artificial latex) used in bras
1960s	Polyester fiberfill used in bras
1968	Rudi Gernreich's No-Bra
1968	Protesters at Miss America pageant stage "bra burning"

Preface: Firming Up the Facts

Popular misconceptions about the brassiere abound. Its history is loaded with myths in which the names of Caresse Crosby, Howard Hughes, Herminie Cadolle, and even the apocryphal Otto Titzling command center stage. Previous writers have focused on the brassiere as an object of seduction, glamour, or oppression, thereby losing sight of the key people and events in the development of the brassiere as a material and social artifact. We hope to replace these tall tales and trivializations with an examination of the brassiere's role in the history of American women. Indeed, it is time to shelve the stereotype of the brassiere as oppressive and to take a more balanced view of its development. Far from being an imposition by men on women, the brassiere emerged in the twentieth century as a major component of underclothing and as a multibillion dollar industry through the efforts of both women and men. Their stories will be told in this book.

Contrary to popular perception, the history of the brassiere began in the third quarter of the nineteenth century. As implied in the title of this book, at that time the brassiere brought women "uplift" in several facets of their lives, including health, fashion, and economic opportunity. Some brassieres lifted breasts that had become pendulous, while others raised firm breasts to artificial heights. Before brassieres were invented, corsets performed such functions, but they pushed from below instead of lifting from above. Forward-thinking physicians and thoughtful lay women observed, however, that corsets constricted the torso, thereby weakening the muscles, compressing the lungs, and interfering with digestion and childbearing.[1] Those who opposed corsets argued for suspending the weight of the breasts, the undergarments, and the outer garments from the shoulders, a considerable feat given that the skirts of mid-nineteenth-century dresses weighed as much as thirty-two pounds. Ultimately early breast supporters brought about the diminution of the corset and its metamorphosis into a slightly less constricting girdle and, later, control-top panty hose.

Opportunities for new fashions emerged with the early breast supporter-brassiere. Corsets provided only limited types of shaping: they either crushed the breasts against the chest wall or cradled them in an inverted wedge design. Partly because of this static undershaping, dress bodices changed only in their waist and shoulder positions and in small decorative details between the 1840s and the early 1890s. Brassieres presented myriad possibilities for shaping, from early 1900s monobosoms to the torpedoes of the late 1940s and early 1950s. Variable shaping by darts, seams, gathering, bias cuts, and gussets, not to mention elastic materials and wiring, allowed brassieres to keep up with changes in the silhouette of women's clothing, thereby enhancing the many fashions introduced during the twentieth century. Outerwear styling led the way, followed almost immediately by adaptations in brassieres and corsets or girdles.

The scope of women's economic achievement broadened with the coming of the brassiere. Women held almost half of the more than 1,230 U.S. patents awarded for breast supporters between 1863 and 1969. Some of these required advanced engineering, including Hilda Ericson's shaped, perforated latex brassiere.[2] Others, including Olivia Flynt's 1870s breast supporter, were firmly anchored in the dressmaking tradition. Women's firsthand experience of the complex problems of fit, comfort, and wear-life in brassieres turned to their advantage in devising innovations.

Women have always held important positions in the brassiere industry, not only as designers but also as financial managers, promotional specialists, merchandising wizards, and production managers. As consumers who actually wore brassieres, women designers and manufacturers brought a dual perspective to their roles and were able to critique the product more perceptively than their male colleagues, which gave a potential advantage to firms headed by women. During the twentieth century, the development of new styles became increasingly complicated by issues of product positioning, available materials, and cost factors related to materials and assembly as well as the vagaries of fashion.

Between the late 1870s and the end of the 1960s, women built businesses around the production of brassieres, as sole proprietors or with family members, and some of these companies still thrive. Olivia Flynt, Caroline Newell, Gabrielle Poix Yerkes, Margia Childs Hamlin (Marja), Olga Erteszek (Olga), and Herma Wiedle Dozier (Fancee Free) are just a few women whose companies prospered by producing brassieres. Maidenform's success drew upon the creative talents and marketing genius of William and Ida Rosenthal. Ruth Kapinas's patented designs for Foundettes made Munsingwear a serious contender in the brassiere business.[3] In general, these family-run businesses gradually expanded into large corporations. During this process they became more rationalized and acquired the hierarchical structures of management and unionized labor, while losing their personal stamp.

No individual inventor or business team was able to solve the problems of designing and producing a truly functional and comfortable breast supporter. Breasts come in many shapes and sizes A to I. Breasts can echo the forms of saucers, eggplants, cones and many asymmetrical configurations.[4] Add to this the variable relationship of the breast to the torso and shoulders, and fitting problems can become daunting.

Brassieres must do more than fit a multitude of bodies, however. They must accommodate the same body as it changes through the monthly cycle and through the life cycle. They must provide for movement of the torso and arms in many directions without chafing or binding and without slipping out of position. As if that were not enough, brassieres must also retain their own structure through multiple wearings and launderings; must not abrade in contact with clothing; must remain, as a rule, inconspicuous beneath the outer clothing while harmonizing with the desired silhouette; and must be priced to sell to many customers. No wonder hundreds of attempts have been made to design the ideal breast supporter over the past 140 years.[5]

* * *

In tackling a subject as ample as the brassiere, we needed to set some boundaries. We have chosen to stay close to home, to write about the development and marketing of brassieres in the United States. In doing so, we acknowledge the contributions of inventive people of many nations, especially through the United States patents secured by citizens of Canada, France, Britain, Germany, Australia, and Russia. We focused on the years between the 1860s and 1970, with an overview of 1970 to the present.

Only a second book could do justice to the complicated mergers and acquisitions, international fashion influences, and technological changes of recent decades.

Our chosen period of emphasis permits an examination of most of the aspects of technology and taste that shaped present-day brassieres. From the first patent in 1863, breast support graduated from corsets and corsetlike bodices to brassieres. In each decade, brassieres exploited the newest materials, from featherbones to spandex and fiberfill. At some points in the brassiere's evolution, fashion encouraged a heavily structured approach to breast support and coverage. At other times, dressmaking techniques held sway and soft textiles predominated.

For the most part, we have limited our discussion to brassieres as independent undergarments, with only passing mention of corselettes, which combined brassieres and girdles, or brassieres that were built into bathing suits or slips. At the couture level, brassieres even became integral parts of dresses. During the late 1940s and early 1950s, outerwear brassieres of casual cottons and luxurious lamés were popular. Early 1900s "brassieres" did not have cups, but are included in our discussion because their intention was to support the breasts.

Hundreds of companies have produced brassieres in the United States from the 1880s to the present. We specifically mention more than sixty firms, some of them long-lived and others that achieved only a brief fame. In addition to textual discussion, we have listed all brand names (Appendix A) and summarized prominent companies (Appendix B). We have given greater attention to some companies than others, not out of partiality but because their archives or other documents were available to us. In a few cases, we have been able to establish details about a company by direct conversation with the owners or their descendants. Far less can be deduced about the history of a company if all that remains are published advertisements and one or more patents. Our hope is that this survey will stimulate further scholarship on individual firms and that companies will be willing to open their archives to serious researchers.

In an attempt to capture the experiences of consumers, we placed an informal questionnaire in retirement centers and gave them to individual women in Rochester, Minnesota. About sixty replies were received from respondents aged fifty to over eighty. These do not constitute a scientific sample but do offer clues to brand preferences, wearing practices, and attitudes. Quotations from completed questionnaires and insights from occasional published articles are incorporated in Chapters 5 through 8. Producer information predominates in this book, partly because of the paucity of extant consumer data. We mention the opinions of women customers whenever possible, but much of that information is lost to the historical record or was not gathered formally in the first place.

Some previous writers have presented fashion as a burden from which women ought to have been "set free." We perceive fashion and the businesses that provided fashion goods in a different way. Women used fashion as entertainment, self-creation, and everyday art. As consumers, women were free to reject unacceptable styles, including the long skirts of 1922 and the sack dresses of 1957.

Finally, in writing about this most distinctive of women's garments, we have attempted to amalgamate fashion with business, technology, and many aspects of women's everyday lives, including their work, recreation, and health. Because these various topics inevitably involve technical vocabulary from different disciplines, we have included a glossary of terms to assist the general reader. We have allowed the historic viewpoint to permeate this account as much as possible, believing that latter-day sociological and psychological analyses of the brassiere already abound in the scholarly literature. Rather than following an all-encompassing theory of history, we have taken an eclectic approach that we believe offers the necessary flexibility for dealing with a long period. We hope that you will find in this story of the brassiere as much enlightenment and entertainment as we have had in writing it.

1 The Birth of the Brassiere

The breast supporter made its debut in 1863, when Luman Chapman patented his corset substitute (Figure 1).[1] Its innovative "breast puffs" and "elastic shoulder-brace straps" were designed to eliminate "friction" on the breasts, which was considered a harmful feature of conventional corsets. There is no evidence that Chapman ever manufactured his supporters in a large quantity. He may have been a professional corsetier, living in Camden, New Jersey, when he patented the supporter, but even the patent application is not informative on this point. Chapman had moved to Philadelphia by the time he obtained a second patent for a more conventional corset. Like many of the inventors of breast supporters who followed him, Luman Chapman offered women a more comfortable and healthful alternative to the constriction of fashionable corsets.

If Chapman was the father of the prototypical brassiere, followers of dress reform were its many mothers. Dress reformers vigorously opposed the constricting corsets and bodices, voluminous petticoats or bustles, and long, heavy skirts of the 1840s through 1890s (Figure 2). However, they differed on what should replace the fashionable styles. Some believed that imitations of Greek and Roman dress promised more comfortable and attractive apparel. Others, calling themselves Pre-Raphaelites, advocated a return to the beauties they saw in early Renaissance dress and art. Janey Morris was one leader in Artistic Dress in late nineteenth-century England. She and her circle preferred loose, drapey styles, colored with vegetable dyes and decorated with embroidery. William Morris, Janey's husband, owned a firm that offered such goods. Another reform-minded emporium, Liberty & Company, of Regent Street, London, purveyed styles inspired by Japanese and other Asian garments.[2] One controversial group of reformers in the United States promoted wearing "the American Costume" in the 1850s. Only outerwear was affected; corsets remained part of their ensemble. Later generations have called this costume the

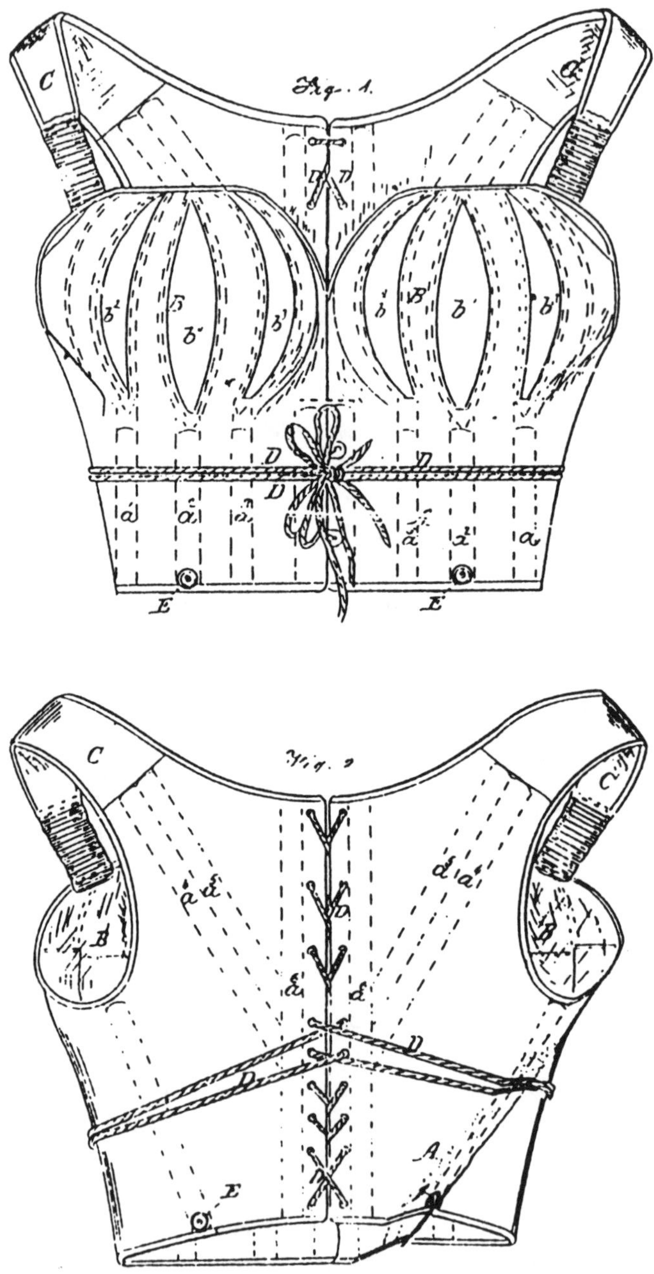

Figure 1. Patent illustration of the first breast supporter, designed by Luman L. Chapman of Philadelphia, U.S. Patent 40,907, awarded 15 December 1863.

Figure 2. A tightly corseted young woman from Mt. Carroll, Illinois, in the 1880s.

"bloomer" because of Amelia Jenks Bloomer's campaign for this ensemble in her reformist newspaper, *The Lily*.[3] Consisting of a midcalf-length dress worn over full-cut Turkish trousers or straight-legged "pantaloons," the American Costume was adopted by only a tiny percentage of women in the early 1850s. Despite its brief and limited popularity, the American Costume caused a sensation, giving newspaper reporters a field day. Popular songs and doggerel verse took potshots at the bloomer. Dancers sashayed around the ballroom to the Bloomer Schottische. Satirical cartoons intimated that wearers of such dress would soon adopt cigars and other masculine habits, cowing the formerly dominant sex.

Public ridicule and general outcry drove all but the most committed wearers of the American Costume to return to fashionable long skirts for street wear.[4] The stalwarts included water-cure physicians such as Mary Walker, Harriet Austin, and Ellen Beard Harman, who wore the American Costume for many years.[5] Political activists, including Elizabeth Cady Stanton, put aside the revolutionary attire because it provoked hostility, making men and tradition-minded women more resistant to arguments for woman suffrage. Suffragists deemed improved public relations worth the inconvenience of wearing conventional clothing.

Shying away from the furor raised by dramatic departures from tight waists and long skirts, a fourth group of reformers concentrated on redesigning women's underclothing, which they thought was the root of all evil in womenswear. Typical styles promulgated by underwear reformers included the chemiloon or chemilette, a one-piece combination of corset-cover and drawers, which resembled a jumpsuit with short sleeves, medium to short legs, and scooped neckline. Suspenders to hold up petticoats and stockings were also part of the kit.[6] Paramount in hygienic underclothing, of course, was a replacement for the odious corset, with its dozens of metal bones or "stays." Some of the "hygienic waists" closely resembled corsets with the stays removed and broad shoulder straps or complete shoulder yokes added. Mrs. Fletcher's Emancipation Waist belonged to this type. In 1874, Lucien and I. DeVer Warner, brothers with some medical training, produced a "sanitary" corset closely modeled on the style patented by Lavinia Foy.[7] Other alternative undergarments were designed to replace the corset's functions of supporting the breasts and holding up the stockings.

Hygienic styles of underwear began to be advertised and marketed in major cities in the United States, including New York and Boston. One New York entrepreneur, Mrs. Fletcher, sold less constricting underclothing for strong-minded women, beginning in 1874.[8] Boston was a major center of the Dress Reform Movement, even in the 1870s. The 1895 Dress Reform convention attracted luminaries of the movement such as Dr. Anna Galbraith, Frances Russell, Mabel Jenness, and Annie Jenness Miller.[9]

Boston thus provided a hospitable milieu for the production of a proto-brassiere. Olivia Flynt, a well-to-do Boston dressmaker and dress reformer, developed an idea for corsetless support in 1876, patenting a "bust supporter . . . especially adapted to ladies having large busts" (Figure 3).[10] Her design was meant to replace the corset, "enabling beauty of form to be preserved without lacing or otherwise injuriously pressing or binding the body." As Figure 3

O. P. FLYNT.

BUST-SUPPORTER.

No. 173,611. Patented Feb. 15, 1876.

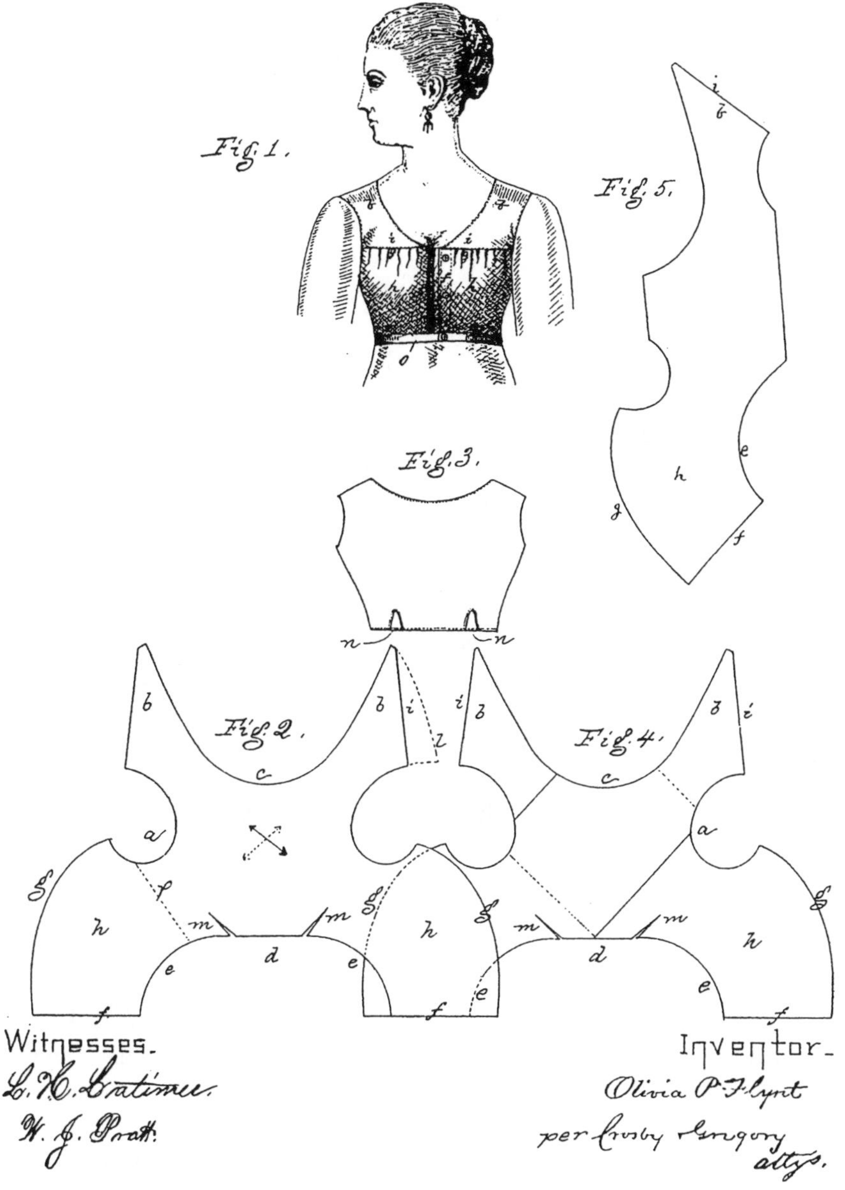

Figure 3. The first bust supporter known to be produced in the United States, patented by Olivia Flynt.

shows, Flynt created a subtle design. The lower concave edge encircled the torso just below the breasts; the convex outer shapes were gathered onto the straight-edged upper shapes, providing fullness over the breasts, and using bias stretch to eliminate the need for shoulder seams. In the garment shown in Flynt's advertising, a cloth extension with buttons was sewn on below the breast, lengthening the camisole portion to provide support for other garments.

Flynt sold her system of underwear, including breast supporters, from her Boston workshop. By 1881 she was offering custom-fitted supporters by mail order. At this time, mail order was in its infancy. Aaron Montgomery Ward's pioneering efforts had begun only in 1872. Department stores such as Bloomingdale's in New York sent out catalogs by the mid-1880s and Sears set up a mail-order pocket watch business in 1886.[11] According to Flynt's promotional catalog, her customers lived throughout the United States; her clientele also included Russian and English visitors. Her products must have delivered some of the promised benefits, because even in the 1890s health reformers commented approvingly on her designs.[12]

In her booklet *Manual of Hygienic Modes of Under-Dressing for Women and Children*, Flynt wrote that she had been manufacturing improved underwear since the late 1860s. She extolled the ability of her Flynt Waist to replace "several other under-garments usually worn at the same time" and to support "the heaviest bust from the shoulders, thereby relieving the individual of the discomfort of its weight." Flynt claimed that her "waist" could hold up the stockings, drawers, petticoats, and even the dress skirt from the button-studded cloth extension below the supporter proper. This waist came in styles for wearing with décolleté party dresses as well as maternity wear, and it even came with padding for use by customers in whom "sufficient development is wanting."[13] To accommodate those who could not visit her Boston atelier, Flynt sent three samples of varied sizes, allowing the client to choose the best. Payment, including all cost of mailing, was to be remitted by money or postal order, check, or registered letter. Prices ranged from $2.50 to $7.18, depending on the material—cottons of various qualities, linens, or silks—and whether boning was included. Flynt preferred not to use bones, but provided them on request. Her products were comparatively costly, at a time when skilled laboring men earned between $10 and $20 per week and even a clergyman's annual stipend was just $1,500, or about $30 per week.[14]

Olivia Flynt shared the market for reform-style breast supporters with Annie Jenness Miller, another campaigner for women's dress reform and publisher of *Dress: A Monthly Magazine Devoted to the Practical and the Beautiful in Women's and Children's Clothing, Physical Culture, and Kindred Subjects*. She patented and produced a "model bodice . . . designed especially to take the place of the corset." Its intent was "to support the bosom and give a smooth line to the waist [bodice]." Jenness Miller contended that her model bodice met the requirements of fashion, with no steel inserts and with only "a few slender bones of pure whalebone [to] keep the garment in place."[15] The Jenness Miller garment did approximate a fashionable late 1880s silhouette with less constriction of the torso. Her model bodice and the dress styles she featured would have met the needs of women who chose to remain conventional in appearance while pursuing unconventional careers or social goals. She continued to advertise her model bodice for three years, along with other hygienic undergarments and women's products.

Olivia Flynt's supporter, patented in the 1870s, harmonized reasonably well with the slightly raised waistlines of that decade. When elongated bodices came into fashion in the 1880s, Flynt's garment lost any relationship to high style. A Flynt waist was also incapable of reducing the waistline to produce the fashionable hourglass silhouette. Who, then, would continue to buy these revolutionary garments? The likely wearers would be women sufficiently educated to be cognizant of reform dress, self-confident enough to defy fashion, and financially able to purchase professionally designed and fitted garments.[16] Then, as now, feminism encompassed many shades of opinion. In the 1870s, Abba Gould Woolson defined reform dress in terms of ready-to-wear, which she believed would free women from time-consuming and labor-intensive home sewing or obtaining custom-made apparel.[17] One group of reformers tenaciously maintained that dress reform undergirded all other reforms for which women might crusade. These women continued to promote dresses and undergarments that freed them physically and psychologically from the impediment of high fashion, even as other feminists reverted to conventional styles of dress.[18]

Although dress reform excited public furor, it was hardly the most revolutionary cause embraced by American women during the nineteenth century. From the 1820s through the 1850s, middle- and upper-class women with some measure of leisure and the yen to improve American society did charitable and educational work to uplift the "deserving poor." They campaigned with speeches, pamphlets, and newspaper articles for temperance and the abolition of slavery. Highly dedicated reformers produced food, apparel, and needlework for fund-raising at "antislavery fairs."[19] After Lincoln issued the Emancipation Proclamation and the Civil War ended, activist women concentrated their attention on banishing Demon Rum from the land. Indeed, many of the women who agitated for votes for women plainly intended to use their suffrage rights to close the bars. Reformers never tired of painting grim pictures of how women and children suffered from alcoholic husbands and fathers. Abuse and neglect, poverty and degradation were their lot. Temperance, meaning total abstinence, and woman suffrage were Amelia Bloomer's main themes in her speeches and her editorials for *The Lily*. Ironically, she refrained from giving speeches on dress reform so that full audience attention would be focused on her pro-suffrage, antiliquor messages.[20]

Other "strong-minded" women's preoccupation with the hygiene of clothing can best be understood as part of the movement toward health reform in which women played prominent roles.[21] Many Americans of the 1800s yearned for better health: fewer illnesses, more vigor, and longer lifespans. The orthodox medicine of the era seemed powerless to help. Drastic therapies such as violent purging and catharsis, bleeding, and application of mustard plasters often made the sufferer worse, driving patients toward what Norman Gevitz termed "other healers." These included such medical sects as botanical medicine, based on herbal remedies; hydropathy, which used water to treat disease; homeopathy, which employed minuscule doses and operated on the principle of "like cures like"; and eclecticism, which combined botanical and regular therapies.[22] Adding to the melange of approaches were the scores of home hygiene manuals published from the late eighteenth century onward. Often these books were based on one of the schools of sectarian medicine.[23] Authors and physicians allied to these schools campaigned for a simpler diet high in fiber, but low in meat, condiments, fat, and stimulants. Exercise was part of this regimen and, quite logically, so was a style of dress that encouraged physical activity.

Most self-help publications directed their preachments to women, because women took the major responsibility for care of the sick and ministration in life crises in American households. Some women sought a larger scope for their curative abilities and, encouraged by health reform, began to campaign for admission to medical schools.[24] Mainstream schools were largely limited to the "sterner sex," but institutions founded by medical sects welcomed women students. Gender equality harmonized with their other unorthodox views. Women committed to orthodox medicine often had to travel to Europe to study at such schools as École de Médicine and the Maternité, both in Paris.[25] Some of these well-educated women returned to the United States to staff the newly established women's medical schools, including the Women's Medical College of Pennsylvania, founded by Quaker women in 1850.

Formal education of nurses in the United States began even earlier than that of women physicians. Dr. Joseph Warrington began to offer classes at the Philadelphia Nurses' Society in 1839. Ann Preston, a Quaker physician, organized a training school for nurses at the Women's Hospital of Philadelphia. Nurses' training burgeoned after the Civil War. In 1872 and 1873, nursing schools opened or began full functioning at the New England Hospital for Women and Children in Boston, Bellevue Hospital in New York City, the Connecticut Training School, and Massachusetts General Hospital. What had been an untrained "calling" became a profession.[26] The first organization for nursing in the United States was formed "for the establishment and maintenance of a universal standard of training" in 1893. Even women who embraced neither medicine nor nursing became better informed about the functions and care of the human body through classes on physiology and hygiene offered to mothers, teachers, and other nondegree students by the women's medical colleges. Ladies' physiological societies reached middle-class women with information about health.[27] A growing cadre of women sought to improve their health habits, including wearing some degree of reformed dress.[28]

Influenced by the movement toward more healthful choices in dress, inventors continued to patent ideas for breast supporters. Seemingly none of the pre-1890 innovations in proto-brassieres enjoyed commercial success. Mortimer Clarke's 1884 version used elastic or rigid material to enclose the breasts. His arrangement of straps braced the back in a configuration that resembled present-day sports bras. Tabs with hooks hung from the sides of the lower band, providing for attachment of other articles of clothing. Idalia Weed's so-called corset had narrow shoulder straps; its slightly curved front was shaped by short vertical stays, extending two inches below the breasts and ending in an elastic band slightly above normal waistline position. Of all pre-1890 patented designs, Weed's most nearly resembles twentieth-century brassieres.

Despite several Americans' ingenuity in design, breast supporters offered no immediate competition to corsets. As long as most fashionable women demanded the viselike fit of typical 1870s and 1880s bodices (see Figure 3), looser, more flexible substitutes for the corset made no inroads. Some women who yearned to shed the corset were undoubtedly deterred by the social opprobrium of being a "loose," uncorseted woman. Unfettered clothing had an all-too-close association with prostitutes. Other women may have been constrained by financial exigencies from changing their customary dress. Business crises rocked the United States between 1873 and 1877, and recurred periodically in the 1880s. Reversals of fortune meant the impoverishment of many middle- or upper-class women, some of whom might have otherwise ventured to purchase reform styles of dress. Only when a broadly popular change, the princess dress, reshaped outerwear silhouettes in a socially approved fashion, during the more prosperous early 1900s, could the forerunners of the brassiere appeal to more than a minority of American women. Then the wearing of brassieres moved beyond the educated, reform-minded, and well-to-do first adopters to many upper- and middle-class women.

2 Brassieres Win a Niche in Fashion

The tiny clutch of inventors who devised breast supporters and the women who wore them in the 1880s would have been amazed to walk into a 1917 corset department and see brassieres prominent among the displays.[1] By the mid-1910s, brassieres rather than corsets had become the source of increased business in foundation departments, according to the trade press.[2] In the *New York Times*, Macy's trumpeted: "A New Brassiere Department Just Opened."[3] The softening of women's dress silhouettes and the reduction in weight and bulk of their clothing helped pave the way for the acceptance of brassieres. Expansion of women's work, recreation, public roles, and health care further disposed them to trade in old-style corsets for these new foundations. Within this period, two phases are evident: 1890 to about 1905, when regional firms sold breast supporters by mail order, and 1906 to 1917, when brassiere manufacturers of varying sizes distributed their wares regionally or nationally through retail chains, specialty shops, mass merchants' catalogs, and department stores.

Le Bon Marché opened in Paris about 1850, inaugurating the era of the department store. Early department stores in the United States grew from the expansion of existing fabric (dry goods) or specialty stores. Starting about 1860, American department stores applied the Parisian innovations of clearly displayed fixed prices, an atmosphere that welcomed "lookers" as well as buyers, and attractively displayed merchandise of many types. Jordan Marsh and Company in Boston and A. T. Stewart in New York vie for the honor of being the first U.S. department store, although several of the stores that ultimately departmentalized opened between 1827 and 1858. Department stores attracted an enthusiastic following by offering elevators, rest rooms, restaurants, telephones, and package delivery. Luxuriously appointed stores, notably Marshall Field in Chicago and John Wanamaker in Philadelphia, drew milling crowds that gawked, socialized, and often made purchases. Department stores' policies evolved further just after World War I, inducing major changes in the manufacture of all apparel, including brassieres.

In the early 1890s, breast supporters lacked the efficient production techniques and wide patronage that would recommend them to department store merchants. Instead, these garments—variously labeled "short stays," "bust girdle," or "strophium"—appeared in minuscule advertisements in the back pages of women's magazines, especially *The Delineator* and *Harper's Bazar* (which became *Harper's Bazaar* in December 1929). Most of these were for mail-order sale, although a few represented patterns a woman could sew at home. Their arrival on the market related directly to a new trend in evening and hostess gowns. In their quest for novelty, some fashion designers had recycled the high-waisted silhouettes of the 1790s and early 1800s in heavier fabrics and darker colors (Figure 4). Styles included less formal garments suitable for daytime wear as well as party dresses. These Empire styles never seriously challenged the prevailing mode of an elongated, cinched waist, puffy leg-of-mutton sleeves, and flared skirt, but they offered an appealing option to the Aesthete, the athletic, emancipated New Woman, and the pregnant woman. Wasp-waisted corsets spoiled the silhouette of Empire gowns, but protobrassieres filled out the abbreviated bodices perfectly. The Empire vogue had begun to peter out by 1897; only dressy tea gowns for daytime parties and a few housedresses kept the high-waisted effect. Yet breast supporters continued to sell.[4]

Specialized companies produced breast supporters. The Delsarte Manufacturing Company advertised in 1893 and 1894 its "strophium" and "bust girdle" or "bust corset," a distinction Delsarte never explained. In the late nineteenth century, the name Delsarte evoked a system of physical culture and expressive facial exercises used by some budding actresses and devotees of fitness. The unconstrained support of breasts by a "bust girdle" instead of a corset harmonized with the Delsarte system's goals. According to one promotional leaflet, Delsarte exhibited these wares successfully at the 1893 Columbian Exposition, held in Chicago.

Delsarte apparently lasted only a couple of years, but Ferris, Classic Corset Company, Mrs. C. D. Newell, Sahlin, and Chicago Corset Company marketed their various breast supporters for long periods. Ferris's Bust Supporter, seen in 1894 in *Ridley's Fashion Magazine*, continued to be shown as late as 1907 in Marshall Field's spring catalog. The catalog's price of $1 was average for supporters, and it was "particularly adapted to those who desire a shapely form without wearing a corset." Full-length "waists" were advertised under this label into the mid-1910s at a cost of up to $3.50. Classic Corset Company advertised its Grecian Bust Girdle in national periodicals between 1901 and 1903, but

Figure 4. An evening dress in the Empire style; pattern offered to dressmakers and home-sewers by *The Delineator*, January 1893. Courtesy Butterick Archives.

the firm appears to have been making this protobrassiere even earlier. Made of heavy cotton jean, fine batiste, or netting for summer, the "bust girdle" was equated with a "corset rest."[5] It was recommended for golf and other athletic activities, for pregnant and nursing women, and for vocalists, readers, and lecturers, who needed unfettered use of their lungs. Classic Corset Com-

Improved Bust Support
By its use the weight of the breasts is removed from the dress-waist to the shoulders, giving coolness and dress comfort, ventilation, a perfect shape bust, and free and easy movement of the body. Made with skirt and hose supporter attachments, high or low bust. Catalogue Free.
When ordering send bust measure.
Sizes from 30 to 38 . $1.00
" " 40 " 45 . 1.25
AGENTS WANTED
MRS. C. D. NEWELL, 1087 N. 41st Court, Chicago

Figure 5. Consumer advertisement for Caroline Newell's bust supporter sold by mail order, 1895–1908. Courtesy Butterick Archives.

pany's enterprising Chicago manufacturer and patentee, Louise Stitt, arranged to have Gimbel Brothers in Philadelphia handle the mail orders from women in the eastern states.[6]

Caroline Newell's product (Figure 5) showed great staying power, appearing in small advertisements from 1895 through 1908.[7] Newell made claims of comfort and easy movement for her Breast Support Form. She also stressed "ALL DEFICIENCY OF DEVELOPMENT SUPPLIED," a theme mentioned by other advertisers. Newell's protobrassieres supported the breast and, by means of flexible steels or featherbone, added to what nature had bestowed.[8] Robert L. Dickinson, a Brooklyn gynecologist and indefatigable crusader against corsets, commended Newell's design because it supported the weight of the breasts from the shoulders and was "reasonable in price" at $1 to $1.25.[9]

Several early producers prospered by offering conventional styles of corset as well as breast supporters. Rose Sahlin's wrapped-style, long-line Bust Form Corset changed proportions with the shifting lines of prevailing fashions; by 1913, it was long and slim-hipped.[10] Sahlin's sensitivity to fashion changes gave her an advantage over Newell, Stitt, and other potential competitors. Franz

Reinhardt's 1901 patented design launched what became the Chicago Corset Company into the manufacture of brassieres.[11] Reinhardt's Kabo Bust Perfector was advertised by name in the fall 1900 Sears, Roebuck catalog.[12] The Kabo merely smoothed the outline of the corset top, rather than giving support, but another Chicago company, Gage-Downs, produced a Bicycle Waist that resembled a long-line brassiere with elastic sides and shoulder straps. It was marketed to athletic women. The Bicycle Waist and a slightly shorter version, the Bust Supporter, came in sateen and summer netting and were sold in waist sizes of 18 to 30.[13]

The woman who could sew could secure a supporter very cheaply, though with substantial cost in time and labor. *The Delineator*, a magazine devoted to professional and amateur sewing, carried many advertisements for ready-mades and also sponsored its own styles of breast supporter, offering patterns for 20 cents. Recommended fabrics included cotton brocade, "coutelle," or other firm woven material. *The Delineator* also contracted with the R. R. Appleton Company of New York to produce finished examples for between $1 and $2. This garment, intended for use with "short-waisted effects," had buttons at the lower edge to connect it to an Empire petticoat for wear with "Empire Styles, Tea Gowns, Wrappers, Lounging Robes, and other loosely fitted garments" (Figure 6).[14] A combination of darts and seams produced a close fit. Conventional corset features persisted in this style, including stays or bones and back lacing, but the buttoned front and adjustable shoulder straps presumably offered improved convenience and comfort over standard corsets. When the Empire dresses waned in popularity, *The Delineator* switched to advertising longer-lined "bathing corsets" that extended down to the waist like later long-line brassieres.[15]

Manufacturers continued to tout their supporters' benefits to health and comfort. These undergarments evidently did relieve wearers from the strictures of conventional corsets, to judge from the longevity of several companies that produced them. What protobrassieres could not deliver was the currently fashionable figure. Only a true corset could mold the tiny waist, rounded hips, and arched back admired between the late 1890s and about 1906.

Chicago seems to have been a mecca for companies that made breast supporters. A booming city with well over one million people, Chicago offered a pool of labor, so important to the needle trades. As a railroad hub and mid-continental port, Chicago was the ideal location for shipping goods around the United States. Mail-order titans Montgomery Ward and Sears, Roebuck had located their facilities in Chicago, and many smaller catalog outlets were based there.[16] Thus it would have been an advantageous site for any manufacturer hoping to win a contract from a mail-order house. No records survive to

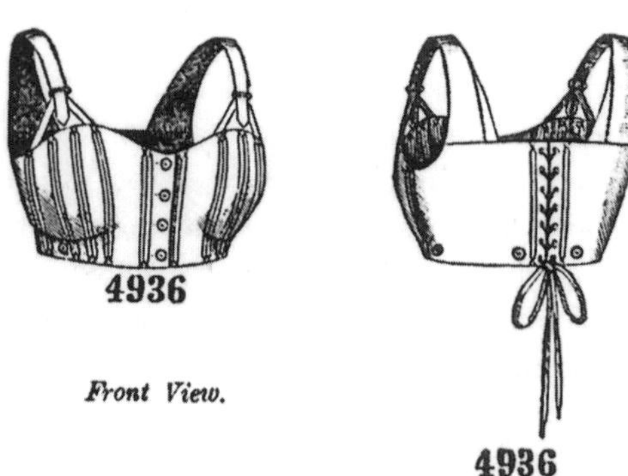

Figure 6. Fashion plate pattern for "Empire Stays" and petticoat to complement dress style in figure 4, January 1893. Courtesy Butterick Archives.

document who supplied Sears with the unbranded styles that appeared in their catalog alongside the Kabo. The Windy City continued for many decades as an important regional center in brassiere manufacturing but yielded national preeminence to New York and Newark, New Jersey, during the early twentieth century.

The appearance of Ferris and Classic Corset models in store retailers' catalogs was remarkable in an era when department stores often disdained branded merchandise. In the early 1900s, Marshall Field and Gimbel Brothers may not have deemed the breast supporter trade worth chasing with merchandise carrying their own store brands; perhaps they wanted to confirm their credibility as sources of goods for a wide range of discerning patrons in urban and suburban households. It is even more surprising that the general catalogs produced by Montgomery Ward and Sears, Roebuck included brassieres. Ward specifically targeted farmers and their families, while Richard W. Sears and A. C. Roebuck went after the patronage of low-income Americans. Neither customer pool included many obvious prospects to buy the early brassieres. Nonetheless, catalogs aided in the acceptance of breast supporters by educating hesitant women about their use. The fall 1903 Sears, Roebuck catalog purveyed

> an improved breast support for low or high busts. Made of strong, light material called Tampico fiber. By its use the weight of the breast is removed from the dress waist to the shoulders giving coolness and comfort in warm weather, producing a perfect shaped bust and free and easy movement of the body. They are just as essential for a slender person as for a stout one and meet a long felt want for every woman and girl from the age of sixteen.

Sears, Roebuck's breast supporter/brassiere prices ranged from 19 to 88 cents, with a few designs reaching 98 cents by 1917. Smaller catalog retailers, including Bellas Hess & Company, of New York, offered brassieres at 25 to 59 cents.[17]

Up-and-coming chain-store retailers also participated in disseminating protobrassieres. J. C. Penney, originally called the Golden Rule Store, sold its first breast supporter over the counter in Wyoming in 1902.[18] Wyoming was the only state that from its beginnings had granted women suffrage in state elections. This level of women's emancipation and the need for practicality, rather than the pursuit of fashion, may account for early acceptance of protobrassieres in this rural area.

None of the first manufacturers of breast supporters managed to prosper after 1910. Protobrassieres had harmonized only with little-worn styles, adopted by resolute reformers or women who prized physical freedom above high fashion. In contrast, women who followed the latest designs could live with the new brassieres. Dresses and shirtwaist-skirt ensembles of the 1900s featured front blousing that exaggerated the full, low bosom; sleeves ending in soft fullness at the wrist; a narrow waistline; and a flared skirt that trailed the floor in back. Any woman who wore an older-style supporter had to renounce this silhouette and pay a relatively high cost of $1 to $2 for the privilege. Brassieres, like corset covers, accommodated the modish silhouette and retailed for as little as 19 cents.[19]

Contributing to the greater expense of prototypical brassieres was the element of handcraft. They were made to measure, using either the bust or waist circumference. By contrast, corsets had been among the first items of women's apparel to be factory made, in fixed sizes, beginning in the 1860s.[20] Breast supporters needed more frequent washing and thus wore out more quickly than corsets did, adding to their ultimate cost.[21] Older manufacturers also lost patronage by failing to offer multiple styles, varied materials, or new designs. Early supporters were utilitarian, whereas brassieres of the 1900s boasted all sorts of enticements, including lace, embroidery, and "dainty" fabrics of thin silk or sheer cotton. Offering a less radical departure from existing styles of undergarment, brassieres enjoyed higher sales than earlier supporters.

Most of the manufacturers of protobrassieres seem to have expired by 1908. In their place grew companies that bore the names DeBevoise, Poix, Warner, Gossard, and Benjamin and Johnes, which employed factory production methods and sold fixed-size garments, of varied and changing styles, through corset departments, specialty stores, and catalogs.[22] These companies became powerhouses of manufacturing, serving the next generation of brassiere wearers.

That generation arrived, along with the very name "brassiere," when in 1904 the Charles R. De Bevoise Company first labeled its product a brassiere (Figure 7) and in 1905 Gabrielle Poix described her invention as a brassiere in the text of her patent.[23] The word *brassiere* was the Norman French term for an infant's undervest or woman's bodice, and thus was probably familiar to the first American users of the word.[24] Gabrielle Poix's family prized its French heritage. The De Bevoise family were Dutch but had descended from the French Huguenots who had fled religious persecution in France to settle in the Protestant Netherlands and England. As the DeBevoise product shows, the 1905 brassiere resembled a camisole, with just a few bones to stabilize its shape and control the position of the breasts.[25]

New directions in women's dress fashions reinforced the broad appeal of the new brassieres.[26] Pouchy bodices began to lose their charm about 1905, preparing women to accept svelte lines in both the bodice and the skirt. The princess dress, smoothly fitted from shoulder to hem by subtly curved seaming (Figure 8), had been shown as an alternative fashion as early as 1901, but by 1907 princess styling emerged as a major fashion trend and was popular with Ameri-

BRASSIERES AND COMBINATIONS
FROM DE BEVOISE
FOR DESCRIPTIONS OF FASHIONS SEE PAGE 824—A

Figure 7. Consumer advertisement for DeBevoise brassieres and combination undergarments. *Vogue*, 23 May 1907.

Figure 8. Fashion plate with smooth-waisted princess style gowns; note monobosom silhouette. *Vogue* 31 May 1906. © Vogue; Condé Nast Publications, Inc.

can women. Princess dresses were made by many companies in every style from silk evening gowns to daytime "wash dresses" of cotton or linen. Conventional straight-fronted corsets literally had no place under the trim lines of princess dresses, but brassieres combined neatly with low-topped corsets to create the streamlined silhouette.[27] Advertisements and fashion editorials demonstrate the connection between brassieres and princess silhouettes. "No woman should indulge in a princess dress unless her figure is shapely and graceful," remonstrated the copywriter for the Fairy Combination Bust Form and Corset Cover.[28] A viable market for brassieres began to develop.

Princess lines gave way in about 1910 to the Directoire fashion, which was yet another revival of the early 1800s silhouette with its raised waistline and long, tubular skirt. Softly draped bodices and layered skirts of various lengths and widths dominated women's dress styles from 1913 to 1917. All of these fashions, lightweight and loosely fitted, looked best over a brassiere and a straight-hipped corset that extended only a few inches above the waistline. The best brassieres were cut on the bias (diagonal) of the fabric for extra smoothness. By 1917, brassieres were confirmed as major underfashions, chosen to coordinate with particular gowns.[29]

Although the De Bevoise Company was a prominent brassiere manufacturer, it had many rivals, including Kops Brothers, Benjamin and Johnes, Gossard, Model, G. M. Poix, Nature's Rival, and Ovida.[30] These firms dominated the advertising in fashion magazines, and probably the sale of brassieres, well past the 1910s. Among the turn-of-the-century manufacturers, only Ferris continued to coexist with the new breed of brassiere company, perhaps because Ferris concentrated on corsets, with brassieres as a sideline. During this era Warner also specialized in corsets. Although Warner sold its first breast supporter in 1902, brassieres seem to have been a secondary part of its product line until the 1920s.

Each firm occupied a particular niche in the brassiere market. Brief profiles of a few of these businesses reveal some of the variety of brassieres marketed during the early twentieth century.

Poix and Model appealed to fashionable young women by offering youthful designs for perky breasts. G. M. Poix, based in Brooklyn, New York, labeled its line the A. P. Brassiere Directoire, making a direct connection to the Directoire line in dresses. A retrospective account of the company relates that Mme. Augustine Poix, Gabrielle's mother, was "a well-known couturiere . . . catering to a high class clientele." In 1905, Mme. Poix enlisted the help of her young daughter in designing a fitted bodice that would secure the desired undershaping for her gowns. Spurred by the customers' enthusiasm, shy Gabrielle showed her "brassieres" to the corset buyer at Altman's, a classy New York department store. As the market for these underpinnings expanded, the G. M. Poix Company began to specialize in brassieres.[31] The Poix ads of the 1910s showed a few live models, but generally they used elegant sketches of coy young women in fancy styles that sold for $1.50 to $4.50. Fine print in the advertisements referred to prices as low as 50 cents and as high as $25! G. M. Poix had only one serious rival. Started about 1915 in New York, Model Brassiere Company gloried in a fashionable image, clearly intended for chic young things (Figure 9). Model kept its prices to 50 cents to $7.50, placing them within reach of many purses.[32]

DeBevoise, Benjamin and Johnes, and Nature's Rival exhibited fashion awareness but seemed geared to a slightly older or less fashion-conscious woman. Between 1905 and the late 1920s, the Charles R. DeBevoise Company occupied a prominent place in the brassiere industry from its plant in Newark, New Jersey. Despite a rather conservative presentation, it produced almost-backless and strapless designs, along with more standard brassieres. DeBevoise claimed to produce hundreds of styles, probably counting each variation of fabric and trim as a style; not more than twenty visibly distinct models appeared in advertising. DeBevoise dominated the market for cautiously fashionable garments, but had one emerging competitor in Newark: Benjamin & Johnes, makers of Bien Jolie brassieres.

Most conservative in styling was Kops Brothers, a New York firm whose wrap-around designs and extensive use of corsetlike adjustments may have appealed to mature women.[33] Waldemar and Daniel Kops devoted their efforts to incessant patenting rather than fashion innovation. Singly or together they secured at least forty-one patents between 1904 and 1931. Kops' advertisements rarely appeared in the high-fashion press. They probably reached their customers through newspapers, store flyers, or household periodicals.

In the early years, brassiere sales seem to have been more regional than national, with Chicago companies supplying midwestern stores and perhaps building on the earlier Chicago patronage for protobrassieres. Clarence Mayer started up Nature's Rival in about 1916, beginning with fairly staid designs, but gradually becoming more daring.[34] H. W. Gossard Company offered Chicago women a wide range of corsets and brassieres, including styles for pregnant and nursing women. Gossard traded on excellence in finish and fit, with each size "modeled on a living figure."[35] New techniques of promotion supported Gossard's sales. The *Gossard Corsetiere and Merchandiser*, a monthly company magazine that reportedly reached over 5.5 million readers, featured film stars' testimonials, a technique overlooked by other manufacturers. Gossard offered retailers prepared advertising copy and dummies for display purposes.

Kleinert, Lane Bryant, Camp, Jeanne Walter, and Ovida all served special

To The Slender Woman, Who Thinks, "I Don't Need A Brassiere!"
PARDON us, but you do need a "Model" Brassiere to smooth away that ugly "corset ridge" and to give your figure those svelte, sweeping, ultra-modern lines.
The Brassiere that is best for the slender woman is a *loose-fitting* or *semi-fitting* or *unboned* "Model," which has displaced the clumsy, crumply "corset cover," now out of fashion.

Model your figure with a
Model
TRADE MARK
brassière
50¢ to $7.50
Illustrated Style Book Free
Model Brassière Co.
Dept. "H"
200 Fifth Avenue, New York

First Prize Panama-Pacific Exposition. Highest Award ever given to any Brassiere in any Country!
Bandeaux Brassieres—all kinds of materials—white or flesh color 50c up.
Fiftieth Anniversary Year
Harper's Bazar, September, 1917

Figure 9. Consumer advertisement directed to slender women for Model brassieres as a substitute for corsets. *Harper's Bazar*, September 1917.

clienteles. Kleinert Company, now best known for dress shields, manufactured maternity breast supporters with leak-resistant linings in the early 1900s, selling them through Sears, Roebuck and other mass merchants' catalogs. Kleinert may also have supplied dress shields to G. M. Poix and DeBevoise, which included shield-style brassieres in their lines.

The S. H. Camp Company of Jackson, Michigan, began operation in 1908, specializing in maternity and postoperative brassieres and corsets. Only Camp advertised regularly in the *American Journal of Nursing*, *Journal of Obstetrics and Gynecology*, and *Corset and Underwear Review*, rather than in fashion or household magazines. Camp traded heavily on the medical benefits of its products, with secondary attention to the demands of fashion.

Comfort and fashion played equal roles in the undergarments and outerwear made by Lane Bryant for her maternity clientele. Bryant's products included a brassiere patented by her second husband, Albert Malsin.[36] Trained in Europe as an engineer, Malsin also received patents for a maternity dress with expanding waistband and a two-piece ensemble that camouflaged the enlarging abdomen.[37] Lane Bryant's sale of dresses and wraps along with foundations set this company apart from all competing firms.

By the start of the twentieth century, women avidly sought to maintain a fashionably slender figure, making them receptive to new diets and rubber undergarments that promised "easy" reducing. Dr. Jeanne Walter offered "medicated" Para rubber undergarments to women who were determined to sweat off unwanted pounds. At $4.50 to $6, these were pricey, yet they continued to be advertised for many years, basing their appeal on reducing without diet, exercise, or medicine.[38] Ovida Company promised similar results with a reducing brassiere of woven elastic fabric, dubbed "Elastreco."[39] Reducing brassieres could have been bought only by comparatively wealthy women. Between 1917 and 1919, a typical family with one child had an annual income of $1,505, of which $238 was spent on family clothing.[40]

These prominent firms represent only a fraction of the manufacturers of brassieres. *A Directory of Textile Brands and Trademarks* listed fifty-two brands of brassieres on the market in 1918.[41] Although some companies offered two or three brands, this still totaled an impressive number of brassiere manufacturers in more than a dozen cities. Small towns such as Bridgeport, Connecticut, and Lima, Ohio, had just one or two firms, whereas Newark, New York, and Chicago boasted multiple manufacturers.

In some respects, it was relatively easy to launch into the manufacture of brassieres. They were made of lightweight woven fabrics typical of corset covers and drawers, including cotton broadcloth, batiste, lace, washable silk, or cotton net. Broadcloth and corset-weight coutil were used to fashion heavy-duty styles, firm enough to control the curves of the breast, the sort of product in which Kops Brothers originally specialized. The shapes of early brassieres were also relatively uncomplicated: princess-style seams and some darts shaped the garments over the breasts. Lacings or surplice closings, overlapping in back or front, were popular expedients for adjusting body circumference and compensated for imprecise sizing. Hardware was limited to a few hooks in the front-closing styles.

The features that made brassieres easy to manufacture also favored continuation of home sewing as an option. *Vogue*, *Delineator*, and *Ladies' Home Journal* carried simple patterns for brassieres and bandeaux between 1893 and the 1920s.[42] Pearl Merwin, author of *The American System of Dressmaking*, devoted one lesson to a brassiere, which she described as "a positive necessity for a full bust and fleshy forms."[43] Clearly, it was far easier to sew a brassiere at home than to produce a corset, which required special sewing machines and industrial equipment to assemble.

Nonetheless, the trend clearly favored ready-made brassieres. As they were gaining experience in styling and fit, brassiere companies simultaneously devoted great effort to clever advertising and marketing to build a clientele for this relatively unfamiliar product. Only those manufacturers with strong advertising could persuade reluctant department stores to offer them shelf space.[44] Advertising claims became more diverse, appealing to different customers, and marketing embraced an array of techniques. Trade and popular press used a two-part nomenclature in the early 1900s. "Brassiere" designated a camisole, without sleeves or with small cap sleeves. Styles labeled as "bandeaux" approximated the styling of late twentieth-century brassieres, with narrow shoulder straps. Ovida's composite bandeau and brassiere was an anomaly.

In the early 1900s, advertising appeals for brassieres and bandeaux tried to combine claims for healthfulness and comfort with assurances of "a perfection of bust outline" so desired with "tailor-made gowns or shirt-waists."[45] Golf and tennis were mentioned as sports that required the flexibility of a brassiere, in lieu of a stiff corset. Swimwear was also not complete without a brassiere: Mme. Meyers emphasized, "You will never realize the full enjoyment of surf bathing without the freedom and comfort afforded by this garment."[46] Even though Ferris made stodgy styles of brassiere, these were shown in advertisements being worn by women riding bicycles or swinging exercise clubs.[47]

By the 1910s, however, brassieres and bandeaux existed for one purpose: to mold the breasts to the shapes required by fashionable dresses. Advertisements rarely mentioned health benefits. Macy's 1911 advertising copy admonished readers: "This season's low corsets and close-fitting gowns make the Brassiere more indispensable than ever."[48] Company advertisements in *The De-*

lineator, *Vogue*, and *Harper's Bazar* explained why the brassiere was essential to fashion. Gabrielle Poix wrote that her brassieres hid "the unsightly corset ridges, will not push up the bust when sitting."[49] Her rival, DeBevoise, declared its products "imperative in this day of slender effects as the keynote of smart feminine attire . . . [giving] unbroken lines from shoulder to waist."[50] Advertisers denounced a brassiereless look as "vulgar, unhygienic, and incorrect."[51] Even the slender woman was warned that she, too, needed a Model brassiere "to smooth away that ugly 'corset ridge' and to give [her] figure those svelte, sweeping, ultramodern lines" (see Figure 9). Ovida traded on its products' ability to reduce the bust measurement two to four inches simply by putting one on—an easily substantiated claim, because lifting and confining pendulous breasts would have immediately reduced breast circumference.[52] Alone among brassiere companies, Ovida suggested that its brassiere might be worn *without* a corset.

Fit as well as general silhouette received close attention. According to Gossard, "the better way is to be fitted to your brassiere when you are fitted to your corset."[53] The copywriter implicitly likened this to the need for having a shoe fitted. Merchants, however, carefully weighed the economics of fitting brassieres, because the use of a fitter's time was profitable only if the item were expensive, multiple brassieres were bought, or the resulting goodwill fostered customer loyalty. It took time for a fitter to measure a customer, select suitable garments to try on, and alter the chosen garment for perfect comfort. Only in the 1930s did foundations department staff begin to fit brassieres routinely. Even before formal fitting became the norm, brassieres were purchased through the sales personnel in better department stores and specialty shops. Self-service was for low-end retailers only.

Many brassiere makers promoted their wide range of styles, as designed to flatter different figure types and meet individual requirements without detailed fitting.[54] Benjamin and Johnes lauded their Bien Jolie brassieres: "Fits *your* individual figure, snugly."[55] Warner seems to have pioneered the idea that the immature figure required support by a brassiere. As early as 1917 they marketed a "Growing Girl" design, intended for slender women but with a name that invited youthful patronage and may represent the first advertising of brassieres to teenagers.[56] Perhaps Warner recognized the latent buying power of "flappers," a group composed of teenaged girls in the late 1910s.[57] The name became a byword in the 1920s, expanding to embrace both adolescents and unmarried women in their twenties.[58] Flappers followed fashion eagerly, becoming increasingly important to outerwear producers and brassiere manufacturers.

In an effort to differentiate their products, brassiere manufacturers resorted to using catchy names, such as the tango brassiere, which met fashion's demands for "relaxed lines" and looked attractive under "the diaphanous upper portions of gowns."[59] Benjamin and Johnes coined the brand name Bien Jolie, French for "very pretty," to replace their frumpy-sounding early trademark, La Walohn. Even the catalogs mailed to rural women used French names such as LaPetite, La Tour, and Bonaire for their brassiere styles by 1913.[60] Ovida and G. M. Poix also invoked French associations, implying that their owners were Frenchwomen, skilled in creating chic, beautifully crafted foundation garments.[61] Indeed, craftsmanship offered another selling point for many brands—each asserting that its products outshone all others in finesse of manufacturing techniques. Model Brassiere Company gave details: "(1) Extra large arm shields; (2) removable boning; (3) rustless hook-and-eyes; (4) unconditional guarantee of workmanship and wear."[62]

Along with print advertisements, retail and wholesale marketing of brassieres became more sophisticated in the late 1910s. In *Corset and Underwear Review* in October 1916, retailers were instructed on how to teach corset saleswomen to recommend a brassiere to accompany a newly purchased corset. Each major style of brassiere was presented with a little "story" about its features. The editor recommended placing brassieres that retailed for less than a dollar in a separate part of the department, so that women shopping at that price level could be served efficiently, while freeing one or more saleswomen-fitters to linger longer with the customers who could be induced to spend more. According to the *Gossard Corsetier and Merchandiser*, brassieres were more profitable to sell than corsets. Worn next to the skin, brassieres wore out relatively quickly and needed frequent replacement.[63] Trade writers calculated that a woman might buy four brassieres to every corset that she purchased.

Changing fashions, inventive zeal, and clever marketing only partially account for the success of the brassiere in the early 1900s and 1910s. As it evolved, this newer style of breast support released women from the viselike grip of the straight-front corset, thus providing greater physical flexibility and a modicum of comfort in the paid employment in which an increasing number of women were engaged.[64]

In 1880, 2,647,157 women, 14.69 percent of females over ten years of age, were gainfully employed. By 1890, that number had grown to 4,005,532, or 17.40 percent of the same population.[65] Occupations held by women often required considerable physical labor and stamina. At least 85 percent of women workers participated in three census categories: domestic and personal service; manufacturing and mechanical industries; and agriculture, fisheries, and mining.[66] Women in these types of work needed clothing and underwear that allowed them to move freely.

In the early twentieth century, an even larger proportion of women participated in the labor force. According to the 1910 census, 8,075,772, or 18.1 percent, engaged in gainful employment; by the 1920 census, that figure was 8,549,511, which was an absolute increase but a relative decrease to 16.5 percent of the total. Population grew faster than women in the workforce.[67] Between 1890 and 1910, substantial shifts had occurred in the percentage of women in different types of work. Numbers of women in domestic and personal service had declined sharply, whereas manufacturing, mechanical industries, agriculture, forestry, and animal husbandry experienced smaller percentage drops. The percentage of working women engaged in professional services almost doubled between 1890 and 1920, although this varied by specific profession. The important new category was clerical work, which absorbed 16.7 percent of employed women but had not been used as a broad classification in earlier censuses. Factory employment, however, had increased in absolute numbers of workers compared, for example, with nonfactory dressmaking and seamstress work, which fell almost by half. This probably reflects the decisive swing by consumers toward ready-to-wear clothing to the detriment of the custom-made clothing trade. However, the absolute increase in women in clothing factories was moderate: 265,643 workers in 1920 versus 237,270 in 1890.[68]

Women telephone and telegraph operators more than doubled between 1910 and 1920. Clerking in stores, bookkeeping, and stenography all increased; surprisingly, so did bankers, brokers, and money lenders, marshals, sheriffs, detectives; insurance agents and officials; draftsmen; and chauffeurs.

College degrees, secured by only 2,682 women in 1890, were earned by 13,398 graduates in 1916, giving wider access to the professions. Between 1910 and 1920, the number of women college professors and presidents rose from under 3000 to over 10,000; primary and secondary teachers increased, too. Women physicians declined in numbers (9,015 to 7,219), but lawyers, judges, and justices increased (558 to 1,738) and religious, charity and welfare workers rose almost fourfold during the decade. Undoubtedly the new semiprofessional pursuit of social work, in which women figured so strongly, accounts for the latter increase.[69]

The U.S. involvement in World War I offered women wider, though fleeting, business and factory opportunities and probably also helped account for the doubling of the number of nurses between 1910 (76,508) and 1920 (143,664).[70] Of the nearly 1 million women who performed war work, only a minority were wholly new to the labor force. Others switched from office to factory jobs, and some reentered lines of work that they had vacated upon marrying. A few women served the Allied Expeditionary Force overseas as nurses or telephone operators. Volunteers supported the doughboys through the YMCA or other service organizations.[71]

Women with such a wide variety of occupations clearly required more practical clothing than the more homebound women of 1880. This included less-confining underclothing, of which the 1910s brassiere was an example. Relatively soft and flexible, with few or no bones, it permitted the woman who wished to follow conventional fashion to wear a low-waisted, less heavily boned corset. Women who sat for most of the day at desks or telephone switchboards would have been far more comfortable in brassieres than in tight-laced corsets. Strenuous work was less arduous for the woman wearing a brassiere and low corset. Stooping, stretching, lifting, climbing stairs—all were eased by the new foundations.

Leisure activities also favored the acceptance of brassieres. Women had greater access to sport by the late 1910s. For the fortunate ones who attended college, team and individual sports proliferated. Fashionable noncollegians engaged in golf, tennis, and horseback riding, even riding astride by the early 1900s.[72] Bicycling became a craze in the mid- to late 1890s, settling into an established sport for middle- and upper-class women and men by the 1900s. Bicycle "waists" and "short stays" were promoted for this activity, whose vigor and bent-forward position practically precluded wearing a standard corset; waists gave way to brassieres as the 1900s advanced.[73]

By the late nineteenth century, swimming offered exercise to women of all social classes. Public and private bathhouses had provided women instruction in swimming as early as the 1870s. Both working-class women and middle-class homemakers used bathhouses in the last decades of the nineteenth century. Not content with merely paddling around a pool, a few daring American women followed the example set by English and European "mermaids" and began to compete publicly in swimming meets. For these endeavors a functional style of swimwear was needed, not the clumsy bathing dresses worn on the beach. Skirtless, collarless, and sleeveless one-piece suits were developed, in both woven and knitted fabrics.[74] Sometimes the attire included a breast supporter.[75]

Young working-class women gravitated toward dance halls, amusement parks, and movie theaters after work and on Sundays, despite the objections of family and conservative community members. Before the end of the 1910s, middle-class women and men were socializing in these commercial settings, which had been partially sanitized to attract the family trade. What Kathy Peiss has described as a "heterosocial culture" imbued with "consumerism" flourished, offering women new opportunities for self-expression—including the chance to display fashionable clothing, supported by fashionable undercloth-ing. Motivated by the desire to attract dates and possible suitors, and armed with direct knowledge of fashions from factory or retail work, young employed women offered a large though financially constrained market for the new styles of brassiere.[76]

Some women's leisure was directed toward a more serious pursuit: political activity. Long before they won suffrage, women campaigned for the major political parties in the Northeast, Midwest, and West.[77] The woman suffrage movement splintered and languished in the late nineteenth century, but experienced a renaissance in the early 1900s. By the early 1910s, western state legislatures had granted women the right to vote in state elections. In the effort to secure federal voting rights, the British-inspired National Women's Party engaged in radical protest. America's National Association of Woman Suffrage Associations (NAWSA), led by Carrie Chapman Catt, preserved a decorous but persistent approach to winning votes for women.[78] When the United States joined World War I, NAWSA supported the war effort, in order to claim suffrage as the fruit of their patriotism and contribution to victory.[79]

Along with occupational diversification, recreational opportunities, and political work, women's health care began to change for the better in the early twentieth century. Up to that time, a pregnant woman rarely saw a doctor or midwife until she was in an advanced stage of labor. A few physicians recognized that serious trouble could be averted by examining and instructing the prospective mother early in pregnancy.[80]

Prenatal care became available in some regions in the late 1800s, but this practice took hold only in the 1900s. Along with testing for symptoms of disease, physicians and nurses offered advice about diet, exercise, clothing, and breast care.[81] Recognizing that breast-feeding was crucial to an infant's health, doctors and nurses urged women to nurse their infants.[82]

By the 1910s, writers at the forefront of maternal health instructed pregnant women in the newest methods of breast care. They condemned brisk rubbing with a rough washcloth and application of drying agents like glycerine and alcohol. Instead, they recommended washing with a soft cloth and mild soap to remove breast discharges. New mothers were instructed to keep breasts aseptically clean and support them with a brassiere, a convenient substitute for the cumbersome binder that was regularly used in hospitals.[83] Brassieres gave comfort to swollen, tender breasts and aided in cleanliness of body and clothes. Absorbent pads could held in place by the brassiere. Brassieres were needed even more after the baby was weaned, to preserve the figure, because stretched tissues sagged without support.

Although the early twentieth century witnessed much development of the brassiere, some ideas were simply too advanced for commercial success. These innovations foreshadowed future types and features of brassieres. In response to the fashion for Empire styles of dress, Marie Tucek produced a true push-up "breast supporter" in 1893.[84] Demicups above a wide metal band and straps that attached at the outer border of the cups produced a broad décolletage. Though she called them "pockets" in her patent texts, Tucek had pioneered brassiere cups (Figure 10).

Early brassieres for athletic women were patented by Ethel Quirk, who designated her breast supporter for acrobatic dancing and other theatrical use, and Laura Blanche Lyon, whose 1906 "bust supporter" appeared as soft and unconstraining as a modern sports bra.[85] Lyon's design was essentially a very short camisole with gathering to form the cups. Unlike 1990s pull-on counterparts, this brassiere fastened in back. Brassieres for sleepwear were pioneered by Jeanne Leeman and the underwire concept by the visionary Madeleine Gabeau.[86] By separating the breasts, Gabeau's brassiere clashed with the prevailing fashion silhouette, an ample monobosom without perceptible cleavage. Gabeau's device had soft cups, but the earliest use of the term *cup* in United States literature occurs in two patents issued in 1916, both consisting of elastic webbing, strips of which were arranged to overlap and thereby form "cup-shaped cavities" or "cup-shaped elastic bust sections."[87]

Mary P. Jacob, self-styled "inventor of the brassiere," secured a patent in 1914 for an admittedly innovative but commercially unimportant brassiere design.[88] Her use of bias cut represented a fuller exploitation of an existing feature of the brassiere styling of its era. However, Jacob's chosen design may have been troublesome to manufacture and its use satisfactory only to wearers with small, firm breasts.[89]

Several striking trends emerge in brassiere development between 1890 and 1917. First, patenting activity became more closely associated with successful businesses. Daniel and Waldemar Kops, Gabrielle Poix, Charles DeBevoise, Rose Kleinert, Samuel Gossard, and Alfred Benjamin all produced successful patent applications between 1900 and 1917. Women participated extensively in patenting brassieres and, in their roles as nurses and physicians, advocated wearing brassieres.

Some of the requisites for an effective brassiere were realized during these twenty-eight years: harmonization of brassiere shape with the external silhouette, relative inconspicuousness underneath the clothing, and a price that placed brassieres within the reach of middle-class women. There were even attempts to devise brassieres that could be used in active endeavors and ones that could hold each breast in a separate cup. Yet these were only in the patenting stage by the late 1910s. Much remained to be done, especially in fitting the

BREAST SUPPORTER.

No. 494,397 Patented Mar. 28, 1893.

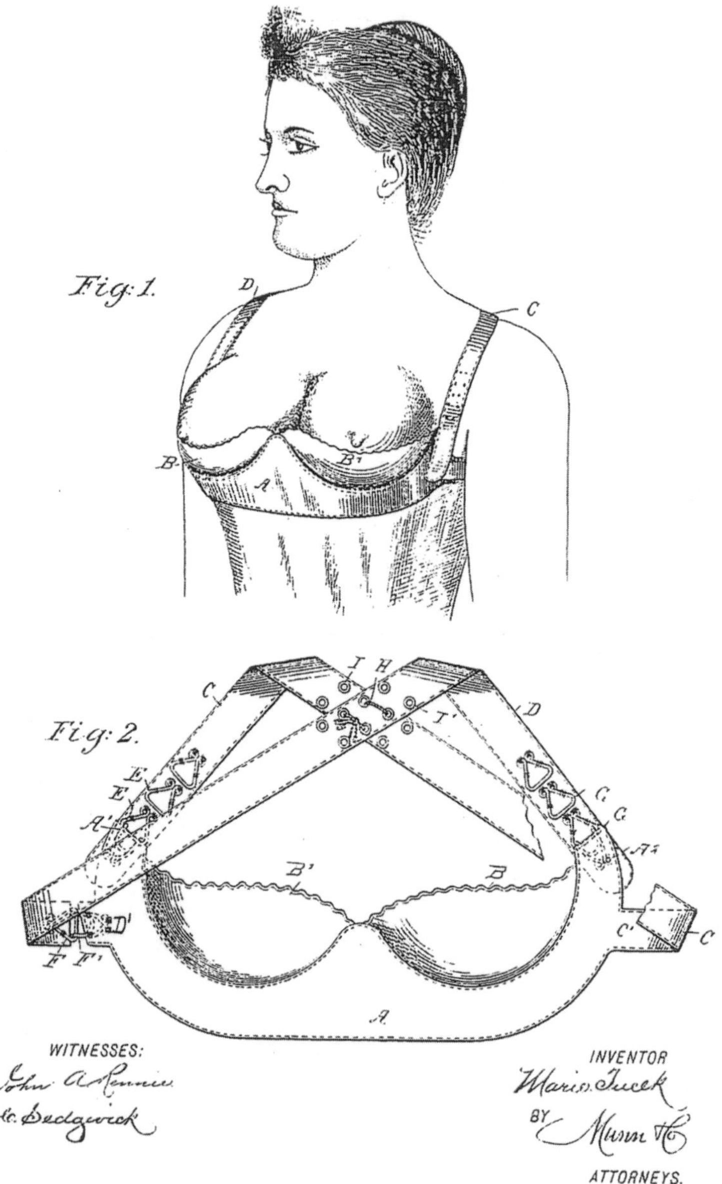

Figure 10. Illustration for first push-up brassiere with separated cups, patented by Marie Tucek, 28 March 1893.

various sizes and shapes of breasts and torsos, as well as providing for movement of the body without chafing or binding. Brassieres may have stayed in position, but they did so mainly because of an excessively tight fit. Each company worked to individual sizing specifications, which frustrated consumers but also built loyalty to a brand once satisfactory fit had been found.

Despite their shortcomings, by 1917 brassieres had moved from being a minority fashion to the mainstream of American womenswear and began to have an economic impact on the apparel industry. Prompted by simplified and systematized production and merchandising arising from wartime exigencies and broad societal enthusiasm for scientific efficiency, that industry underwent drastic changes in the postwar decade.

3 Breasts Lost and Found

Americans who lived through the 1920s looked back on the decade as a watershed—the true beginning of the twentieth century.[1] During this era, people consciously rejected the past and pursued what they considered modernity in many facets of daily living.

For brassiere manufacturers, the years 1918 through 1929 brought unusual opportunities and equally great challenges. New companies, including Maiden Form, Formfit, Lovable, and Lily of France sprang up and became giants of the industry. Some established firms continued to flourish through wise marketing, design, and perhaps a measure of luck. Other stalwarts, including DeBevoise, began to have problems even before the panic of October 1929. Nonetheless, several brassiere companies survived the economic turmoil and contraction to thrive for many more years.

Economic expansion in the United States, though far from universal, put more money in some Americans' pockets. From 1922 to 1927, several industries prospered, notably those that produced housing, electrical appliances, and automobiles.[2] Banking thrived. The economy grew at an annual rate of 7 percent for six years.[3] Between 1921 and 1929 the gross national product increased 40 percent. Banking, insurance, real estate, publishing, and government all hired armies of clerks, more than half of them women.[4] Firms that supplied women's apparel and personal care items, including brassiere manufacturers, could turn a nice profit attracting even modest purchases from hundreds of thousands of businesswomen who had their own incomes.

The flip side of expansion was inflation. The so-called high-cost-of-living eroded Americans' purchasing power in the late 1910s as wartime shortages of consumer goods drove up costs. The Consumer Price Index almost doubled between 1916 and 1920. Then deflation struck in late 1920 and 1921, catching manufacturers and retailers off guard, while giving a temporary respite to consumers. Especially hard hit were businesses holding costly inventories no longer salable at 1910s prices. Catalog behemoths Sears, Roebuck and Montgomery Ward felt the pinch because their core clientele—farm families—were receiving lower returns on their crops.[5] Then prices for manufactured goods returned to a more even keel; inflation remained quiescent through the 1920s. According to the statistics collated by M. Ada Beney, a researcher for the National Industrial Conference Board: "While in 1920 clothing prices rose even higher relatively than food prices, during the period 1922 to 1929 clothing prices remained considerably more stable than food prices."[6]

Brassiere companies maintained relative price stability in part by reducing hand labor, building large demand to reduce unit costs, using standard components made by specialized firms, and knitting brassieres to shape instead of assembling them piece by piece. Prudent manufacturers also heeded calls for limiting the variety of products in a push for rationalization that began during the later war years and gained force through the 1920s.

To survive, producers had to build a large pool of customers, which in turn hinged on sophisticated advertising and the deployment of multiple media, such as radio spots and billboards. The advertising industry grew in influence. Magazines were increasingly important, reaching millions of households. *Ladies' Home Journal*, *McCall's*, *The Delineator*, and *Butterick* all targeted middle-class women, while *Harper's Bazar* and *Vogue* appealed to the upper crust. Frances Donovan, a sociological researcher, credited women's magazines with informing their readers about products and shaping their shopping methods; by the late 1920s, customers came into a store seeking brand-name merchandise.[7] Window and in-store displays were more fully coordinated than ever before. Television had been demonstrated in both England and the United States, but was not yet ready for commercial exploitation.[8] Customers could be lost if advertising was unsuitable or aimed at the wrong clientele, as well as if products were poorly designed or passé. Companies that responded quickly to changing tastes prospered. Those that remained oblivious to shifts in fashion and in the underlying premises of consumption went out of business.

Alert brassiere manufacturers recognized and responded to radical fluctuations in women's fashionable silhouettes. Between 1918 and 1924, the favored body type went from flat to flatter. Skirt lengths almost touched the ankles at the end of World War I, rising to just below the knees by 1924–26.[9] Of course, the true flappers—girls in their teens—bared their knees, at least when they sat down. Their mothers were generally far more sedate, to judge from the contents of family albums and candid snapshots in fashion and society magazines.[10]

The boyish look began to pall by late 1924. Buyers for foundations in elite Philadelphia and Manhattan department stores sensed the new trend: "The flattening idea is disappearing. What people want now is support." In place of binding, young patrons sought uplift, as colorfully expressed by one specialty shop buyer: "Chickens want support, stouts flattening."

Further changes were in store. By 1927, hemlines began to inch downward; trailing panels and pointed "handkerchief hems" foretold a more general descent. Skirts hugged the hips. By spring 1929, daytime hemlines extended four or five inches below the knee and evening dresses grazed the floor.[11] With the lengthening hems came subtle suggestion of waistline indentation and increasing emphasis on the curves of the breast. Fall 1929 brought a higher-waisted, clinging dress style—the latest incarnation of the princess silhouette.[12] Where the dress shape went, the "foundations" were sure to follow, forcing designers to rework their products each season. A columnist for *Corset and Underwear Review* reported in late 1929 that corset and brassiere manufacturers "had to drop work in hand and develop new styles" in the expectation that women would replace the low-waisted dresses in their closets with princess models.[13]

In addition to struggling with shifting styles, manufacturers had to cope with the new lingerie fabrics. Manufacturers such as Kops Brothers, who had worked exclusively with heavy materials, scrambled to adjust machinery and production methods to accommodate sheer textiles, laces, and ribbons. Fiber choices were expanding as well. In the 1920s, the manufactured fiber rayon entered an underwear market that had previously been dominated by naturals, usually silks or cottons.[14] Rayon performed quite differently from silk, though the two had a superficially similar appearance. Fabrics woven from rayon were more likely than silk textiles to stretch in handling. Rayon abraded easily, producing holes, and did not spring back as well as silk when stretched. Yet rayon had virtues, too: softness, absorbency, ready acceptance of dyes, and comfort in wear.[15] Underwear firms that conquered rayon trumpeted this achievement in their advertising. McLouglin Textile Corporation boasted about its LaTosca Lingerie: "It is fashioned by workmen [actually women] especially trained to handle this new material, and styled on living models by an expert designer."[16]

Sheer knitted textiles for fine lingerie were another novelty in the 1920s. Rayon and silk tricot, swami, and milanese appeared in brassieres, panties, and combinations.[17] Carter, Munsingwear, Kayser, and Van Raalte, companies with experience in producing knitted cotton or blended-fiber underwear, began to show brassieres and "singlettes" (brassiere-chemise combination garments) made of these avant-garde fabrics.[18] Throughout the 1930s, knitting companies marketed brassieres made of tricot yardage or full-fashioned styles, shaped in the knitting process, rather like silk and rayon hosiery.

Something more profound than rising skirts and loosening waistlines shook the fashion business between World War I and the stock market crash. Business sages wrote about seismic shifts in retailing, so obvious in retrospect. Despite apparent national prosperity, retail profits languished between 1921 and 1929. According to Joseph Mayer, a department store magnate, customers began to demand aesthetic appeal and fashion in apparel and home furnishings that had previously been slow-changing "staples." By the 1920s these items were bought for their pleasing and *au courant* styling, with serviceability taken for granted. Department stores found they had to change their way of buying and presenting apparel and household merchandise in order to survive. Producers of brassieres were caught between this trend and a revolution in the procurement of merchandise.[19]

Retailers, like other businesses, systematized their methods of securing products in the 1920s. Although scientific methods and efficiency had permeated business thinking before the war, this approach expanded dramatically under the influence of Bernard Baruch's War Industries Board. E. B. Weiss, vice president of Gray Advertising, explained how department store executives began to focus on just a few suppliers for each category of merchandise and to buy goods at a few fixed price levels. "Price lining" reduced confusion and waste and permitted greater assortment of sizes and colors, in a more limited number of lines. Buyers planned their orders to replicate what customers actually bought, based on departmental records of individual sales. Sizes and colors in great demand were stocked fully, while the outliers were carried in a few variants or dropped entirely.[20] Competent buyers did their best to avoid the twin evils of overstocks, which wound up on the sale table, and stock-outs of popular merchandise, which forfeited potential sales.

Apparel makers, including those in the brassiere game, were forced to upgrade styling for fashion-savvy consumers, while concurrently reducing the range of styles they produced. What retailers wanted was dependability, consistency in quality and sizing, and a degree of fashionability that satisfied the store's customers.

Foremost among the challenges facing brassiere producers, of course, was meeting the needs of women whose lives were changing drastically, encompassing more types of paid work, wider opportunities for education, and a greater variety of leisure pursuits. Although hundreds of thousands of women had worked to support themselves or help their families before the Great War, others entered business and industry at the urging of the United States government, first to aid in the defense buildup and then to support the war effort.[21] Inflation as well as patriotism drove women into paid work. Some families needed a second income to buy the necessities. When the war ended, women often lost industrial and public-service jobs to returning soldiers, but continued to dominate the secretarial ranks. Collegiate training opened opportunities in teaching, nursing, library posts, or social work. Between 1922 and 1928, women earning baccalaureate degrees more than doubled, reaching 43,502.[22] None of the lower-level professional jobs offered prestige or lavish salaries, but they did help some women to escape the economic margin where their working-class counterparts toiled in factories or in domestic service.

Office work and the professions required women to present a competent, decorous, well-groomed appearance six days a week. Advice literature on how to obtain a job and accounts of success on the job almost always mentioned business-worthy clothing. Suits and blouses or tailored dresses with coordinating coats predominated among the recommended styles.[23] Writers of advice features routinely urged women to build a wardrobe of basic items in a single color, enlivened by accessories and blouses in contrasting hues. Wool fabrics and silks were recommended for those who could afford them, but cottons and the newly commercial rayon textiles offered less expensive alternatives.[24] Moderate comfort was also required. All of these expectations put conflicting demands on underclothing, to sustain a stylish silhouette while not being too sexy or inflicting distracting physical discomfort. Lingerie also had to be made of lightweight silk or rayon that could be washed overnight and worn the next day without ironing, to keep the women who worked in offices and stores looking (and smelling) fresh each day.[25]

Women who performed heavy or repetitive manual tasks, including factory operatives, farm workers, and nurses, required undergarments and outerwear that gave complete freedom of movement, felt smooth against the skin, and stood up to daily wear. Old-style binders would have been intolerable and a definite hindrance to performance on the job. Blue-collar women required both flexibility and protection in their brassieres, but not the delicacy that served white-collar consumers.

Professional sportswomen, some of whom began to gain fame as tennis and swimming champions, likewise required brassieres that were unconfining but reduced uncomfortable jiggling.[26] Many middle-class women of lesser athletic prowess participated in golf, tennis, and swimming. By the late 1920s, there were about a thousand private tennis clubs and enough municipal courts to meet the demand of 1.2 million players. Golf courses numbered five thousand, with 2 million players.[27] Dance reached probably even more Americans than active sports and was only slightly less athletic. The Charleston epitomized the decade, but the Black Bottom and tango were almost as popular. Classical ballroom steps and even square dancing attracted a following. For all of these amusements, underwear and outerwear had to move with the body—providing another problem for brassiere designers and producers to solve.[28]

Gossard claimed to have met this challenge in a tongue-in-cheek advertising line: "The most active woman in her most active moments won't suffer from dislocation of the lingerie if she wears a Longerlyne [brassiere]."[29]

American women were living increasingly active lives in the public sphere. Work at home was often replaced by work in an office, factory, or school. Women engaged in public recreation, whether at a sport facility, ballroom, or movie theater. Civic involvement also placed women in the public eye. Women of all classes were expected to look attractive, at least on the street, if not when toiling on an assembly line or pushing a vacuum cleaner.[30]

Scrutiny of personal appearance increased at the very time that women were expected to have willowy, elegant figures. Matchstick ladies strutted through the pages of *Vogue*, which reminded its readers that "every smart woman to-day, be she sixteen or sixty, must have the straight figure together with a free, easy grace, a litheness of motion, that were formerly the attribute of youth only."[31] Foundations, including brassieres, girdles, and the popular hybrid corselettes, were worn to enhance women's figures, simultaneously helping the wearer adapt to each nuance of fashionable style. Especially popular were the corselettes that blended the brassiere and girdle into one garment. Absolutely flat in 1919, corselettes began to show cup-style contouring in 1926.

Brassieres were expected to meet women's complex needs without exorbitant cost, because the majority of working women received meager salaries. In the 1930 census report, women's median weekly wage in manufacturing in New Jersey, Ohio, and Rhode Island was $19.13. In Alabama, Mississippi, and South Carolina the median was $8.35. Among women in clerical and business jobs, the annual median wage in the late 1920s was $1,548.[32] Weekly paychecks ranged from $6 for an office girl to $40 for a skilled bookkeeper.[33] The median salary among fifty-five women physicians in private practice was $3,088.[34] Among metropolitan retailers in 1929, assistants to store officers earned as much as $3,000 annually; directors of staff training drew $2,000 to $3,000; and the head of mail order received $2,000 to $4,000.[35]

An annual clothing budget of $500, published in 1926 for the "successful" businesswoman, recommended that she purchase three brassieres, at a cost of $1 each.[36] Even the wife of an industrial worker in New York, whose annual clothing expenditure was expected to range from $52.60 to $63.08, was reported to require two brassieres yearly, at 44 to 58 cents each.[37] These, of course, were standards. The actuality was much different for some women. Factory workers, office girls, and others earning $6 per week could not afford to buy much clothing. Even a 29-cent brassiere, as shown in the catalogs of Sears, Roebuck and Montgomery Ward, was a luxury to unskilled laborers, most farm women, and those supporting families on small incomes.

Price was not the only differentiation among market segments in the brassiere trade. Age groups were becoming distinct: matrons versus flappers. The J. Walter Thompson (JWT) advertising agency conducted interviews of foundation garment buyers in several U.S. cities in 1924 and 1925. Transcripts of these interviews revealed what women of different ages expected from the brassieres they purchased.

The young patrons, dubbed "flappers" by several buyers and by JWT staff, were looking for *uplift* styles of brassiere, in contrast to older customers who wanted the flattening styles. Young women were probably more willing than their elders to abandon the starkly tubular dresses of the early 1920s for body-hugging styles, which required an uplift. Furthermore, firm young breasts would not have protruded in the slim silhouette. A JWT respondent from a fashionable shop reported, "Small sizes sell best—even the little girls wear brassieres now," confirming that the equivalent of a "training bra" was already being produced in the 1920s.[38] A separate research project conducted by JWT gathered responses to a questionnaire from thirty-eight mothers with one or two daughters ages twelve to sixteen. Twenty-six girls wore brassieres and another seven wore corselettes, out of a pool of thirty-nine adolescents. Acceptance of brassieres was evidently spreading among young girls, at least in metropolitan areas.[39]

By contrast, some over-thirty clients often had large, pendulous breasts that impinged on the columnar dresses of the early 1920s. Their breasts would have needed restraining, and they may have been slower to switch to more contoured dresses, such as the 1929 princess style, which drew an enthusiastic reception from young women in their late teens and twenties.[40] A Bronx budget department store buyer noted that recent immigrants from Italy, Germany, and Eastern Europe remained loyal to long-line brassieres in heavy materials.[41]

One traditional distinction among categories of customer diminished in the 1920s. According to a Chicago mail-order respondent to the JWT interviewer, "The rural market reached by mail is only a little less up-to-date than the urban market, thanks to the flivver [Ford], the radio, and national advertising magazines."[42]

Mail-order catalogs had traditionally informed rural customers about the latest styles and expedited their acquisition. Now catalog retailers were threatened by the spread of both "flivvers" and chain stores, such as J. C. Penney, which offered attractive prices in convenient downtown locations. Penney established a wholly owned subsidiary, the Crescent Corset Company, to produce women's undergarments. Its brassieres were originally marketed under Lady Lyke.[43] Department stores also sent out catalogs to regular customers, but their circulation was too small and localized to threaten Sears, Roebuck or

Montgomery Ward. Marshall Field and its eastern counterparts attracted the trade of socialites and urban upper-middle-class women rather than the typical patrons of catalog giants.[44]

Life was changing as rapidly for brassiere producers as for the customers. Only the innovators survived, in particular those who were swift to respond to the desire for uplift styles. As early as 1923, inventive designers began to patent bandeaux with contouring. New Yorker Essye K. Pollack filed what appears to be the first such design (Figure 11),[45] which she says in her application was intended to benefit "women with large and heavy breasts especially . . . following childbirth." Her style may have reached the production stage, because a very similar design, with the addition of a side seam, appears on page 78 of the spring 1926 Montgomery Ward catalog. In any event, her concept was echoed in widely disseminated brassieres.

One of the biggest winners from the emergence of the uplift was a new company, which began life as Enid Manufacturing but by early 1930 had become Maiden Form. The company was incorporated in 1922 by New York dressmaker Enid Bissett and her partners Ida and William Rosenthal.[46] Company archives contain competing accounts of the historic beginning of their production of intimate apparel. In the early 1920s, fashion promoted the flat-chested look with the breasts bound against the chest wall. One popular brand of binders was Boyshform, a name that accurately portrays this company's fashion objective. One account of Maiden Form's origins relates that an actress-customer of Enid Bisset and Ida Rosenthal hated the binders and insisted on a breast supporter that would allow her chest to expand and create a flattering bustline.[47] The name Maiden Form, taken as a product trademark in 1924, offered a direct contrast and challenge to Boyshform.[48] From that time forward, Enid Manufacturing/Maiden Form Company became specialists in intimate apparel.

William Rosenthal protected and promoted Maiden Form's business interests by securing numerous patents for brassieres.[49] The first of these had the stated purpose of providing "a brassiere which is adapted to support the bust in a natural position, contrary to the old idea of brassieres made to flatten the chest."[50] Maiden Form Brassieres began to appear in *Corset and Underwear Review* in 1927 (Figure 12) and in *Harper's Bazar* in fall 1928. The advertisements claimed a "double support pocket," rather than using the word *cups*. However, it did have cups, created by gathering the breast sections onto a flat, rectangular center piece. A snug band extended beneath the breasts. By the time Maiden Form reached a national market, however, other companies had already started to sell uplifts.

Model Company showed an unmistakably contoured brassiere in the Au-

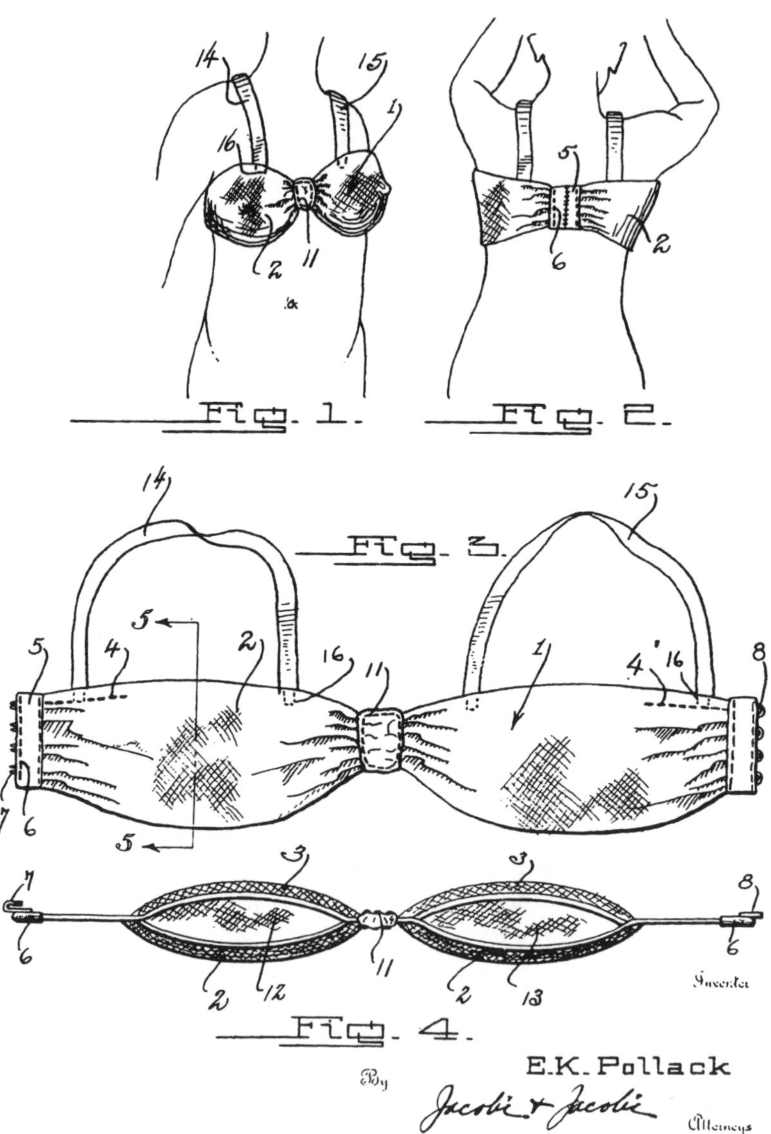

Figure 11. Early uplift bust confiner, a rebellion against flattening bandeau styles, "for women with large and heavy breasts," patented by Essye K. Pollack.

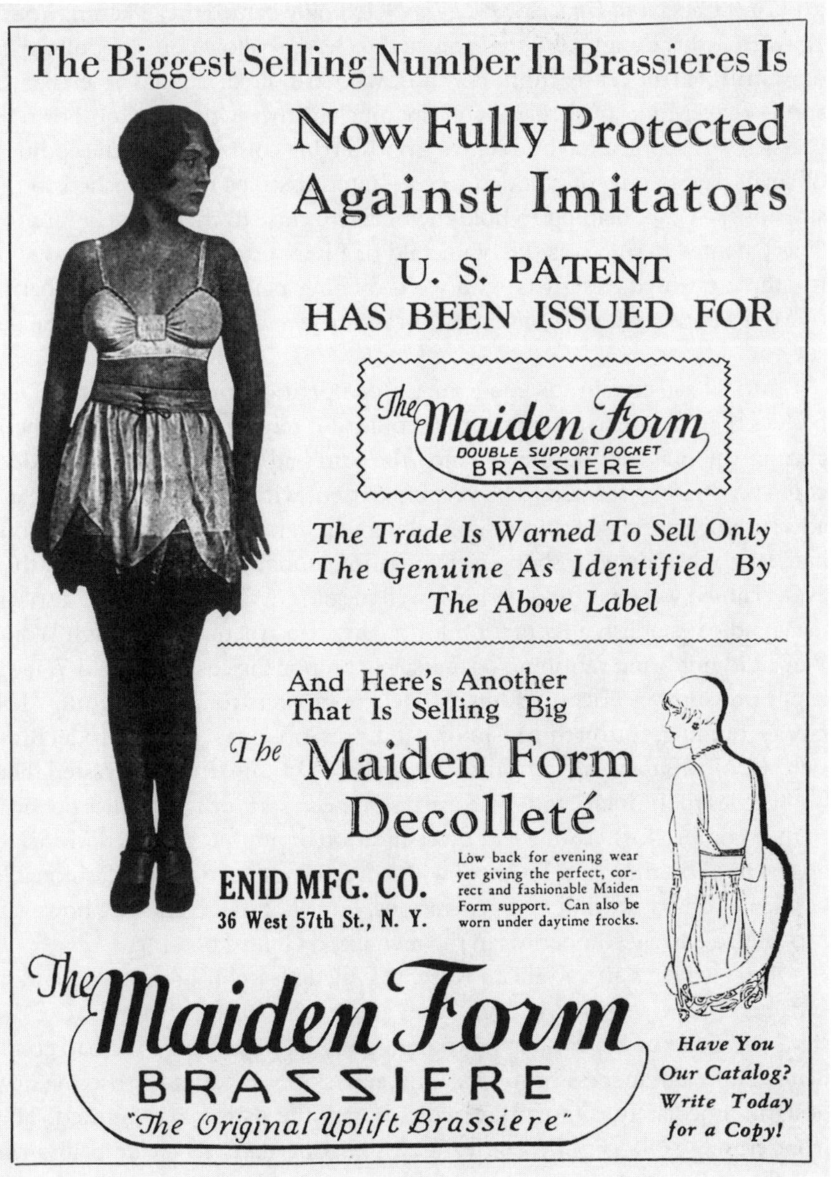

Figure 12. Trade advertisement of an early Maiden Form brassiere, patented by William Rosenthal. *Corset and Underwear Review*, November 1927. Reproduced with permission.

gust 1925 *Corset and Underwear Review*.[51] Tellingly named the "Flaming Youth Brassiere," this design could be adjusted to have shallow cups by pulling up drawstrings in the center front. For those who so desired, it could be left flat. In spring 1928, Model pushed this concept much further with the "Cup-Form"[52] brassiere, still contoured by a center-front shirring cord, but with the addition of small darts, and—the hidden secret—interior straps that branched to the sides of each cup, helping to hold the brassiere close to the chest (Figure 13). This patented design was the brainchild of Elvira Campa McKeefrey, one of the three talented designers who were creating patentable styles on behalf of Model in the 1920s.[53] McKeefrey's brassiere was destined for many years of success.

Model had certain advantages in the competition for the uplift customer: besides their designer-patentees, they could also rely on many years of experience in the brassiere business, which the firm had entered in 1915. Model's company strategy seemed to be keeping current with high fashion. Company advertisements stressed chic designs, along with relative comfort: "Dress your hair, lace or button your shoes, recline, dance, lounge" without restraint; they even claimed wearers could perform well in sports.[54] The Model line also endeavored to establish a reputation for quality construction. Although World War I did not bring rationing of brassiere components, as did World War II, it put pressure on prices, leading Model copywriters to assert in 1918: "The fabrics, binding, cotton thread, hooks-and-eyes, ribbons . . . in the Model Brassiere are of *the same high standard* as last year."[55] In 1919, they contrasted their "16 stitches to the inch" with "the usual skimped 11, 12, or 13" stitches per inch of their competitors.[56] Sufficient diversification of products allowed Model to appeal to "Daughter and Mother" with advertising that depicted fashionable women of obviously different generations. For all of its advantages, however, Model had a lively competitor in the revitalized G. M. Poix, Inc.

Just two days after William Rosenthal filed his uplift brassiere patent, in October 1926, Gabrielle M. Poix Yerkes applied for an equally innovative design, one that put her business into high gear.[57] Yerkes must have had confidence in the uniqueness of her idea, because she began to advertise the new design immediately, almost three years before the patent was granted. This front-closing style (Figure 14) featured radiating darts to create roundness and the suggestion of true cups. Heavily advertised in women's magazines, the design made quite a splash. In a stroke it provided comfort to large-breasted women and nicely adapted to the reemergent curves in women's apparel (Figure 15).[58]

Yerkes's design had one major advantage over the uplifts from Maiden Form and Model—adaptability to use by pregnant and lactating women by means of a front opening. Pollack's brassiere allowed for enlargement of the

June 29, 1926. 1,590,693

E. C. McKEEFREY

BRASSIÈRE

Filed June 2, 1925

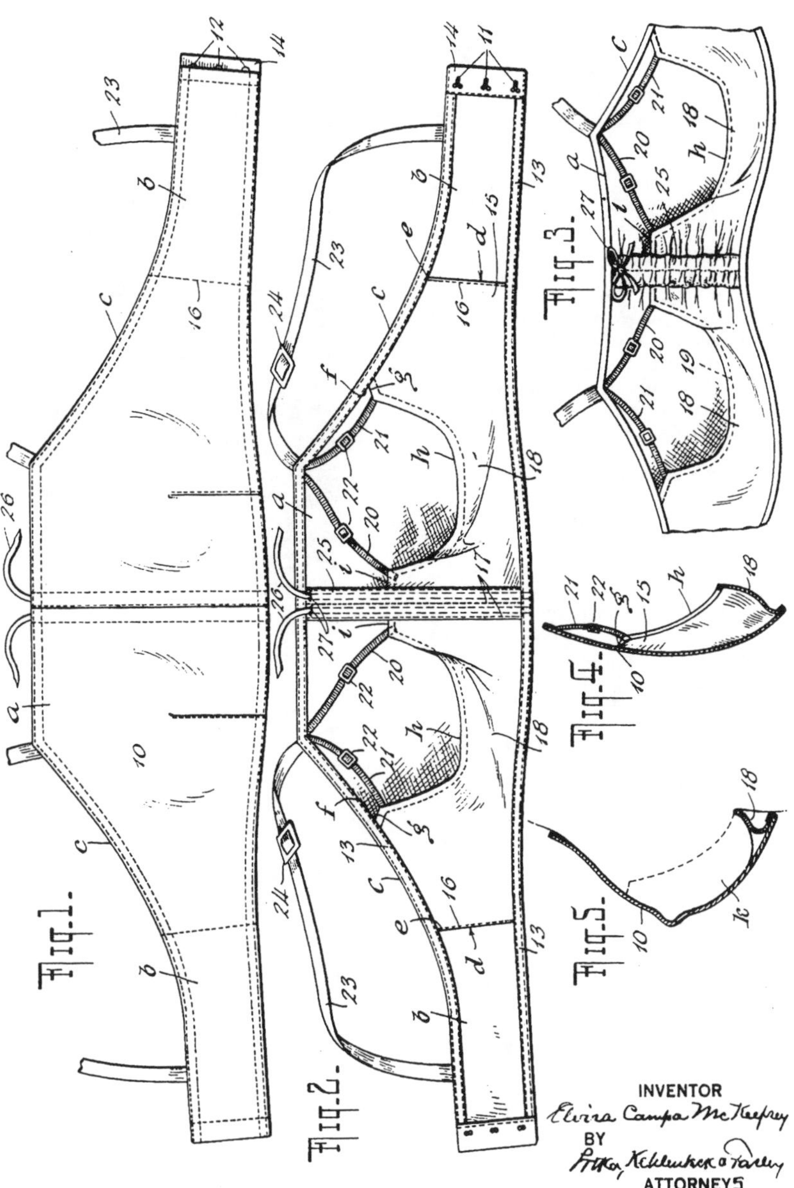

Figure 13. Illustration of an adjustable uplift brassiere patented by Elvira Campa McKeefrey, 29 June 1926.

Stylists Feature It! Doctors Recommend It!

The A.P.-UPLIFT
TRADE MARK
U.S. PATENT NO. 1702922

Is On the Crest of Popular Demand!

To overcome the evils of the flat-chest vogue, Mme. Poix, famous French designer, invented The A. P.-Uplift to relieve and correct constricted, painful, sagging busts. Physicians and maternity centers throughout the United States hailed it as THE reliever and re-moulder of unnaturally confined breasts, and *prescribed* The A.P.-Uplift to thousands of women suffering from tight, bandage-type brassieres.

And now fashion demands the feminine contour, which The A.P.Uplift *perfectly* and *instantly creates!* The thousands who found health and relief in this scientific garment are now augmented by a nation of style-conscious women who find The A.P.-Uplift the most perfect moulder of grace, charm and beauty.

Simple to adjust, dainty, painstakingly made in lovely fabrics, The A.P.-Uplift is being featured by leading stores throughout the country.

You, too, should share in the profits and turnover enjoyed during this crest of popular demand for The A.P.-Uplift.

The A.P.-Uplift is protected by U. S. Letters Patent No. 1702922.

Descriptive booklet gladly sent at your request.

Sizes 30 to 44 bust

No. 373—Pink Batiste (6 to box) per doz. $8.50
No. 284—Pink Tussah Silk . per doz. 12.00
No. 279—Pink Repp . . . . . . per doz. 12.00
No. 285—Pink Mesh . . . . . . per doz. 15.00
No. 276—Pink Double Net . per doz. 15.00
No. 356—Embroidered Net . per doz. 24.00
No. 280—Pink Silk Jersey . . per doz. 24.00
No. 275—Heavy Silk Jersey . per doz. 36.00

Extra Size Model 36 to 52 Bust

No. 279X—Pink Repp $15.00
No. 366P—Brocade and Mesh 21.00
No. 418P—Jersey and Satin 33.00

G. M. POIX, Inc.

99 - 103 MADISON AVE., NEW YORK

Also Manufacturers of

A. P. BRASSIERE DIRECTOIRE & "GIRLISH FORM" CONFINERS & COMBINATIONS

Boston Office—52 Chauncey St., Room 1008

Pacific Coast—D. A. J. Bacon, 833 Market St., San Francisco

Figure 14. Trade advertisement for Gabrielle Poix Yerkes's uplift brassiere, adaptable for nursing. *Corset and Underwear Review*, November 1929.

IN THE SOUTH –
MORE FORMALITY.
BERGDORF
GOODMAN
616 FIFTH AVE. NEW YORK
Above all, this season, gold... gold jewelry, gold gowns, glitter and brilliance. The wardrobe one takes south this season should be distinctly more elegant in feeling than ever before... a mode recognized by the Bergdorf-Goodman ateliers, in the evening gowns photographed here.
(Left) a gown of modernist feeling, in gold and beige metal cloth. (Right) a frock of very delicate gold lace, with smartly long waist and skirt back, over a flesh slip. Both perfect for northern wear now... and indispensable for formal occasions in the south later.

Figure 15. Fashion models in figure-skimming gowns of 1928, with curves evident. *Harper's Bazar*, January 1928.

breasts but not for convenient nursing. It had the conventional back fastening. The "A.P. Uplift" was accepted for advertising in the *American Journal of Nursing* and appeared with a credit line in the 1934 edition of Louise Zabriskie's *Nurse's Handbook of Obstetrics*.[59] Buoyed by the favorable publicity, the Poix company flourished well beyond the 1920s. The features and timing of the design constituted a marketing coup because of the dramatic changes under way in the 1920s in the education and care of pregnant and nursing women.

One pervasive worry of the late 1910s and 1920s was the survival and health of American mothers and their infants. To its shame, the United States ranked fourteenth among sixteen "leading countries" in rate of maternal deaths in pregnancy and labor. Between 1890 and 1913, there had been no real reduction in maternal mortality, even at a time when deaths from typhoid, diphtheria, and tuberculosis had declined sharply.[60] Forward-thinking physicians had been urging their colleagues to give prenatal care since the late 1800s, and by the mid-1910s a crusade to save babies and mothers was in full swing. Throughout the 1920s, scholarly articles and editorials on the techniques and benefits of prenatal care filled the medical and nursing literature. Periodicals for lay readers, such as *Good Housekeeping*, *Parents'*, and *Hygeia*, also carried articles by health professionals on the need for medical supervision during pregnancy and for postnatal attention to both mother and baby. The Sheppard-Towner Maternity and Infancy Act provided the states with matching federal funds for offering classes on prenatal hygiene.[61] Breast care was part of the curriculum, an especially crucial part because of the realization of the health benefits conferred on the infant by mother's milk.[62] For most women, the wearing of brassieres played a role in breast care and comfort.

Medical advice about care of the breasts continued to change in the 1920s. More and more physicians and nurses advocated gentle washing and application of sterile lubricants as safer and more likely to prevent cracking and soreness than had the outmoded abrasives or the oversoftening effects of cocoa butter or lanolin. Cracks or "fissures" of the nipples caused women severe pain and could lead to infection. No antibiotics were yet available to stem the problem once it started. The resulting mastitis or inflammation of the breast represented a serious complication, believed to lead to breast cancer in later life.

Professional attitudes toward brassieres were developing simultaneous with innovations in medical routines of breast care. Nurses Caroline Gray and Mary Alberta Baker mentioned brassieres as part of postnatal routines in their 1915 revision of a classic obstetric text.[63] Unlike nurses, physicians disagreed about the benefits of brassieres. Dr. Frances Sage Bradley, a strenuous opponent, wrote in the popular health magazine *Hygeia*, "Her doctor will undoubtedly condemn the deadly brassiere, responsible perhaps more than any other one thing for the scanty milk supply of the modern woman. . . . After all, the brassiere is only a flapper fad to secure a boyish form. The girl does not realize that it may cost her a bottle-fed baby."[64]

Bradley fulminated against brassieres just as uplift styles were gaining popularity, but she had little opportunity to keep up with changing fashions, working as she did among desperately poor women in rural Arkansas. Her association of flappers with flattening was refuted by the foundation buyers' evidence that as early as 1924, flappers were buying uplifts. Brassieres had medical proponents, too—doctors who merely cautioned against tight brassieres that pulled the breasts down against the chest wall.[65] Physicians such as Charles Harold Lewis specified discussing the suitable use of brassieres during the woman's first prenatal office visit.[66] Carolyn Conant Van Blarcom and Hazel Corbin, two nurse-leaders in prenatal education, approved of brassieres in their writings both for other nurses and for prospective mothers.[67] Indirectly, nurses and physicians were stimulating the businesses of companies producing uplift brassieres.

While Maiden Form, Model, and G. M. Poix were doing a lucrative trade with their varied uplift styles, other established companies thrived in their particular niches. Although not in high demand in coastal markets, Nature's Rival brassieres commanded a steady midwestern following. Communications and shipping were still relatively slow in the 1920s, allowing this regional manufacturer to flourish. A buyer for a Chicago department store commented to the J. Walter Thompson interviewer: "The owner (of Nature's Rival) is well-known, and orders are filled almost instantaneously. Kops [Brothers], like all Eastern houses, are harder to reach."[68] Chicago buyers could obtain merchandise with comparative ease and could replenish stock as needed during a selling season. Maintaining a full assortment of styles and sizes counted heavily with merchants in the competitive atmosphere of the late 1920s.

Kabo Corset Company, another Chicago-based firm, appealed to fairly conservative women and continued to be carried by brand name in mass merchants' catalogs. In the early 1920s, Kabo trademarked one of its styles with the double entendre "Flatter U."[69] By 1929, however, its line included many uplift, cupped styles, including bandeaux and a long-line brassiere. Most forward-looking of Kabo's products at the end of the decade was a bandeau of celanese acetate—a modified fiber, similar to but newer than rayon. Even the cut of this style was advanced, with cups showing arched tops, which would typify the 1930s.

Some manufacturers chose to feature corselettes in their lines. In fact, corselettes commanded a major portion of foundation business in the 1920s and early 1930s. Benjamin and Johnes showed Bien Jolie corselettes continuously from 1924 to 1929. Only one advertisement, from 1929, depicted a bandeau and low-topped girdle.[70] Bien Jolie advertisements offered very little specific detail, aiming mostly for an upper-class image, overlaid with cautious acceptance of new fashions. Bien Jolie's styling tended to only slightly contoured cups, even as some of its competitors were beginning to feature deeper curves. By 1929, Alfred Benjamin had died and Charles Johnes was contemplating retirement. In early 1930, executives formerly associated with Nature's Rival, notably Samuel Yaffe, bought Bien Jolie and reinvigorated the company, which then outlasted Nature's Rival by two decades.

Lily of France, another company dedicated to corselettes, offered a "cup bust and slim hips" in its Duo-Settes. The owners of Lily of France also produced the corselettes of the Mme. Irene Company, emphasizing unstinting quality in both brands. Mme. Irene vanished from fashion magazines in 1930, but the brand continued to be produced, according to advertisements in the trade press.[71] Lily of France presented low-backed corselettes in the late 1920s to accommodate evening gowns that began to show plunging backs instead of front décolletage. When small breasts were "in," it was no thrill to have them peeking out of a neckline.

Niche producers provided brassieres for customers who were worried about their figures. Rubber brassieres as well as girdles and other "reducing" garments continued to populate advertising in fashion magazines. Jeanne Walter's brand remained quite salable, with her core product virtually unchanged from its early twentieth-century form. This "Fifth Avenue" company accommodated new styles by adding to its line instead of retooling existing garments.[72] Its corselette, called a "Reducing Corsage," and a shorter bandeau model appeared in 1929 advertising.[73]

Treo competed with Walter, showing a variation on the "reducing" theme in its "paraknit" brassiere. This brassiere was alleged to have superior elasticity, presumably obtained by combining Para rubber with other fibers. As early as 1919, Treo was sold by brand name in the Sears, Roebuck catalog. The early style was made of strips of webbing, crossed to produce cups. By 1920, Treo had developed an openwork elastic material, combined with an inelastic lower band.[74] Subsequent styles showed a wedge of rigid material separating the shallow cups formed by the paraknit. Responding to fickle fashion, Treo had produced a "finesse" line by 1928, showing corselettes of "patented fabrics of varied tension" to give contour with "no hooks, no bones, no attachments."

Some brassiere companies came to grief in the late 1920s. The casualties of changing styles and business trends included one flash-in-the-pan firm and an old, established manufacturer. Boyshform entered business in about 1918 to provide shaping for the hollow-chested, tubular silhouette that had just begun to be popular.[75] Boyshform claimed optimistically that its utterly flat bandeaux would hold the bust in position without "pressure or pinching."[76] With a name—and perhaps design vision—that was so limited, Boyshform quickly lost sales to rival companies that made uplift styles. An unsuccessful foray into manufacture of rubber brassieres added to the company's woes. Boyshform was forced into reorganization in August 1925 and had declared bankruptcy by 1928. The owner, Walter Pruzan, moved into finance but met with reverses during the 1929 crash. He committed suicide in 1932.[77]

Although it did not collapse, the Charles R. DeBevoise Company experienced a gradual contraction of its business in the late 1920s. In about 1922, DeBevoise began to switch from exclusively live-model advertisements to sketches that emphasized French fashions. In 1924 and 1925, according to the J. Walter Thompson survey, DeBevoise appeared to be doing very well in eastern cities, along with Model and Bien Jolie. Yet there were hints that the company was floundering. In 1925, the firm ceased its two-decade practice of printing an anglicized pronunciation "Debb-e-voice" at the bottom of the advertising copy. Seemingly, they were attempting to capture a potential "French connection" that they had left untapped when beginning business in 1904.[78]

More damaging than failure to play up their French antecedents, in all likelihood, was DeBevoise's strategy of offering styles for too many types of customer—from larger women to "girlish figures." Advertisements alluded to three hundred designs, though some of these may have differed only in minor details.[79] A lack of defined customer and a well-edited group of products may have cost DeBevoise retail accounts in the new milieu of price lining and model stocks. Perhaps, too, the lack of continuing innovation, including patentable designs, caused DeBevoise's sales to flag, especially as the economy faltered in late 1929. Its consumer advertisements disappeared from *Vogue* and *Harper's Bazar* after 1927, but continued until 1932 in the less fashion-conscious *Good Housekeeping*. DeBevoise's commercial advertising, emphasizing "merchandise tie-ups" with other apparel, did not return DeBevoise to its formerly eminent place in the industry.[80] After 1932 DeBevoise advertisements disappeared from fashion magazines, but continued in *Corset and Underwear Review* and the *Dry Goods Merchant Trade Journal* through March 1933. The firm appears to have ceased all advertising in April 1933, but it shows up in city directories into 1935.[81]

Kops Brothers could easily have become a similar casualty of economic uncertainty and changing taste.[82] Despite Waldemar and Daniel Kops's zeal in patenting—with twenty-nine patents awarded to them between 1918 and 1929—the company's brassieres, Nemo Circlets, had a stodgy image. Perhaps the brothers recognized their stagnating business or the limitations of an older clientele and took action. Founded in 1894, Kops formally incorporated under New York law only on March 21, 1924.[83] Simultaneously, the owners switched their advertising account to J. Walter Thompson, a long-established, innovative company known for its market research. In the hope of reversing a downward trend in the volume of their business in retail stores, Kops Brothers commissioned JWT to gather data on corset and brassiere sales in several cities in the United States.[84]

In a concise history of the Kops account, a JWT staff member recounted their findings: "The new demand was for combinations, sheer bandeaux and circlets. The corset industry was becoming more and more like the underwear industry. . . . We have convinced the manufacturer [Kops] that women nowadays do not care so much about the workmanship of reinforced eyelets and extra boning, as they do about the finished appearance of the garment."[85]

JWT advised Kops to stop making heavily boned corsets and brassieres and retool its plants to produce rubber corsets and lightweight brassieres of up-to-date cuts in lace and sheer materials. Their brand name Nemolastic was streamlined to Nemo-flex, and even the advertising was revamped to a jazzier format, with gratifying results. The account history reported that "from just the September and October (1925) advertising, 2,000 letters were received from consumers, many of them asking to buy a certain style direct from the manufacturer."[86] By 1927, Kops Brothers was marketing its own uplift style, with cups fitted with darts and a band beneath the breast.[87] The definite arch shape of the cups represented a fashion-forward trend. By following the market demands, Kops Brothers escaped the fate of Boyshform and thrived into the late 1960s.

The prominent firms profiled here by no means represent the full extent of brassiere production. According to the 1921 edition of *Trademarks, Labels, Prints to the Textile Industry*, thirty-nine companies manufactured brassieres in the United States under sixty-six brand names.[88] Geographic spread characterized the industry, with sixteen firms in New York City, two in Brooklyn; six in Newark, five in Chicago, and single firms in Detroit and Jackson, Michigan; Boston and Worcester, Massachusetts; Bridgeport, Connecticut; Portland, Maine; Cincinnati; Washington; Philadelphia and Meadville, Pennsylvania. Several midwestern firms combined forces in the "Associated Apparel Industries," which included several companies in Chicago and one in Kalamazoo, Michigan.

Census figures reported for 1929 reveal a concentration of production in New York, Illinois, New Jersey, Michigan, Massachusetts, and Connecticut. Smaller output occurred in Georgia, Indiana, Pennsylvania, and Wisconsin.[89] Except for the addition of Georgia and Indiana and the omission of Maine, sites of production changed little during the 1920s. New York and New Jersey continued to be the East Coast's largest centers, while Chicago served the Midwest. Important individual firms, such as Warner in Connecticut, kept those states on the map as brassiere producers. Georgia served the South, with Atlanta as leader.

From the consumer side of the equation, the geography of sales was shifting. Shopping centers in city and suburb began to turn a chore into a form of recreation. The Oak Park, Illinois, shopping center, first in the United States, opened in 1916.[90] Country Club Plaza in Kansas City followed in 1922. Department stores began to open "branches" miles from town centers, beginning with the National Department Store in St. Louis in 1922.[91] New access stimulated demand. Between 1917 and 1927, sales rose 425 percent in clothing stores.[92] In these circumstances, brassiere producers had to continually improve what they produced and market it effectively to stores that reached the largest number of potential customers.

Increasingly, brassiere sales depended as much on promotion as on effective design and manufacturing. Women were faced with many choices of brand and styling, and manufacturers had to advertise in an up-to-date manner to survive. The techniques of advertising were becoming more sophisticated, with human-interest appeals and a clear presentation of one main "reason why," an attempt to introduce the reader to the finer points of a particular brand. Manufacturers provided retailers with print-ready newspaper advertisements, placards and body-forms for counter displays, and layouts for eye-catching presentations in store windows. Further locations for advertising followed in the 1930s.[93]

Among the advertising appeals used between 1918 and 1929 were reduction of body bulk and arrest of aging. "Diaphragm control," essentially a suppression of midriff bulges, represented a major code phrase in advertisements by G. M. Poix and Warner. Fleshiness in the back was also confined by high cut and boning. No ripple of flab was allowed to break the plumbline-straight fall of the dress. Poorly fitted foundations that wrinkled or sagged were alleged to "add years to your figure."[94]

Fashion reached into the formerly neglected category of underwear. Treo dubbed its "finesse" line of corselettes "under-fashions," a term used by lingerie firms into the late twentieth century.[95] Such companies as DeBevoise stressed that their products would help the wearer look elegant in any style of dress designers might concoct.

Along with innovation in production and marketing of brassieres, came equally newsworthy achievements by inventive designers. Almost two hundred patents for brassieres and corselettes were awarded between 1918 and

1929. Some patented styles were too far "ahead of the curve" for commercial acceptance in their own time, but hinted at brassiere trends of the future. Underwires of a modern type were devised by Lewis Fritz in 1923, and straps adjustable by a square metal "ring" appeared in a patent filed by Mary Bollwine in 1928 but not awarded until 1930.[96] Several strapless brassieres and one bust augmenting style represented the efforts of creative designers.[97]

Teresina Maria Negri, resident of Paris, won a U.S. patent in 1924 for a "bust support" that "is made to measure and forces the breasts to fit respectively into the two pockets which it forms without the assistance of any whale bone or any strengthening band."[98] This remarkable design had contouring seams similar to those of 1960s bras. Radical design put it beyond the range of popular taste, and the implied custom sizing would have been too costly to attract a manufacturer in the United States. If Negri's prototype was ever produced in France, the maker appears not to have exported it to North America.

Of greater social significance was a patent secured in 1918—for a "surgical bust substitute" to wear with their regular brassiere by postmastectomy patients. This was devised by Canadian nurse Laura Ethel Mailleue (Figure 16). *Trained Nurse and Hospital Review* reported Mailleue's invention with approbation in 1919.[99] Whether or not this first prosthesis for mastectomy patients was fully effective, it signaled a nurse's desire to help women cope with the physical changes and psychological discomfort resulting from the amputation of a breast.[100] From the 1950s onward, the U.S. Patent Office recognized various designs of brassieres for women who had breast-removal surgery.

Despite the dominance of commercially produced brassieres, women could still sew their bandeaux at home or order them from a custom dressmaker. More than a few women exercised this option, to judge from the many "dressmaker" bandeaux that have survived in museum collections. Created from silk crepe or satin, sheer cotton, net, figure weaves, and lace, some of these brassieres revealed exquisite detailing that gave credibility to curators' speculations that these were made in France.[101] Others combined fine finish with amateurish design and may have been one-off models made by some "little dressmaker" to coordinate with a particular dress. One unique peach-colored crocheted brassiere featured shallow cups with considerable stretch. Made of a composite yarn, it anticipated the commercially produced knitted brassieres of the 1930s.[102]

Custom or homemade types of brassiere persisted through the 1930s, based on patterns offered by *Vogue*, *The Delineator*, and various American pattern companies. By the late 1930s, wiring and other complex components gave manufacturers a decided edge over custom sewers. Even home economists began to endorse the purchase of ready-made brassieres.[103] Indeed, the

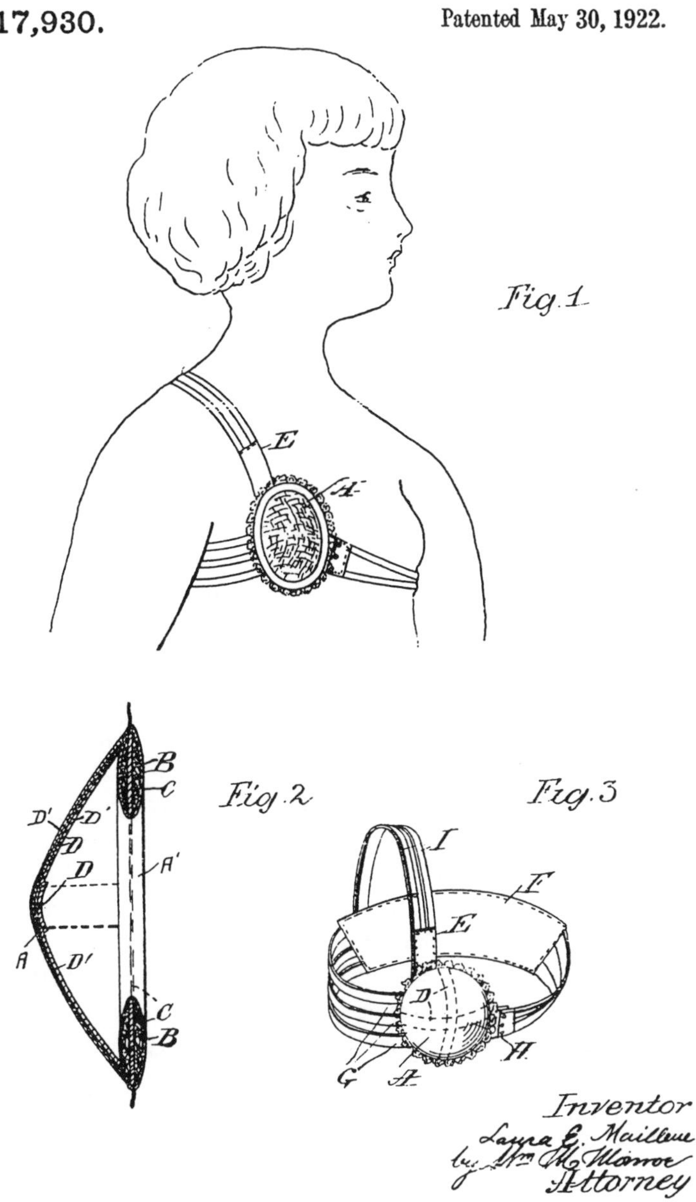

Figure 16. Earliest patented postmastectomy bust substitute. Patented by Laura E. Mailleue.

time was fast approaching when a more heavily "engineered" type of brassiere would require industrial machines and techniques.

Increasing complexity of cut pointed (almost literally) toward the future of brassieres. So did the burgeoning manufacturers of the West Coast. The firm of Hollywood-Maxwell seems to have led the California incursion into the national market in about 1929. In 1925 Madame DesLauriers opened the Lov-é Brassiere Company in Hollywood, where she supplied brassieres to larger, hard-to-fit women. Lov-é prospered in its region and by the 1930s commenced advertising in the national trade press. Reneé of Hollywood began to make a range of women's lingerie in 1921; by 1933, the entire business was devoted to brassieres.

The city of Hollywood was already the heart of the movie industry and was beginning to catch the nation's imagination as a center of beauty, sexiness, and glamour. Film stars such as Theda Bara, Mary Pickford, Lillian Gish, Greta Garbo, and Gloria Swanson enjoyed the adulation of fans.[104] They had many opportunities to put their stamp on new styles of clothing because they were seen by such large audiences. Weekly attendance at films reached 115 million by 1930.[105] Fan magazines such as *Movie Star News* and the entertainment newspaper *Variety* gave movie and theater devotees a chance to look closely at what their favorites were wearing. Oddly enough, brassiere advertisements rarely made reference to film stars as trendsetters, although Gossard had featured unnamed film stars in its advertisements from August 1916 until 1918.[106] Only in the 1930s did companies begin to associate their brassieres with the erotic appeal of the movie star.

Between 1919 and the 1929 stock market crash, the brassiere began to evolve toward its present-day form. Most evident was the establishment of cups, with fixed or adjustable contours, as a standard component of brassiere design. Practical nursing brassieres came on the market. A few brassiere manufacturers began to work with rayon or silk tricot, which provided softness, smoothness, and flexibility. Brassieres of the late 1910s and 1920s were made to be inconspicuous under sheer or revealing apparel, by use of flesh-toned materials and narrow straps.[107] Strapless and virtually backless models were sold at various times. Old-style fasteners had begun to be replaced by hook and eye tapes, like those found on present-day brassieres.[108]

Yet in 1929, many desirable aspects of brassiere design remained to be accomplished. Cups were not yet sized, and straps could not easily be adjusted in length. The delicate brassiere fabrics of the 1920s, such as crepe de chine, could not have withstood frequent machine laundering. Snagging and running bedeviled silk and rayon brassieres. Laundry products were harsh and would have induced fading and loss of garment shape. In an age when the washing machine was not an established household appliance, white brassieres were hard to maintain, leading to the popularity of peach and tea rose colors.

By the mid-1920s, women of middle and upper income seem to have been wearing brassieres quite regularly, to judge from the reports of buyers elicited by J. Walter Thompson Company. Young women appeared highly enthusiastic about this garment. Indeed, they were the most avid consumers of new styles. The brassiere offered women a freer, more comfortable way of dressing, one which harmonized with their busy lives. Whether they would abandon the brassiere as an expendable luxury in the hardscrabble years of the Great Depression remained to be seen.

4 Brassieres Rise, Stocks Fall

"Business Is Wonderful, and Going to Be Better," gushed the editor in a headline in the December 1929 *Corset and Underwear Review*. These sentiments seem absurd in retrospect, because the Great Depression took hold in 1930. Despite widespread deprivation and business failures in the 1930s, retailing held up remarkably well, and the number of transactions in retail stores fell only by about 15 percent.[1] Throughout the Depression, retail departments that sold "foundations"—girdles, brassieres, and combination corselettes—proved to be highly resilient, even buoyant. A March 1930 editorial detailed the situation: "Retail sales in department stores in the various Federal Reserve Districts of the country declined two per cent in January 1930, as compared with January, 1929. Yet in this month sales in the corset departments were more than twenty per cent ahead of January, 1929."[2]

Many foundation departments expanded, moved to more prominent locations in their respective stores, and received facelifts that created an atmosphere of elegance and comfort. Stores in various cities devoted what must have been scarce funds to these departmental makeovers. In the November 1932 issue of *Corset and Underwear Review* alone, Arnold Constable and Sterns (New York), John Wanamaker (Philadelphia), the May Company (Cleveland), Joslyn's (Denver), and The Fair (Chicago) all reported revamping and enlarging their corset and brassiere departments. The money was well spent. According to *Women's Wear Daily*, the major apparel trade paper, in summer 1937, the "corset section in the average department store contribute[d] 6 per cent of the total store net profit."[3] Corset departments regularly excelled in profitability. Manufacturers of brassieres and other foundations did not immediately share in the prosperity of the retailers.[4] However, once producers began to adopt improved business methods, they reaped a portion of the consumer dollars being spent on undergarments.

Credit for keeping foundation retailers afloat amid the wreckage of other businesses goes mostly to shifts in the shape of women's fashionable clothes and ideal body type, made practicable by new fiber technology. The trends in dress styles that had been launched in 1926–29 accelerated in the 1930s. What began as a gentle suggestion of the feminine figure became a tightly defined silhouette (Figure 17). Waistlines reappeared, after almost a decade in hiding. By the mid-1930s belted, sashed, and otherwise nipped-in waists were typical in dresses for day wear as well as for evening.

Breasts gradually arose where flatness had prevailed. The round contour of 1930 was succeeded in 1932 by pointed breasts, a shape referred to as the Belle Poitrine. *Corset and Underwear Review* credited "Western buyers" and unnamed "Hollywood stars" with early promotion of this pointy look, but the trend soon spread beyond America's movie capital.[5] Buyers for foundation departments from around the United States made semiannual treks to New York and San Francisco to attend showings by brassiere and corset manufacturers. This helped to disseminate the latest styles, including the Belle Poitrine. Cone-shaped breasts predominated as the ideal for adult women from 1935 into the early 1940s, when an aggressive breast profile, later dubbed the torpedo, was in vogue. Some college women scorned the Belle Poitrine and by 1935 opted for more sinuous contours, perhaps because gentle curves harmonized well with their standard classroom outfit of sweater-plus-skirt.[6] As early as the 1920s collegiate women wore pullover sweaters and sport skirts to classes, but the trend became firmly entrenched by the 1930s. In 1929, saleswomen in foundation departments were coaxing young shoppers to buy brassieres by comparing their silhouettes in sweaters with and without uplift.[7] Older adult women wore sweaters, too, and also dressier equivalents—the knitted suits and two-piece dresses that became a staple of city day wear. Even golf ensembles sometimes featured sweater-skirt sets.[8]

Skirt lengths began the 1930s about six inches above the ankle, but rose a few inches by 1935 and crept up to just below the knee by 1939. Slim skirts prevailed through 1935, after which fullness slowly increased, in the form of flare, pleats, and gathers. Back emphasis in skirts enjoyed fitful popularity between 1936 and 1939; fullness was concentrated in the center back, with flounces and other projections evoking the bustles of the late 1800s in a softer form. Even a bouffant, petticoat-supported style made a brief appearance in 1939–42, before wartime shortages and restrictions put it on hold for almost four years. In evening wear, back emphasis of another sort was hugely popular among the fashionable elite: a plunging décolletage that flirted with the callipygian cleft (Figure 18).[9] The bodices of some gowns managed an almost backless effect and a few designs accomplished the tricky feat of low front *and* back.[10] Occasional evening dresses were totally strapless, although these seldom displayed

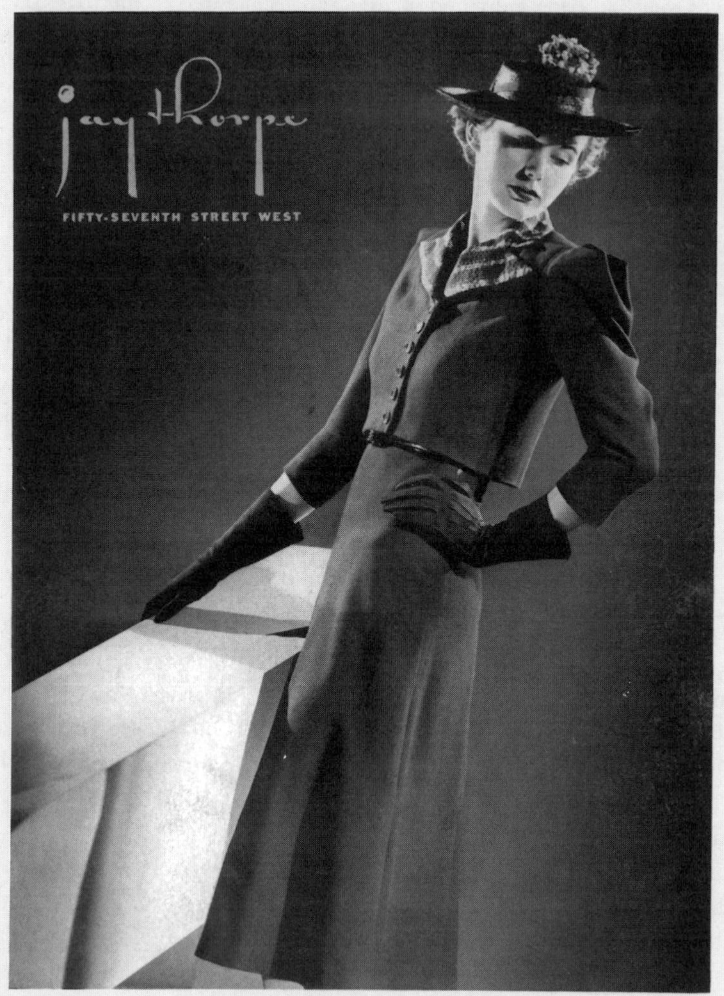

MARCH 15, 1937
jay thorpe
FIFTY-SEVENTH STREET WEST
TO BE YOUNG IN A SPRING WORLD WEAR THIS BOLERO SUIT-FROCK
WITH BODICE AND REVERS OF FLOWER-STRIPED PRINT . . 65.00.
THE HAT BAR ADDS A GAY SAILOR WITH MATCHING POSIES . . 20.00.

Figure 17. Fashion model in fitted bolero-suit with tucked shoulder emphasis and definitely fitted waist. *Harper's Bazaar*, March 15, 1937.

Figure 18. Fashion model in backless evening gown 1934. Edward Steichen/© *Vogue* Condé Nast Publications, Inc.

the depth of cleavage seen in models with straps or a halter. Bias cuts, created with nearly miraculous skill by such French couturieres as Madeleine Vionnet and Alix, fostered the trend toward clinginess in formal wear and in some daytime frocks.[11]

The most pervasive and enduring fashion trend of the 1930s, however, was emphasis on the upper torso. Collars, shoulder flanges, cowl drapery, intricate pleating, gathering, or tucking all made the bodice the centerpiece of the costume. From time to time from 1932 through the end of the decade, shoulders jutted outward and sleeves ballooned. Not since the 1890s had the chic woman's bodice shape been so imposing.

Elite fashion continued to look to Paris, notably the ateliers of Coco Chanel, Elsa Schiaparelli, Madeleine Vionnet, Mainbocher, and Jeanne Lanvin. Those who could not afford Parisian models took their fashion cues from the costumes in lavish movies, which were still affordable entertainment. Some of the most characteristic fashions of the thirties reflected the personal style of Hollywood stars such as Greta Garbo, Jean Harlow, Marlene Dietrich, Joan Crawford, and Ginger Rogers. Militaristic details like epaulets and officer-style hats cropped up in the mid-1930s as European tensions built. Fashions with ties to South and Central America emerged in the late 1930s and intensified during the early 1940s, when these nations counted among those "friendly" to the Allied cause. Carmen Miranda's turbans and bare-midriff tops typified the look, but intense colors also paid tribute to south-of-the-border style.

Figure-revealing clothing required complementary styles of foundations. *Vogue* warned readers: "Your can't bluff much about your figure under the merciless clothes of to-day [but] something very definite can be done in the way of local assistance by the new inexpensive girdles and brassieres."[12] Women had to update their brassiere, girdle, and corselette wardrobes every two to three years, even if that meant skimping on the amount spent on their dresses or suits. Dr. H. Paul Nystrom, professor of marketing at Columbia University and an acute observer of apparel trends, admonished retailers:

> Most customers have less buying power than formerly. . . . Women are shopping, not for fun but for values now-a-days. . . . Customers are harder to please . . . [but] more than ever, they are interested in fashion. . . . In spite of the declines in purchasing power, there has been no decline at all in the interest in the fashionableness of goods. . . . Many consumers have been forced to buy cheaper and cheaper goods, but they apparently expect more style in these new goods than in the old.[13]

Relentless advertising had awakened women to the style potential of brassieres, and they were becoming increasingly selective about which models they would buy. Furthermore, the pool of customers for foundations was expanding. Young women whose only underwear had been a garter belt and panties began to experiment with bandeaux and girdles. Girls of fourteen to nineteen years of age spurned the old-fashioned heavily boned corsets, but eagerly accepted the new under-fashions made possible by a fortuitous development in fiber technology.

In October 1931, Lastex came on the market, and foundation manufacturers seized it like a life preserver. Percy Adamson had proposed the concept of Lastex to the New York-based U.S. Rubber Company, and when the idea came to fruition, he set up Adamson Brothers to distribute it.[14] This innovative material consisted of an extruded latex core filament, wrapped in double layers of cotton, rayon, or silk. In contrast to natural rubber, Lastex offered light weight, resiliency, improved washability, and durability. Unlike Latex, rubber split easily when sewn on an industrial machine, causing manufacturers headaches. The new yarns adapted well to being knitted and woven into fabrics for girdles and brassieres. Two-way stretch was born. A further bonus was Lastex's improved stability over natural rubber, which degraded in products within a few months. The layers of fiber over the core improved resistance to perspiration. However, girdles and corselettes of Lastex wore out more quickly than earlier ironsided corsets of coutil and featherbone. This stimulated replacement sales and enhanced the profitability of Lastex products.

At first this new material primarily affected the production of girdles and corselettes, but it also provided improved back fastenings for brassieres. Warner's A'lure brassiere line, introduced in 1933, consisted of pieced sections of Lastex.[15] Porosity and relatively light weight made Lastex a better choice than rubber for summer brassieres.[16] Responding eagerly to the new designs and fabrics, "juniors," the composite group that included teenagers and young adults, led an upsurge in sales of foundation garments. *Women's Wear Daily* went so far as to claim: "Lastex wiped out the depression for the foundation garment industry by raising the unit price with increased profits for manufacturer and retailer."[17]

Of course this was an exaggeration, but clearly Lastex blunted the effects of the Depression for some manufacturers and many retailers. In *Corset and Underwear Review*'s December 1929 "State Street" column, which reported trends among Chicago retailers, a buyer was quoted thus: "Our business in the corset department has increased fifty per cent, and this added business can be credited in a very large degree to the young girls." Youthful customers at Charles Stevens and Brothers in Chicago requested elastic or soft satin girdles, sometimes accompanied by matching brassieres. Merchants quickly discovered that young women purchased foundations more frequently, which made up for their preference for less expensive individual undergarments.

In a climate of widespread consumer acceptance, most brassiere producers managed to survive and even prosper. Evidence in *Corset and Underwear Review*, various fashion magazines, and patent records suggest several routes that led to success—mainly centered on service and product.

Retailers were also avid to gain and hold clientele, especially through service. As Frances Donovan explained, in her study of saleswomen and their milieu, "Customers can get what they want in any store; the service is then the determining factor that makes them choose a certain store and return to it again and again."[18]

Service in the foundations department depended heavily on fitters, who might also be saleswomen or might specialize in fitting in large and elite stores. Although corsets were routinely fitted before 1930, store personnel began to fit brassieres in the 1930s, as styles proliferated and customers became more exacting.[19] A customer would approach the counter in a foundations department and explain what type of brassiere or corset she was seeking. She would be escorted to a private fitting room, where she would be measured and shown various styles that might meet her requirements. Those styles were not chosen at random. Saleswomen-fitters were trained by departmental managers or manufacturers' representatives to analyze women's figures and steer them toward the most appropriate and satisfactory brassieres and corsets. Women who qualified as fitters had to pin out any excess length or width in the chosen corselette or brassiere until a comfortable fit was achieved. She might also sew the alterations or might give it to another staff member to finish.[20] The result came close to a made-to-measure garment. A woman recalled observing her grandmother being fitted for a brassiere in the 1930s by a professionally dressed and well-coiffed fitter—obviously someone of respected status in the store.

Alliances between producers and retailers could be especially effective in training fitters. They shared the costs of training and the resulting profits. Gossard reported that 150 "graduates" completed its five-day course in fitting; diplomas and postgraduate seals were awarded following a written examination.[21] Camp and Company conducted training sessions to teach fitters how to analyze the needs of maternity and surgical clients and to suggest the most beneficial designs—from the Camp line, of course. Camp retained the services of Dr. Rhoda Grace Hendrick as consultant in the design of their braces, corsets, and brassieres. Actual training in anatomy was important for surgical fitters. They needed to be able to interpret the physician's prescription while ensuring support to the client. Sears, Roebuck and J. C. Penney sponsored traveling trainers. These missionaries of fit made as many as two hundred trips per year around the country. Following a sales meeting, fitting demonstrations were open to the public; up to two hundred women customers attended these meetings and fully 25 percent made purchases. Leading Lady awarded certificates to those who successfully completed their course in fitting. Department stores and some specialty shops installed one or more fitting rooms to give privacy to the shopper and her fitter. Catalog companies, including Sears, Roebuck, printed directions for self-measurement to help the woman ordering by mail to achieve a satisfactory fit. One 1932 Sears advertisement showed MGM actress Maureen O'Sullivan in a proud-bosomed pose, announcing her 34–28–37 measurements and urging Sears customers to "Be sure to measure" before ordering any foundation garment.[22]

Stores clearly had the bottom line in view in employing fitters. Returned merchandise and adjustments on sales amounted to 12 percent of gross sales in U.S. department stores in the mid-1930s. Fitters minimized returns by ensuring that the customer had a comfortable corselette, corset, or brassiere before she left the store.[23] They clearly earned their pay.

In an effort to woo faithful patrons, corset department saleswomen went beyond technical know-how and made it their business to know customers' names and to keep files on each woman's preferences in foundations.[24] Recognizing the power of peer influence in sales, stores also tried to employ both young and older clerks and fitters who would be empathetic to their respective age-mates.[25]

At the business level, retailers were the customers of the manufacturers. Prompt deliveries to stores were the type of service these clients required. Manufacturers who went out of their way to keep retailers in stock showed healthy account books. Producers pleaded with retailers to cooperate with them in securing good service by placing orders early, so that they could be met at the start of a selling season. Manufacturers, leery of heavy inventories, were unwilling to make up goods ahead of orders. Vogue Brassiere Company offered forty-eight-hour delivery. Fay-Miss Brassiere Company, founded in 1927, bettered those terms with the promise of twenty-four-hour delivery to retailers.[26] Fay-Miss thrived and secured a lasting place in the world of uplift uder the name Bali.

Brassiere producers contended with coaxing accounts to place prompt orders and also struggled with new patterns of decision making in retail stores. Departmental buyers had once wielded unchallenged power, but by the 1930s they had to secure approval of their decisions from general merchandise managers. These men understood statistics, but were ignorant of merchandise and customers' preferences, according to a complaint in *Corset and Underwear Review*. They curbed reorders that would have allowed stores to keep fast-selling styles in stock.[27] Producers continued to deal with merchandise managers, and were advised to cultivate a positive relationship with them, in addition to wooing the buyer and the promotions personnel.[28] Lovable Brassiere Company's sales representatives courted Sears, Roebuck's merchandise manager Louis Pfeifle over several years, first in Chicago and then in New York, in order to win an account with the mighty mail-order house.[29]

Sound service at retail and wholesale levels meant little unless a company could offer new, alluring designs, using improvements in fibers, innovative components, and advanced methods of fabrication. Imagination could transform the nature of a business. Creative designers provided some companies with an "ace in the hole," as exemplified by Ruth Kapinas at Munsingwear, Ariel LeMay at Camp, Elvira Campa McKeefrey at Model, and Abraham and Victor Becker at Western Corset Company.[30] Other manufacturers thrived on one compelling innovation. Hollywood-Maxwell introduced Whirlpool stitching in 1934 (Figure 19). This much-imitated technique of stabilizing the shape of cups was patented in 1935 by a former dentist and founder of Hollywood-Maxwell, Joseph R. Bowen.[31] Concentric rings of stitches became a staple of brassiere design through the 1950s.

Although some retailers and manufacturers were doing well, the economy as a whole was in dire straits. President Herbert Hoover had tried in vain to turn the economy around. In 1932 Americans elected Franklin D. Roosevelt in the hope that he would be more successful. The Great Depression was at its worst, and the new president attacked it on several fronts with his New Deal policies. Key to these efforts were two acts, one setting up the Agricultural Adjustment Administration to rescue the depressed farm economy and the National Industrial Recovery Administration (NRA) to stimulate industrial activity while keeping the volume of output in line with consumption.[32] Initiatives were made specific to particular industries.

Part of the National Recovery Act was an executive order for fair competition in the brassiere and corset industry issued on August 14, 1933, making 1934 the "Year of the Blue Eagle," named after the emblem of the NRA. The stated purpose of the order was to increase employment. It introduced the thirty-five- to forty-hour work week, along with a minimum age of employment (sixteen), minimum wages, and requirements for sanitary workplaces. Wages for this industry were fixed nationally at $14 per week, which translated into 35 cents per hour for forty hours. Prior to this act, manufacturers in the textile trades paid vastly different wages, depending on geographic area, ethnicity and gender of workers, and other variables. Under the NRA, every aspect of the apparel industry was regulated: advertising limits, delivery charges, discounts, rebates, labeling, display charges, pricing at wholesale and retail levels, packaging, and even piracy. In 1934, 2.5 million firms displayed the NRA eagle banner.[33]

With 557 NRA basic codes, plus 208 supplemental ones, the administrative system became unmanageable. While attempting to guarantee workers a wage with which they could maintain a family and home, the NRA failed to protect consumers, and prices rose sharply. The business community, which had originally urged passage of the National Industrial Recovery Act, began to oppose it and, in May 1935, the Supreme Court invalidated the system. Nonetheless, industries maintained shorter work weeks and greater numbers of employees.[34] The economy began to stabilize and then rebound perceptibly.

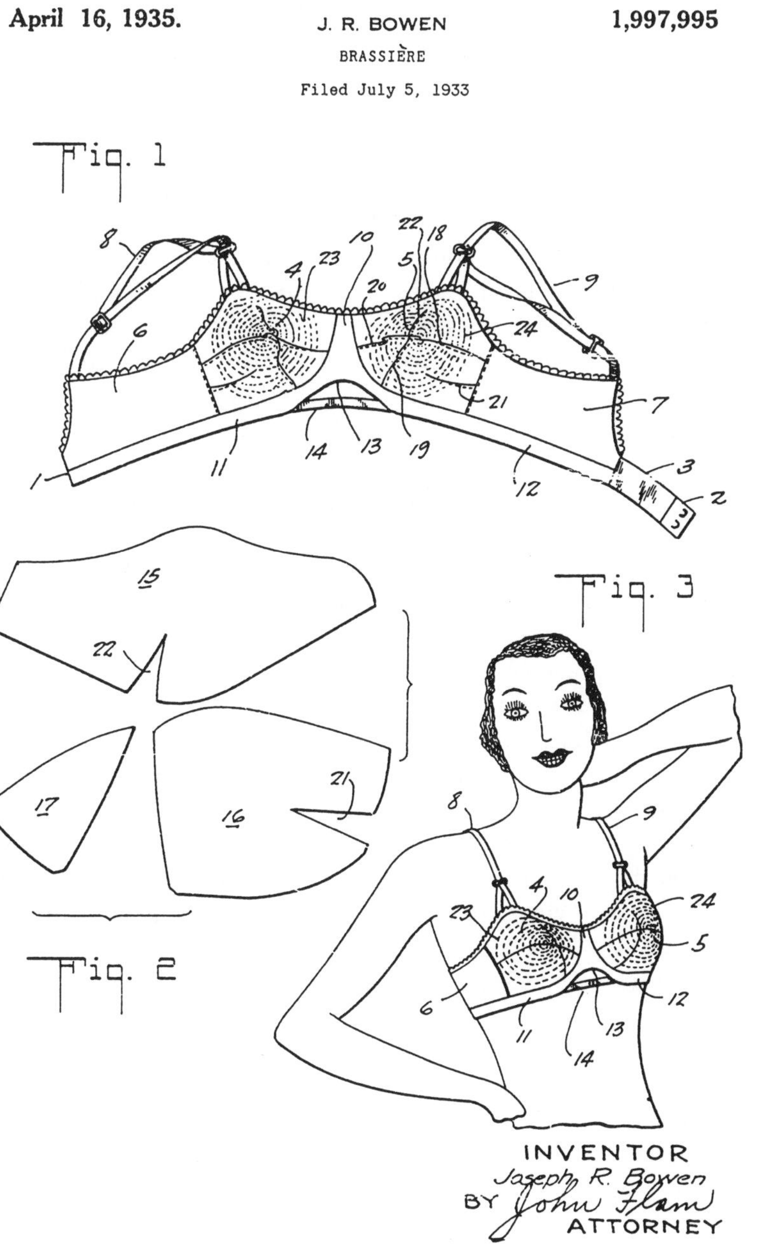

April 16, 1935. J. R. BOWEN 1,997,995

BRASSIÈRE

Filed July 5, 1933

Fig. 1

Fig. 2

Fig. 3

INVENTOR

Joseph R. Bowen

BY John Flam

ATTORNEY

Figure 19. Patent illustration of brassiere with Whirlpool stitching, designed by Joseph R. Bowen for Hollywood Maxwell.

Like government officials, industry leaders were trying to come to grips with the frightening new economic realities. Andrew J. Haire, editor of several apparel trade journals, lamented in his *Corset and Underwear Review*: "One of the paramount evils in the corset industry is that today we are all making too many styles and changing them too often, copying the best sellers of other manufacturers and trying to beat their values."[35]

In another editorial, Haire urged producers to manufacture foundation garments only in response to orders and to gear expenses and operating programs to the amount of merchandise that could be sold at a profit.[36] In other words, they could survive only if they improved profit on unit sales rather than striving for high volume sales. According to Haire, they needed to play up quality in their products, rather than trading on rock bottom prices.[37] These steps may seem painfully obvious, but they were news to some foundation companies. Some readers must have heeded Haire's advice and begun to embrace efficiency measures. To recover fiscal health, they followed the example of profitable retailers in cutting down product lines and instituting strict cost accounting for their businesses as a whole. Just as stores offered depth of size ranges in a smaller number of brands, manufacturers also began to focus on their most profitable styles and to drop all others. Manufacturers worked to particular "price points," meaning wholesale price levels. In the most efficient companies, fit and workmanship were held constant across all price levels; only the quality of fabrics and trims varied.[38]

Success rates from stricter business practices seem to have been quite high. Only a few brassiere companies disappeared, notably Jeanne Walter and Ovida. The emergence of Lastex killed the sale of rubber "reducing" garments, partly because the old-style rubber products could not readily be redesigned for the new uplift effects. Weight loss through diet and exercise also undermined the appeal of sweating off pounds. So perhaps did the odor that must have accompanied wearing such undergarments! DeBevoise flailed around, trying without success to market its brassieres to a broad spectrum of customers. The brassiere maker who claimed to have been first in the trade, beginning in 1904, ceased business in April 1933.

In the teeth of economic adversity, including a relapse into depression in 1937–38, several new brassiere companies emerged, cultivating customer bases that varied in age, income, taste, or special requirements.[39] Notable among them was Vanity Fair Silk Mills, which had started as a supplier of fabric to other underwear companies but began to make brassieres and panties of its own in 1934. Lightly structured knitted brassieres were Vanity Fair's specialty. Another future star in the brassiere firmament opened for business in 1927 under the coy name Fay-Miss Brassiere Company. The firm enjoyed such success with its Bali design that by 1941 the producer had adopted the name of the garment. Besides being exotic, the name Bali was an excellent advertising gimmick, suggesting the similarity between the silhouette produced by Bali brassieres and the "pear-shaped, moon-pointing breasts of a Balinese virgin."[40] This quip did not come from a Bali advertisement, but a 1939 magazine spread by Bali made the explicit claim that its products would help a woman to have the lovely breast profile of a woman of Bali. In the lower border of some ads, the discreetly vague figure of a topless Balinese charmer toted a basket of fruit on her head (see Figure 29).

Venus Corporation, New York, served nursing mothers with a closely defined product—a single style with only minor modifications. Venus's West Coast competitor, the Western Corset Company, was founded in late 1932 by Abraham Soundel Becker and Victor Becker. This team gave their firm a valuable edge by continually patenting improvements to their Beautee-Fit brand of maternity brassiere. Existing firms that had made corsets brought out brassiere lines between 1930 and 1941; one example was A. Stein and Company's "Perma-lift."

Women were influential in many of these businesses, but were often not the sole owners. Design was evenly divided between men and women. For every Gabrielle Poix, there was a William Rosenthal. Many companies were family held or in the hands of a small group of associates, such as the teams that managed Model Company, Maiden Form, and Lovable. Sometimes women discharged unexpected roles: Ida Rosenthal left the designing to her husband, William, while she managed the financial and promotional aspects of Maiden Form.

During the years of depression and war, the California brassiere manufacturers played up the Hollywood connection for all it was worth, and that was quite a bit. Movies kept their appeal as affordable entertainment in grim times.[41] Movie costumers such as Travis Banton and Howard Greer showed couture designs in the fashion press and all sorts of casual fashions were being reported as California Style. Hollywood-Maxwell, Mabs of Hollywood, Renée of Hollywood, Heléne of Hollywood, and Tre-Zur exploited American women's dreams of looking like film stars. Movie personalities populated advertisements for many types of consumer products because they were familiar to millions of fans. However, major brassiere makers did not feature individual movie stars. Hollywood-Maxwell claimed that its brassieres were "used exclusively in Paramount Pictures" but did not show a named actress in the accompanying picture.[42] Maureen O'Sullivan was not shown in her brassiere in the Sears advertisement and was not directly connected to the corselette represented. Moral codes for the film industry restricted undress on screen, and this enforced modesty may have made stars afraid to be photographed in their undergarments. In fact, an element of anonymity pervaded the models in brassiere advertising.

California was not the only up-and-coming area in the manufacture of brassieres. Until the 1920s, the South had not produced a national brand name in brassieres. This changed when the Atlanta-based Garson Company started in business, at first making wash dresses that it sold door-to-door. Its customers asked for undergarments, so in 1926 Garson produced a brassiere called "The Flapperette." By 1928, Garson was specializing in the manufacture of brassieres for sale to retailers under the brand name Beauti-Form. Challenged by another holder of that trade name, the fledgling company trademarked the name Lovable in 1931 and concentrated on producing brassieres for "price-conscious" customers. One of Garson's early contracts was with the Lerner Stores chain, to which they later added Macy's and Sears, Roebuck. These mass merchants sold a variety of Lovable styles, many of which retailed for substantially less than $1.

When the NRA was passed in 1933, negotiators for machine operators in the brassiere industry settled on a weekly wage of $14. In Atlanta, Garson was paying $9 per week, although the regional average was $5. As the wage rose, so did Lovable's productivity, satisfying both labor and management.[43] Beginning in the 1930s, Garson showed itself color-blind in its employment policies, with fully integrated factories and lunchrooms. Other companies' degree of racial integration remains unknown. Lovable also marketed to African American women, but used the same advertisements featuring white models in all publications.[44]

The International Ladies' Garment Workers' Union was active in brassiere companies. Maiden Form is one example of a unionized shop that began as a tiny enterprise employing fewer than a dozen workers, many of whom were relatives and friends. As the company grew, unionization became appropriate.

In addition to offering new products, modernization of physical facilities and methods of operation gave competitive advantage to several manufacturers. Dr. H. C. Parmeley, editor of *Business Week*, contended that the Depression had not changed the business pattern: "Those [manufacturers] who win will win because they have the most modern plants and most up-to-date facilities, because they have revamped their production equipment, and . . . have put aggressive ingenuity to work to develop new markets and new products."[45] In part, the introduction of Lastex in 1931 and nylon in 1939 made retooling essential. Nylon (see Chapter 6) was entirely synthetic, unlike rayon and acetate, which were cellulose-based. New fibers required handling different from the

1920s lingerie standbys of silk, cotton, rayon, and acetate. Unfortunately, the trade press gave little information about the changes in plant machinery embraced by specific companies, beyond mention of adding floor space or sewing machines.

Productive capacity meant little without cultivation of loyal patronage. Brassiere makers' customer base spanned a wide range of ages when the new users, some of them teenagers, were added to the generation of "fortyish" women who had begun to wear brassieres in the early 1900s. Most manufacturers wisely chose to concentrate on one segment of the age spectrum of customers. These choices are revealed in the images of the photographed or sketched models, the brevity or coverage and control of the brassieres; and their daring or cautious styling. Whichever age group a company aspired to attract, their advertising followed the motto: "Sell Them Youth."[46]

Firms that resolutely pursued the teens and young adults in the 1930s included Hollywood-Maxwell, Bali, Formfit, Maiden Form, Model, Nature's Rival, Vanity Fair, Hickory, and Venus Foundations (Chicago).[47] Added to this lineup were most of the knit-brassiere producers, particularly Carter, Kayser, and Vassarette. Their lightly structured knitted brassieres and corselettes would probably have appealed to women who needed gentle shaping of curves rather than substantial support. Smooth-textured, knitted-to-shape brassieres adapted especially well to clinging bias garments or knitted apparel popular with young, trim women. Carter advertised a knitted mesh brassiere called a "mouldette," for "children from ten to fifteen years of age."[48] Training brassieres were not creatures of the 1950s! The idea of marketing to prepubescent girls started at least two decades earlier.

In our informal survey of women over fifty years of age, respondents gave several reasons for wearing their first brassiere, including the desire to achieve a fashionable look, submission to peer or maternal pressure, or the need for support. Only a small number of women mentioned comfort as an inducement to start wearing a brassiere.

A few major firms sat on the fence about their target customers and tried to reach both older and younger clientele, with mixed success. Kabo, Lily of France, Kops Brothers, Munsingwear, G. M. Poix, and DeBevoise fell into that category.[49] Of those companies, Warner, Lily of France, and Munsingwear enjoyed the greatest success, perhaps partly due to clever marketing. Warner, Bien Jolie, and Gossard included designs for mature figures, but pitched most of their advertising to women who were young and firm. Youthful models populated Van Raalte's advertising, but some of them were large women, unusual at that time for a specialist in knitted brassieres. Camp and Leading Lady focused on specific clienteles. Camp designed for pregnant and nursing mothers and postmastectomy and surgical patients, whereas Leading Lady designed for maternity use and large-breasted women with cup-sizes D through I. Venus Corporation (New York) used simple line drawings of their nursing brassiere, instead of showing them on a figure, probably because the inside structure of the cups, with extra padding over the nipples, represented their major selling point. Although 15 percent fewer babies were born in 1933 than in 1929, maternity brassieres were in sufficient demand to be catered to by Venus Corporation, Camp, Leading Lady, Form-O-Uth (later Anne Alt), and Maiden Form.[50]

The few high-priced, semicustom manufacturers active in the 1930s divided on the age question, with Pauline Gordon featuring girlish styles and Ruth Merzon and Edith Lances catering to matrons.[51]

Girls in their teens were the darlings of several manufacturers and retailers. So potent was the adolescent market that the term *teens* appeared in the trade and consumer advertising as early as 1930, years in advance of widespread societal attention to "teenagers" as a defined group.[52] Carter's brassiere and girdle advertisement included a design called TeensV in its 1935 line. Carson Pirie Scott, in Washington, D.C., located a special junior foundation department next to the junior dress department, so that each could stimulate sales in the other.[53] Mass merchandisers' catalog illustrations also appealed to the young customers with sketches of girlish figures.

Manufacturers tried to entice young patrons by showing skinny shoulder straps and strapless designs, delicate fabrics, strong colors (red, blue, gold, black), smooth cups, and flexibility of shaping. By 1934, Carter offered a brief, pull-over-the-head style called Banjo that used Lastex. G. M. Poix produced Cuties, essentially silk-tricot-covered pads set into a bandeau, for the young customer or the adult woman who wanted more up front.

Until the mid-1930s, the full word *brassiere* always appeared in advertising. However, the young things who wore up-to-date bandeaux truncated the name to go with the wispy garment. Among college women across the United States, according to a *Harper's Bazaar* survey conducted in 1934, *bra* was the going expression, just as *p.j.* substituted for pajama and other slang terms described fads in hats and informal togs.[54] For instance, denim "beer jackets" and jeans offered a casual option for extracurricular activities in 1936–37. College campuses nurtured a definable fashion culture, even in a decade of financial stringency. *Vogue* reported campus styles annually, beginning in late summer 1934, when cashmere sweater sets, leopard coats, monogrammed dresses, and white raincoats were among the must-have fashions.

Warner must have tuned into youthful trends, because in February 1934 it ran an advertisement that reported "The 'bras' is all important." By 1935,

Warner officially marketed its A'lure Bra, truncating the word in the trade name. Other companies climbed on the "bra" bandwagon, with Carter, Kleinert, and Van Raalte using the diminutive in 1936 and Fay-Miss touting its Bali Bra in 1937. Curiously, Fay-Miss had christened this style the Bali Upper at its debut in 1936. A few companies, including Maiden Form, persevered in calling their garments "brassieres" through the 1930s. Others, including G. M. Poix, preferred "bandeau." Perhaps "bra" seemed too slangy for long-established companies that wanted to keep the respect of matrons.

Mature customers and women of all ages with large or pendulous breasts were offered long-line brassieres, built-up backs, firm bands under the cup, wedge-shaped inserts of cloth between the cups, wide straps, power Lastex, and light boning. Customers old and young sought low-backed brassieres to wear with evening and day dresses with back décolletage.

Formfit Company hit on a sizing feature calculated to capture the enthusiasm of women with ample bosoms. In October 1932, this maker announced production of small, average, and full cups in each band size (e.g., 34) of a particular style. S. H. Camp and Company, however, pioneered in relating the size and pendulousness of breasts to letters of the alphabet, A through D. Camp's advertising designers depicted letter-labeled profiles of breasts along with a frontal anatomical sketch of a woman's breast in the February 1933 issue of *Corset and Underwear Review* (Figure 20). Gradually the concept of defining the breasts' volume caught on. In 1937, Warner began to feature cup sizing. Previously, Warner and other companies seem to have relied on stretchable cups to accommodate different depths of breast. Model and Fay-Miss also offered the option of A, B, C, or D cups in the late 1930s. Catalog companies used Small, Medium, Large, and Stout designations instead of letters through the 1940s. Munsingwear designer Ruth Kapinas wittily nicknamed the alphabet options "nubbins, snubbins, droopers, and super-droopers."[55]

Despite jokes, this new feature in sizing improved women's chances of obtaining a reasonable fit—impossible when only the total circumference of the bandeau varied, e.g., 32 to 40 inches. Warner also was working on the band in their bandeaux: a stretchable undercup band appeared in their advertising in fall-winter 1938. Multisized bands, created by several "eye" positions in fasteners, became common in the 1930s, as did shoulder straps adjusted with a D-ring.[56] Wearers got to decide just how high they wanted to hoist their "poitrine." Not incidentally, specialized firms producing just hook-and-eye tapes, straps, and even adjusting-rings sprang up to supply brassiere makers with standard components, allowing them to concentrate on designing and producing the body of the bra.

Ironically, the Cuties marketed by G. M. Poix for young, small-breasted

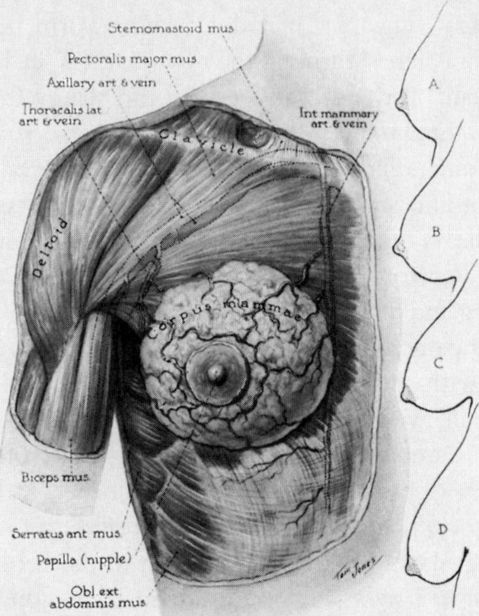

The

Blood Supply of the Female Breast

Right—Profiles of Common Types of Breasts from the Small Breast of the Young Girl to the Pendulous Breast of the Older Woman.

Leading physicians everywhere recommend Camp Supports. Better department stores in the corset and surgical sections find this a very profitable line, opening up a new avenue of sales. Fitting manuals are furnished the stores. Write for information.

Physiological Supports

S. H. CAMP AND COMPANY

Manufacturers, JACKSON, MICHIGAN

CHICAGO	NEW YORK	LONDON
1056 Merchandise Mart	330 Fifth Avenue	252 Regent Street, W.

Figure 20. Anatomical drawing of breast tissues under the skin, with first breast profiles to illustrate cup size by letters. *Corset and Underwear Review*, February 1933. Reproduced with permission.

women, were inspired by a product that was definitely not cute—the first patented brassiere attachment to enclose mastectomy pads (Figure 21). This represented one of Gabrielle Poix Yerkes's more perceptive innovations. As physicians' diagnosis of breast cancer became more accurate, numbers of mastectomies increased, often in combination with radiation therapy or radium implants. Doctors prescribed and women sought special brassieres after treatment. Yerkes may have tried to develop this aspect of her business because the fashionable side seemed to be contracting. Whether the mastectomy adaptation was widely produced is open to question, because no image appears in consumer, nursing, or trade magazines. Possibly Camp dominated this market, as an offshoot of its other medically related brassieres and corsets. Camp Company offered retail fitters special sensitivity training for working with mastectomy clients. The Chesterman-Leeland Company of Philadelphia also manufactured Junoforms prostheses.[57]

Even though 1930s brassieres were far removed from their early image as healthful substitutes for corsets, physicians had begun to recognize the place of bras in the arsenal of weapons against disease and discomfort. William S. Bainbridge and Paul S. Seabold published professional papers about prescribing bras for cystic conditions.[58] Mindful of the tendency to commit hasty surgery, Bainbridge admonished colleagues: "The patient has the right to demand this painstaking effort, this exactness of diagnosis. A criminal is presumed (under the law) to be innocent, until proven guilty. A mammary gland should have the same privilege."[59] Fred Lyman Adair, a nationally known proponent of prenatal care, recommended using bras to alleviate pendulousness in women who had weaned their infants.[60] In the 1930s, as today, few physicians related health issues to apparel.

Price as well as age appeal and special requirements distinguished the various manufacturers in the 1930s. Not only the Lovable Company but also Maiden Form, Bien Jolie, Dorothy Bickum, and several producers of knitted brassiere set their price range to appeal to women on tight budgets. In 1935–36 Kayser and Carter were able to offer styles as low as 59 cents and 75 cents, respectively. Vanity Fair had a model priced at $1 in 1935. Bien Jolie and Maiden Form offered models at $1 and $1.50, though some styles and fabrics cost $2 to $3.50. Warner's A'lure line in Lastex retailed for $1.50 to $5. Hollywood-Maxwell's whirlpool styles fetched $2. Catalog sales appealed primarily to the budget-minded woman, with prices below $1 in many cases. House brands such as Charmode for Sears, Adonna for J. C. Penney, and Joan Browne for Montgomery Ward retailed for the lowest prices, even though they were manufactured by brand-name companies. Half a dozen producers specialized in making sale merchandise and "specials" for department stores at prices close

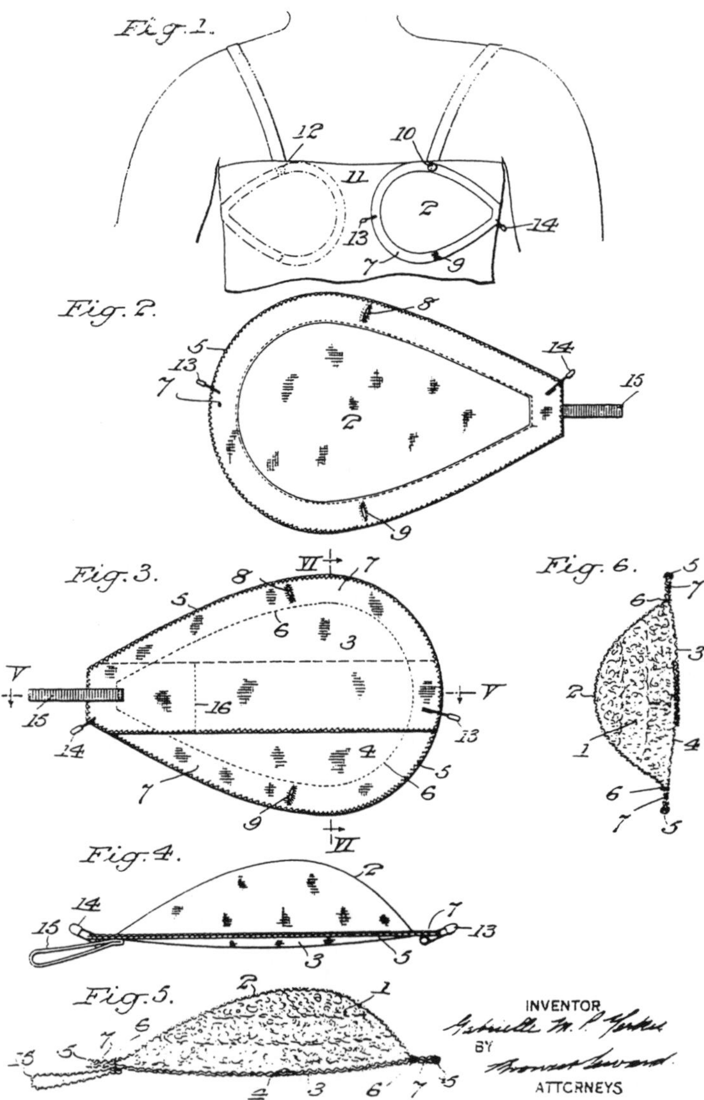

Figure 21. Illustration of bust forms, for postmastectomy patients, to be worn with a brassiere. Patented by Gabrielle Poix Yerkes.

to those of mass merchants.[61] In general, fancy materials, long-line shaping, and maternity or surgical features raised the prices to $5 or higher. Most costly were the offerings of custom or semicustom firms, including Edith Lances ($2–$7.50) and Ruth Merzon ($4 and up), both based in New York City.[62]

Overall, a substantial proportion of women could afford some type of brassiere, particularly as the worst stringencies of the Depression eased in 1935–36 and from 1939 onward. To say this is not to minimize the destitution of millions of American women in the 1930s but to acknowledge that millions did have jobs and could buy at least some clothing each year. Data are available only for 1939, when 56 percent of women had incomes between $100 and $999; 23 percent fell below $100; and 17.4 percent received between $1,000 and $4,999. Census records showed 12,540,278 women in the "Experienced Labor Force, 1940."[63] These figures probably reflect an improved economy as military production began to revive manufacturing. During the worst years of the Depression, women had often suffered cuts in already low pay, but because they worked more in service and teaching than in manufacturing, they endured a smaller percentage of outright layoffs than did men.[64] However small their clothing budgets, women would have strong incentives to spend a few dollars on undergarments that gave shape to the outer silhouette and rescued them from frumpiness.

To ensure that women would not forget about brassieres as they scrimped to buy clothes, brassiere makers honed their promotional techniques. For example, in 1932 Maiden Form became the first intimate apparel maker to advertise in city buses, targeting New York shoppers and out-of-town visitors. The company made even splashier appeals seven years later, when it bombarded visitors to the hugely popular 1939 New York World's Fair with seventy neon signs, which lighted various entrances to the fairgrounds. In a more conventional vein, the trade press reported numerous runway fashion shows of models in brassieres and corsets, sponsored by both individual manufacturers and retail departments. Alert companies gave serious attention to their advertising copy in newspapers and magazines, to make words and picture work together, to be catchy and informative. *Corset and Underwear Review* regularly showed a collage of effective advertising layouts from the previous month or two. Timing of ads was likewise important; efficient promotion coincided with the start of a new season in outerwear. In spring and fall and at Christmastime women might be persuaded to buy brassieres, to complement new dress purchases. New outlets for advertising were assiduously sought: Model bragged about appearing in "that smart weekly, *The New Yorker*." Even packaging became a form of advertisement: Formfit used clear cellophane wrappers to show off its brassieres to women while protecting them from dust and soiling. One Dallas retailer arranged tables full of brassieres to entice prospective purchasers and a Richmond department store kept its bras in trays, for easy presentation.[65]

Despite the international trade wars that characterized the Great Depression and contributed to its prolongation, brassiere sales were not confined to a domestic market. Nations less devastated by the Depression than the United States offered attractive opportunities for expansion. By 1934, Maiden Form had extensive dealerships in Latin America and within a year were selling in places as far-flung as Thailand and South Africa. Lovable maintained offices and production facilities in Canada, Great Britain, South Africa, and Japan. However, not all of the brassiere trade flowed from the United States to other countries. Londoner Rosamond L. Kennedy obtained a U.S. patent for a brassiere that she named the Kestos,[66] after the Greek goddess Juno's sexy garment in the *Iliad*. Kennedy's design consisted of overlapping triangular cups, with shallow darts and slender ties that wrapped around the back to button at the sides. Patented and sold in Britain in 1928, Kestos appeared in U.S. trade and fashion magazines in 1930. After that year, advertising in the United States was confined to individual store spreads, although Kestos figured in editorial features in national magazines. Perhaps their advertisements overstepped Americans' sense of decorum, because at least one Kestos sketch clearly showed protruding nipples.[67] According to Maureen Alden, the Kestos sold extremely well to English women through the 1950s.[68]

The French brassiere house Cadolle purveyed premium quality brassieres through elite stores in the United States. Cadolle Company had been in business in Paris since the late nineteenth century, when it was founded by Herminie Cadolle, who is said to have shown a forerunner of the *soutien gorge* at the 1889 Paris Exposition. Herminie's descendant Marcel Cadolle held two U.S. patents in the 1930s, showing innovative shaping of uplift cups, in one case by insertions and in another by darts.[69] Imports of foundations were as skimpy as the products themselves, however, partly because of curtailed imports and heavy tariffs, not to mention limited demand for costly undergarments.

Kennedy and Cadolle exemplified overseas designers with unique ideas, but there were American innovators, too. When Lastex hit the market in 1931, manufacturers quickly exploited its potential in girdles and all-in-ones. In brassieres, the breakthrough took a few more years and was, arguably, the work of one woman, Ruth M. Kapinas. Kapinas had studied at the New York School of Fine and Applied Art and then had begun working for New York lingerie designer Carol Quick. Eventually, Kapinas established her own line of handmade lingerie, which she sold successfully to I. Magnin, Neiman Marcus, John Wanamaker, Jordan Marsh, and other retailers around the United States. In

1931, she closed her company to accept an invitation to join the Munsingwear firm in Minneapolis.[70]

Kapinas began to experiment with Lastex fabric, designing wool and Lastex swimwear and obtaining two patents for girdles. Then she harnessed the potential of Lastex to create the highly successful Bando-Lure brassiere design for Foundettes, Munsingwear's soft foundations line based on rayon and Lastex. Instead of making preshaped cups, which were normal in brassieres of the 1930s, Kapinas used "the cut of the stretch fabric, in tension with the bust" to form cups and create "a silhouette of lifted, separated breasts."[71] Eliminating the usual seam under the breast, Kapinas devised a horizontal reverse curved seam, rather like an S-shape, which lay along the upper curve of the breast. "In a complex feat of engineering, the tension of the breast on the fabric caused a hammock-like uplift."[72] In contrast to propping the breast from below, this tensional uplift produced a comfortable brassiere that adapted to the size and shape of each breast (Figure 22). One surviving working model of Kapinas's shows that she worked by draping and pinning different pieces together in a three-dimensional prototype. Her talents also ran to mathematics, resulting in designs that were absolutely precise in their sizing.

From 1937 through 1940, Munsingwear sold designs of the Bando-Lure group, which gave entree to upper-level retail stores that had not previously been customers of Munsingwear.[73] Indeed, the line helped Munsingwear to reach "seventh place in national corset sales in 1936."[74] Impressed by the popularity of Bando-Lure, Gossard and Hickory paid Ruth Kapinas the unwelcome compliment of knocking off her design. Sears, Roebuck arranged with Munsingwear to produce an authorized, less costly equivalent with a seam under the cup. The president of Munsingwear began to pressure Kapinas to borrow design elements from rival firms to use in *her* styles, so she resigned. A few months later Kapinas joined Vanity Fair, for whom she designed from 1939 to 1943, before retiring from business for health reasons.[75]

Although Kapinas was not given the limelight she deserved at Munsingwear, S. H. Camp frequently trumpeted the design and teaching skills of Ariel Nichols LeMay. Like Ruth Kapinas, LeMay held at least one patent for a brassiere. Her patent stated that her design was to "provide the requisite uplifting support . . . to elevate breasts, which are abnormally lowered due to weakened and torn muscles and tissues."[76] She constantly received notice in Camp's news briefs in *Corset and Underwear Review* especially as a medically sophisticated instructor of sales personnel in the intricacies of assessing and fitting the needs of maternity and surgical clients. LeMay's dual function as designer and public relations specialist in this family-held firm probably contributed to her visibility.

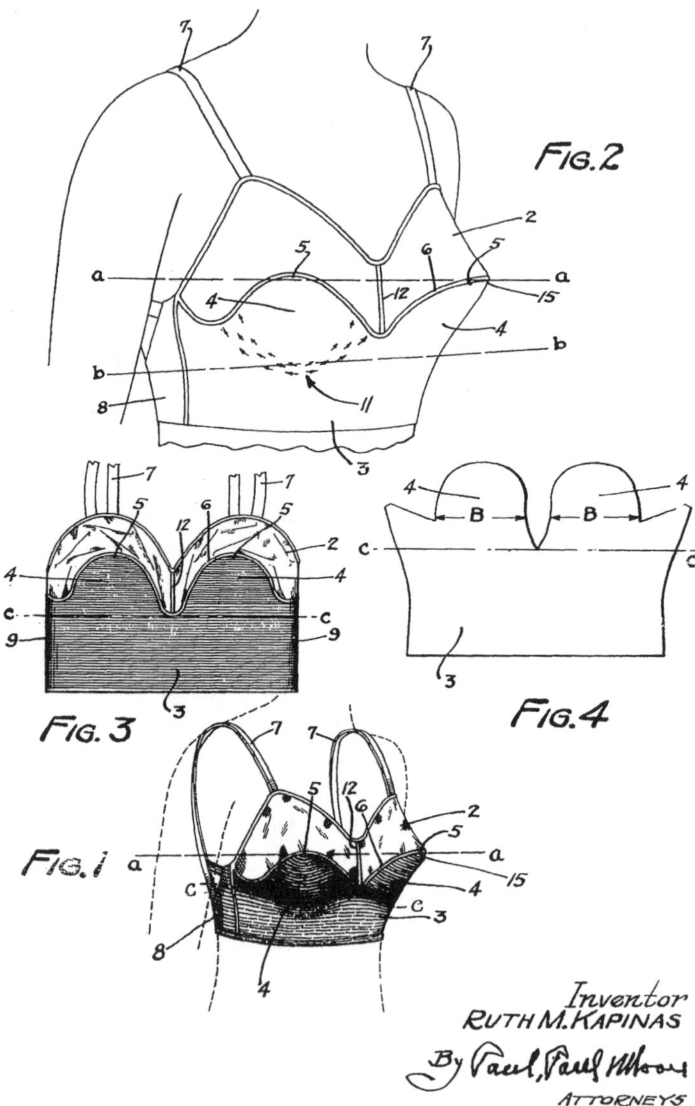

Figure 22. Patent illustration by Ruth Kapinas for Munsingwear Foundette featuring Lastex fabric.

Whereas medical knowledge inspired LeMay's designs, Elvira Campa McKeefrey entered the employ of Model Company in 1920 *as* a model. Noticing her intelligence, the factory supervisor added her to the designing staff. She rose to be head designer and, starting in 1936, became one of the four partner-owners of Model.[77] McKeefrey held four patents, including one for the Scanties line—a brassiere joined to a girdle and a slip. Her other patented designs translated into the bias-cup that became a staple at Model and a 1936 style that emphasized breast separation while giving independent support.[78]

When the dismal decade of the 1930s gave way to the horrendous years of World War II, brassieres and their producers had undergone a transformation. No longer did firms cluster in the New York-New Jersey-Connecticut metropolitan area and Chicago's environs. Southern California boasted a cluster of companies specializing in brassieres, both glamorous and pragmatic. Many more such firms would soon spring up. Vanity Fair of Reading, Pennsylvania, had launched into brassiere production, as had the Lovable Company in Atlanta.

Older firms languished, to fade from existence or be acquired by sprightlier rivals. Recent arrivals such as Bali, Vanity Fair, Formfit, Hollywood-Maxwell, Beautee-Fit, and Lovable would prosper and dominate the business in the coming decades. These survivors had learned to mix attractive products with imaginative promotion and had rationalized their brassiere lines, weeding out any style that did not generate sufficient profits. Each successful producer had specialized, sometimes in brassieres with a particular functional or fashionable image, often in one price range or customer age group.

To a surprising degree, designer-patentees and manufacturers had defined the "modern" brassiere: structured cups in graduated sizes and adjustable bands and straps. Even wires had made a tentative appearance, in a strapless style shown in 1934 by the custom firm of André.[79] These tendencies would soon close the door on the home sewing of brassieres. Already commercial patterns for brassieres had become sufficiently complex to challenge amateur sewers; cheap commercial bras removed the incentive to do it yourself.

Unfortunately, the companies that had kept brassieres in women's wardrobes during the Depression could not relax and enjoy their growing prosperity. War had erupted in Europe, and American isolationism was slowly giving way to the realization that sympathy for countries invaded by the Nazis would eventually have to be matched by material help. Preparedness became America's watchword. Sobriety and stringency began to constrain the makers and marketers of American women's foundations.

5 Dutiful Brassieres

Brassiere manufacturers suffered as many ulcers in the early 1940s as they had in the 1930s, though for diametrically opposed reasons. After nearly a decade of coaxing women to spend part of their small clothing budgets on brassieres, they grappled with the problems of producing enough high-quality brassieres to sell to newly flush consumers. Between 1941 and 1945, millions of women worked for pay as members of the U.S. armed forces or as factory workers or office staff.[1]

Outbreak of hostilities in Europe, especially the invasion of Poland, awoke Americans from their isolationist slumber. The crisis energized the U.S. government and spurred some of the populace to come to the aid of countries attacked by the Axis powers. A small number of American women became involved in late 1939, volunteering as nurses in British hospitals.[2] By the end of the war, 76,000 women or 31.3 percent of American professional nurses served in the U.S. nursing corps. After the Japanese attacked Pearl Harbor on 7 December 1941, the vast majority of Americans responded with vehement patriotism. Almost 500,000 women joined the armed forces of the United States, including WAVES (Women Accepted for Volunteer Emergency Service), WAAC/WACs (Women's (Auxiliary) Army Corps), Marine Corps Women's Reserve, WASPs (Women Airforce Service Pilots), and the Women's Reserve of the United States Coast Guard.[3] Service women "did their bit" both in the United States and in the European and Asian theaters of war. Besides these military volunteers, hundreds of thousands of their compatriots assisted the American Red Cross, the United Service Organization (USO), and the Land Army.[4] Even women who did not undertake the major commitment of new jobs served the Civil Defense organizations in motor services, as ground observers of planes, and as air raid drill wardens.[5]

This was the first war in which the U.S. Quartermaster General directly provided women's uniforms, covering several items of apparel. Regulations for clothing were written for each branch at the time it was approved by Congress, and every branch was different. The Quartermasters' records preserved at the Military History Institute Library in Carlisle Barracks, Pennsylvania, offer only sketchy information about military women's clothing. Women at officers' ranks, including nurses, social workers, medical doctors, physiotherapists, and dietitians received only their outer uniforms and had to provide their own undergarments with the exception of cotton knit vests.[6] Red Cross workers, who did not have military status but were treated as officers, also bought their own underwear.[7] Women in lower ranks were issued undergarments in colors that varied according to the branch of service. A November 1942 advertisement for "Warner's alphabet bras" in *R.N.*, a nurses' magazine, implied that Warner could provide regulation brassieres: "New colors, too—Nurse's white, Army tan, Air Corps grey, and Civilian nude." Dr. Martha Putnam, who had enlisted as a clerk in the Women's Army Corps in 1942, recalled that "everything was olive drab."[8] The Navy women, however, wore white brassieres and girdles.[9] Mera Galloway, correspondent for the young women's magazine *Mademoiselle*, wrote about her WAAC experiences, including obtaining her uniforms. A Des Moines department store issued clothing to the WAACs stationed at Fort Des Moines, including "gloves, socks, stockings, pyjamas, girdles, bras, panties, slips—all of excellent quality by famous-name manufacturers."[10] Once the supply lines were opened, WACs at least were able to replenish their undergarments through the Quartermaster's department.[11] Brassieres and corsets had been designated "essential" parts of the wardrobe. One droll postwar cartoon showed a brassiere and girdle hanging with military jackets, heavy boots, and visored caps in the window of an army surplus store.[12]

For the duration of the war, tens of thousands of WAAC/WACs, WAVES, nurses, and Red Cross workers added a martial note to the American apparel landscape. As usual, *Vogue* offered advice on clothing management and style, exhorting women to wear the uniform properly, without decorative doodads or civilian makeup and hairstyles. However, *Vogue* recommended that when off duty, women dress as civilians. The editors suggested colorful and sprightly clothes that would cheer up men on furlough, who longed to look at something other than khaki, olive drab, and navy. Bright and snappy clothes were also believed to maintain the wearer's own morale.[13] That extended to brassieres and girdles. One department store buyer who had done a brisk business with WAC customers, opined that "women soldiers" wanted to remain feminine and "civilian underneath. Thousands of women pride themselves on fine corsets and brassieres, and there are many such in the WAC ranks who enjoy new girdles and want to wear them during the evening. They are expected to wear control garments to maintain their appearance, and thus need extra ones to change into."[14]

Important though they were as a consumer group, military women's numbers were dwarfed by the hordes of civilian war workers. Before the United States entered the war, industry had begun to gear up to supply Britain with the promised Lend-Lease armaments and equipment. After eight years' slump, factories were humming. Indeed, the Depression paved the way for speedy conversion to war production. Idled factories and workers were available aplenty. Long unemployment rolls melted away under the hot competition for manpower. Months before the bombing of Pearl Harbor, men were being urged to enlist in the U.S. armed services. Yet the Allies recognized how crucial American-made hardware was to victory. President Roosevelt publicized his armament targets, hoping to hearten Allies and alarm the enemy by his formidable numbers. For 1942–43 alone he ordered the production of 185,000 airplanes, 120,000 tanks, and 55,000 antiaircraft guns.[15] Such demands for output forced manufacturers to recruit women to replace men in factories and offices.[16]

Before World War II unmarried and lower-class women had dominated the female workforce.[17] Between 1942 and 1945, substantial numbers of married, middle-class women went to work, although the majority of housewives, especially those with small children, stayed home. Girls who had just completed high school were exhorted by magazines such as *Mademoiselle* to take war jobs—as members of the Signal Corps, machine tool operators, censors in the post office, and myriad other posts. Women labored at tasks that were physically demanding and sometimes dangerous. The fictive Rosie the Riveter's real-life coworkers have left vivid accounts of assembling ships and airplanes amid dirt and din. Most of them did less skilled tasks than riveting, however, leading David Kennedy to suggest that "Wendy the Welder" would have been a more representative prototype.[18] Strenuous work called for protective and supportive undergarments and outerwear (Figure 23). In addition to factory and office workers, 1.5 million women entered the Women's Land Army, performing agricultural tasks to help farmers meet their labor needs.[19] In 1941, 25 percent of American women held jobs; by 1945 the figure was 36 percent. In total, 19 million women participated in the civilian or military workforce for some part of the war.[20]

Factory workers varied in what they wore on both the outside and the inside. Modesty, convenience, and safety all required women to wear divided garments to an extent not previously accepted (Figure 24).[21] Pants moved beyond the confines of the farm, the dude ranch, the beach, and the soiree to become daily attire. Some women, especially those from small towns in conservative re-

Active women need support

To keep your war-job energy at its peak, your supporting garments must be well-constructed and comfortable. This girdle and brassière are individually designed for the wearer.

Figure 23. World War II factory worker with brassiere and girdle illustrated as worn with coveralls, encouraging purchase for patriotic reasons. *Women's Home Companion*, May 1943.

Figure 24. Consumer advertisement for Gossard foundations directed at World War II female workers. *Mademoiselle*, May 1943. Reproduced with permission.

gions, wore pants for the first time in their lives and discovered how mercilessly bifurcated garments revealed their figures. *Women's Wear Daily* continually featured new designs of pants in its issues for March and April 1942. Even *Vogue* vouchsafed its sophisticated, wealthier readers "A Primer on Pants," detailing desirable fabrics, fit, cut, and "How to Wear Them" in its 1 April 1942 issue.

Supportive undergarments also helped hundreds of thousands of "Rosies" to dress efficiently and safely. Recognizing an opportunity to market their products, the foundation companies collaborated to conduct a survey of women in war plants to determine their use of, need for, and complaints about brassieres and corsets or girdles. Results of these surveys, published in *Corset and Underwear Review* between September 1943 and January 1944, revealed some of the experiences of women producing airplanes, ships, guns, and ammunition in Seattle, the San Francisco area, Southern California, Cleveland, and Chicago.

Anonymous reporters from each region described prevailing clothing practices in armament factories. In San Francisco factories, denim and leather attire was reportedly typical. Northern California industrial workers sported "sturdy, well-fitted slacks and jeans, overalls and coveralls" along with flat-heeled safety shoes, socks, hair protectors, tucked-in blouses, and no loose scarves or ties around the neck.[22] Sweaters were interdicted as dangerously loose outer garments or too provocative in "form-fitting" styles. California Industrial Accident Prevention laws required that hair and eyes be completely protected for anyone working around machinery. Some plants mentioned in the survey mandated uniforms, such as coveralls. Women who engaged in outdoor work, notably shipbuilding, found that they needed to layer two or three pairs of long stockings under their slacks for adequate warmth in damp coastal winter weather. Long johns proved very difficult to obtain, and were only available by mail order. Chicago war workers wore slacks, bandannas, goggles, and socks with their work shoes.[23]

The proportion of interviewees who reported wearing a brassiere reached almost 100 percent in Seattle, 75 to 88 percent in San Francisco (depending on the company), 80 to 90 percent in Southern California, 82 percent in Cleveland, and 89 percent in Chicago. More than half of the women respondents in Cleveland seemed to need long-line or medium-length brassieres because, according to the report: "A large percentage of the population here is of foreign extraction with problem figures rather than the more slender type like the average American girl."[24] Evidently these first-generation immigrants, often from Central or Southern Europe, were large-breasted women who had not yet caught the dieting fever. In Chicago, about 8 percent of workers surveyed were "colored." The report made no mention of whether black women had special needs for fitting of brassieres, as did the immigrants.

In addition to presenting bald statistics, this series of articles offered glimpses of attitudes toward foundation garments. The November article reported, "The predominance of the brassiere is an outgrowth of a dress habit in Southern California; everybody from 13 to 90 wears brassieres, except perhaps a very few flat busted women. Even many of these are using a corrective type to help the development of their breasts."[25] Furthermore, California increased its population 72 percent between 1940 and 1950.[26] No wonder more than thirty brassiere manufacturers were doing business in Southern California by the 1940s. *Corset and Underwear Review* acknowledged the importance of this market by running a retail column on California to complement the long-standing features on New York and Chicago.

Retailers actively courted factory workers' business. Knowing that women who juggled home duties and a plant shift had scant time for shopping, some department store managers arranged to have brassieres and girdles brought to the factories or to the women's homes for inspection and fitting. Factory health personnel became de facto allies of the retailers and manufacturers. Nurses, doctors, and other health workers kept alert to strain injuries and absenteeism and if a woman was not wearing a brassiere and girdle, they tried to persuade her to do so. One 1942 cartoon showed a woman in coveralls reaching for a very pointy uplift brassiere and saying to the clerk, "I'll take it. We girls must do our best to keep 'em flying" (Figure 25).

Those manufacturers, such as Lockheed, who required brassieres to be worn on the job often cited "good taste" as the reason, but others perceived that the physical support relieved potential fatigue from forty-eight-hour work weeks.[27] Still other observers noted improved morale, deriving from workers' sense of being well groomed. Something sturdier than a dainty rayon brassiere was needed for hazardous tasks. Breast protectors for industrial war work included a plastic brassiere, produced by the Willson Company and intended to be worn over a conventional brassiere by women doing heavy factory work.[28] Strauss Company of Pittsburgh offered

> a set of flesh-colored, moulded, vulcanized fibre breast protectors . . . in three sizes, with adjustability between the cups to give the necessary width at the breast separation. These have extended ledges at the bottom of the cups to provide a base to resist blows. Light web straps hold the breast cups and are adjustable at the back. These may be detached and laundered and the cups may be sterilized. It is recommended that they be worn over a brassiere.[29]

Respondents to the undergarment questionnaires offered a few criticisms of the brassieres then available, although they were far better satisfied with bras than with corsets, which were being made of nonstretch materials, due to war-

"I'll take it. We girls must do our best to keep 'em flying."

Figure 25. Cartoon from *Corset and Underwear Review*, December 1942.

time shortages of rubber and its substitutes. Cleveland factory workers vented strong dissatisfaction with foundation garments, mainly centered on rising costs, accompanied by poorer wearing quality and decreased comfort over prewar garments. Some women tried foundations and then discarded them out of disgruntlement with the comfort features of the designs. Brassieres' least satisfactory feature were the straps, which were not sturdy or adjustable enough to suit users. One Chicago respondent complained about poor wearing quality in the entire brassiere. Indeed, intense physical activity would have put stress on all parts of the brassiere, shortening its life span. These complaints echoed a 1942 survey of the general population, in which respondents overwhelmingly flagged the straps as problem-ridden but asked for more sizes, better cut and shape, more support, and different materials.[30] Many of these problems could be resolved only with the ending of wartime controls and shortages.

Women had the cash to buy foundations as good as the industry could produce. The Office of Price Administration restrained consumer prices, and the National War Labor Board regulated wage scales during the war. Annual salaries for typists and stenographers were $1,260–$1,440; office machine operators averaged $1,440; accounting assistants, $1,440–$1,800; junior home economists, $2,000–$3,500; federal government jobs for illustrators and photographers, $1,620–$5,600. Land Army workers' wages ranged from $300 to $600 yearly, plus room and board.[31] By war's end, weekly earnings among workers averaged a 65 percent increase. In real terms, incomes rose by 27 percent between 1940 and 1945.[32] There were dramatic increments, too, for a few women. One African American woman reported going from a $3.50-per-week domestic job in the South to a $48-per-week factory job in California.[33] Many women supported their families, with little cash for personal wants, but others had discretionary money that allowed them to keep up their spirits and appearances by buying whatever inner and outer finery they could find.

Women who performed physical labor were encouraged to purchase more expensive brassieres (at 89 cents each) than those required by clerical workers (at 59 cents each).[34] Due to price controls and social pressure, wartime inflation remained in check, at 28 percent, compared with the 100 percent rise in prices in the United States between 1914 and 1918.[35] Brassiere prices held fairly steady in the 1940s, although nylon brassieres commanded premium prices of $2 and higher in 1941–42. The Chicago report from a *Corset and Underwear Review* survey of war workers revealed in the January 1944 issue that women at the Bendix Aviation Corporation bought an average of six brassieres every year, paying approximately $1.50 for each. Even the price-conscious Lovable Company ventured a few higher-priced nylon styles in the 1940s, selling for $3.95 and $5.[36]

Just when millions of women had wartime wages to spend, manufacturers were hard-pressed to make acceptable brassieres and girdles. For the legions of U.S. companies that manufactured armaments, vehicles, food, and other necessities for the troops, the 1940s were palmy days indeed. But several winters (and summers) of discontent confronted the brassiere companies. The War Production Board (WPB) severely taxed manufacturers' patience and adaptability by curtailing allocations or completely commandeering metal, natural rubber, cotton, and even rayon. Silk went the way of all Asian imports—into the void. Years before hostilities erupted with Japan, embargo lists included silk fiber and fabric, which had been highly profitable exports for the Japanese.

Manufacturers' inventiveness carried them through tough times, sustained by a vehement determination to defeat Mussolini, the Japanese, and—above all—Adolf Hitler. Patriotism for the United States in the face of a visible menace stiffened the resolve of business people to work within the constraints of the WPB and support the fight as steadfastly as other citizens.[37] Furthermore, brassiere companies, like much of the apparel business, counted many Jews among their owners and employees. They could hardly renege on cooperation in this fight, when the lives of millions of their European coreligionists were already forfeited or in grave danger.[38]

Problems of supply began to brew months before the shooting started. Dorothy Bickum, long-time corsetiere and colorful entrant into the bra business stated the manufacturers' dilemma humorously in her September 1941 ad in *Corset and Underwear Review*:

Blame It on Adolf!

These days bring their problems a-plenty,
With orders exceeding supply;
Deliveries of fabrics uncertain
And prices still soaring toward sky.

We booked a near record for Fall business
On Kobweb Nylons and the rest
Of Dorothy Bickum's youth girdles.
We're thankful, and this is no jest.

We're harried by present conditions
And trying to serve all in stride;
Maintaining the features and fabrics
That make D.B. garments our pride.

We ask your indulgence and patience,
Your good will we value 'bove all.
It was Adolf who started this mess,
Blame him for your problems this Fall!

Even though foundations became recognized parts of women's uniforms, their "first line of defense," this did not confer the production priority enjoyed by outer uniforms and munitions.[39] Shortly after the attack on Pearl Harbor, the WPB took control of national rubber supplies, with a justification that was impossible to refute. To build a Flying Fortress required 1,000 pounds of rubber; a medium tank, 1,750 pounds; and a battleship, a staggering 150,000 pounds.[40] New supplies of rubber could not reach the United States, because 90 percent of imports came from East Asia.[41] By May 1942, the quantity of elastic permitted in foundations was reduced to 50 percent of what had been used before the war. WPB regulations specified that brassiere straps could contain only two and a half inches of elastic, and elastic insertions in the body of the bra could measure only six square inches in bandeau styles and eight square inches in long-line brassieres.[42] Rubber yarns became as gold by March 1943.

Neoprene, the most promising of the experimental synthetic rubbers, offered brassiere producers some hope in the summer of 1943, but the optimists chased a mirage. After struggling to convert this new compound into usable yarns, spinners could not obtain the supplies of cotton and rayon to cover the neoprene. Shortage of labor and machinery to crank out the required elastic fabrics presented further obstacles. In the end, the military also appropriated neoprene, and the discouraging cycle began again with the less-useful "Buna S" substitute.[43] Conditions were "less worse" for brassiere makers than corsetieres, according to Sam Yaffe, president of Bien Jolie: "new adjustable features have overcome the fitting problem temporarily created by the elimination of most of the rubber."[44]

Metal was sufficiently precious for Yale Hook & Eye Company's Leo Roseman to turn his ingenuity to creating ladders of cloth to form the "eyes" in the brassiere bands, limiting the metal to the hooks.[45] Supplies became so tight that department stores were coaxing women to salvage and turn in the metal from their worn-out corsets and brassieres to be melted down for reuse. Textiles began to run short, too, due to both demand and price controls that made extra production unattractive, even when the fiber was available. Fielding larger and larger armies, the United States consumed vast quantities of tents, tarpaulins, uniform linings, tire components, and parachutes. Into those supplies went the cotton and rayon cloth and yarn desperately needed by brassiere and foundation makers. Requisitions included 35 million yards of duck, a heavy woven cotton textile suitable for tenting.[46] English cotton broadcloth gave way to Mexican cotton, such as the plaids and ginghams used by Maiden Form (Figure 26). Nylon, the Great White Hope of foundation makers, had largely disappeared from brassieres and had gone into cordage, mosquito netting, and parachute canopies. Kapok, a silky fiber from a tropical tree, replaced rubber in bra pads, supplemented by milkweed fuzz as kapok supplies also ran short.

Hampered by the WPB's ever-changing regulations and allocations, brassiere and girdle suppliers did their best to fill large orders; however, many materials were no longer available and specifications could not always be met.[47] Maiden Form's archives include a "Declaration of Essentiality" requesting permission to secure needed materials. This document stated:

> Since May 1942 the company has been substantially engaged in the manufacture of various items on direct contracts from the Army and Navy, including mattress covers, insect

Figure 26. Trade advertisement for Mexican cottons used by Maiden Form as substitute for English broadcloth during World War II. *Maiden Form Mirror*, March 1943. Reproduced with permission.

bars, mosquito bars, and bush shirts. It has also filled large orders for brassieres and garter belts, placed by the Philadelphia and Jersey City Army Quartermaster Offices and by Army Post Exchanges.[48]

Indeed, producing nonfoundation items for the military saved the livelihoods of many brassiere and corset makers, because at least then the government supplied the cotton textiles.[49] So they began to churn out "parachutes for flares, pup tents, camouflage tents, aviation suits, and cartridge belts."[50]

Some firms took military involvement even further. After the war Maiden Form was free to boast that they had been commissioned by the U.S. government to conduct a secret project for the army—to design, produce, and test a vest for carrier pigeons, so that paratroopers could carry the birds safely to earth.[51] Many of the elements of a brassiere—straps, curved shape—appeared in the pigeon vest (Figure 27). Carrier pigeons were required in instances when radio silence was observed, as it was immediately before the D-Day invasion.

One strategy available to all manufacturers was to simplify their lines, efficiently producing fewer, more basic styles.[52] In fall 1941, before the real crunch hit, two trade organizations collaborated on a system for standardizing hook and eye tape.[53] These moves parallel what other American industries were doing—eliminating variety but securing economies that kept the lid on business costs and prices.

Aggressive—if not precisely martial—shaping characterized wartime brassiere designs. Contoured inner or outer rims, push-up insets in the lower cup, concentric stitching, and inverted-V divides showed that these bras meant business! Straps often forked into a two-part support at the top of the cup. In some designs, the straps passed through the cups themselves, forming a vertical inset that would uphold the heaviest breast. Sexiness for evening meant as much plunge as could be managed with minimal nonfabric stiffening, since metal and rubber could hardly be obtained and plastics were not yet practicable. Military vocabulary was recruited to describe the 1940s brassiere silhouette, the Torpedo, which turned breasts into a pair of nosecones. Long after peace broke out, the Torpedo lingered, influencing brassiere design until the late 1950s.

Speaking of sexiness in brassieres, actress Jane Russell told the truth about Howard Hughes's brassiere design in her autobiography. During the filming of Russell's first movie, *The Outlaw*, Howard Hughes designed a brassiere that did not show through her blouse.

When I went into the dressing room with my wardrobe girl and tried it on, I found it uncomfortable and ridiculous. Obviously, he wanted today's seamless bra, which didn't exist then. . . . So I put on my own bra, covered the seams with tissue, pulled the straps

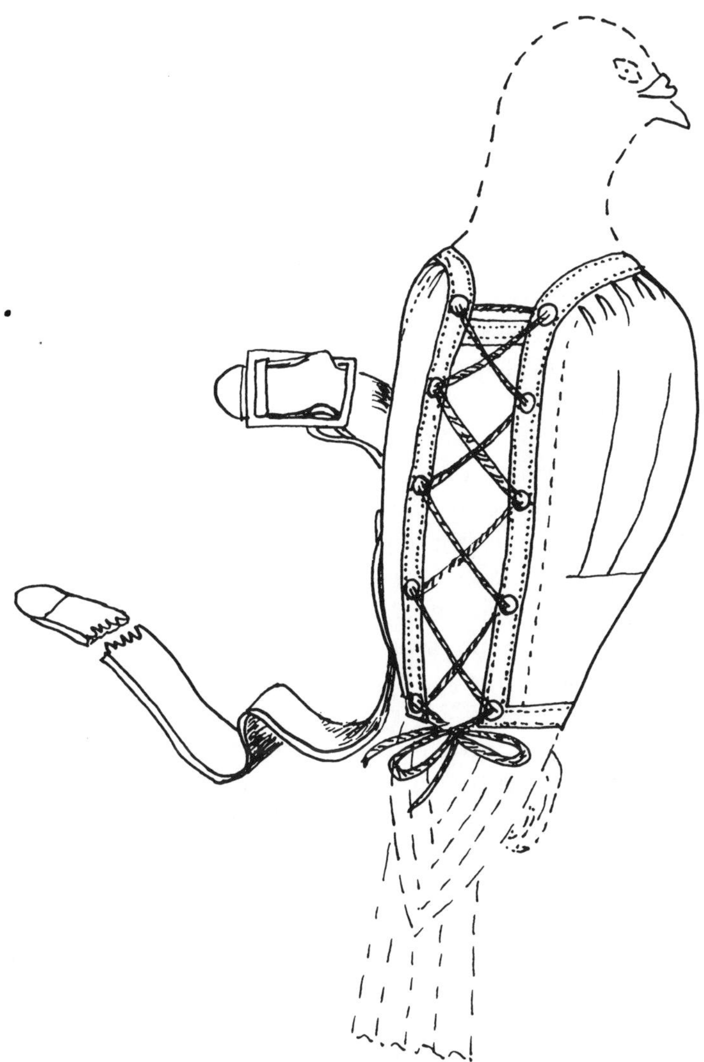

Figure 27. Drawing from blueprints of Pigeon Vest made in secret by Maiden Form for U.S. paratroopers' use in World War II. Label exhorts that birds be held in vest no longer than six hours. Maidenform Archives at the National Museum of American History Smithsonian Institution. Reproduced with permission.

over to the side, put on my blouse, and started out. . . . I *never* wore his bra. And believe me, he could design planes, but a Mister Playtex he wasn't.[54]

The movie industry had access to materials unavailable to other industries. Shortages of components were not the only problem faced by ordinary brassiere makers. The federal government preempted trains and trucks for transportation of both troops and matériel. Manufacturers never knew when components would be delivered or when products could be shipped to retailers. Even retailer-to-consumer deliveries were curtailed or eliminated. "Cash and carry" took on a civilian meaning, as shoppers were pressed to tote their own purchases.[55] The WPB halted production of sewing machines, along with other consumer machinery.[56] A company that needed to replace machines or expand production was out of luck. Repairmen found more remunerative work fixing jeeps than tinkering with sewing machines.

Labor mobility proved wonderful for workers but misery for employers. Employees moved "from plant to plant, from city to city, even from region to region" despite industry efforts to curb the practice of companies' pirating people from their competitors.[57] Apparel producers could never compete with shipbuilders or aircraft manufacturers. Attrition was particularly acute among "young women who are capable of quickly learning new occupations connected with metal trades."[58]

Brassiere and corset advertising was also recruited to the American war effort. Unnamed government officials met with retailers and manufacturers to persuade them to frame advertisements that highlighted their store or company instead of presenting product-specific statements. Service messages that emphasized "why we fight" held favor, as did plugs for war bond purchase, promotion of store services in fitting and reconditioning corsets, tips on how to prolong the wear-life of foundations, and exhortations to buy only as needed. Wartime stringencies made it unpatriotic or at least in bad taste to appeal to hoarding instincts, emphasize luxury, list specific styles and fabrics that might not materialize, or promote sales. Washington declared taboo anything that could stir up inflation or provoke serious shortfalls of merchandise.[59] Trade advertising, as well as that for consumers, embraced themes connected to war. Over a picture of women emerging from an armaments plant, the H & W Company advertising director wrote: "Bombs Are More Important than Bras! . . . These Are Some of Our Girls. . . . Please Be Patient If Deliveries Are Late!"[60]

Business people themselves accepted the need to restrain consumption because they feared empty shelves, which would cause a complete cessation of trade. Another bugbear threatened, namely, that the government would ration corsets and brassieres as they had rationed shoes. In a sense, rationing already operated, but at the level of what producers could procure instead of what consumers could buy.[61]

Fashion coped with the stringencies of wartime life, but the raging conflict inevitably destroyed the familiar system of disseminating new styles. After eighty years of looking to Paris for fashion leadership, the United States was truly on its own in developing apparel designs by autumn 1939. The French couture continued to function, but mainly to attire French Vichy collaborators and the women companions of German Nazi officers of the occupying army. Export of couture to North America ceased. Desperate, the Chambre Syndicale de la Couture Parisienne sent one member, Elsa Schiaparelli, as a refugee to New York to keep alive Americans' loyalty to Paris.[62]

The American apparel industry managed admirably, despite the wartime dearth of imported designs, bringing out of the shadows talented creators such as Maurice Rentner, Valentina, Claire McCardell, Norman Norell, Jessie Franklin Turner, Nettie Rosenstein, Jo Copeland, Anthony Blotta, Elizabeth Hawes, Philip Mangone, and Tina Lesser. Before the war, many of these people had worked anonymously behind manufacturers' labels, but now they enjoyed a measure of celebrity that continued into the 1950s and 1960s. Gilbert Adrian, a well-known Hollywood designer and husband of the movie star Janet Gaynor, began to turn out couture fashions. The New York fashion press, led by Virginia Pope of the *New York Times*, and Lord & Taylor retail executive Dorothy Shaver spearheaded the effort to publicize the work of American designers. New York apparel companies' management and the International Ladies' Garment Workers' Union members united behind a campaign to present Gotham as a hub of high style.[63] Previously, Seventh Avenue in Manhattan had been the nerve center of manufacturing but had looked to Paris for styling cues. In a 1944 editorial *Vogue*'s columnist entertained doubts that New York's apparel designers and manufacturers could ever match French creativity.[64] Perhaps the writer was looking in the wrong places for imagination or was too impatient for change. American sportswear began to set new standards of comfort with style, especially in the hands of McCardell and Lesser.

Entire issues of *Vogue* were devoted to American design. Previously, the hefty spring and autumn issues of fashion magazines had reported only the showings in Paris. New York fashion houses featured many creative American designers in their runway shows. Television, which had been tested in several U.S. cities by 1940, carried a fashion show in 1941, sponsored by Abraham & Strauss and Bloomingdale's and broadcast on WNBT.[65] This event was to have initiated weekly fashion coverage, but sustained commercial use of TV went on hold until the end of the war. However, one CBS show did manage to air on April 9, 1942, showing "Pre-Order" and "Post-Order" styles, illustrating what could and could not be made under L-85 rules.[66] These regulations were created to conserve fabric and labor for military use and to restrain inflation. In the absence of TV, radio offered a well-established medium for messages; Bien Jolie, Bali, Formfit, and Edith Lances all reached the public through the New York metropolitan area station WOR.[67] California style, continuing to attract national coverage, offered the only serious competitor to the New York fashion scene.

One persistent misunderstanding of fashion history is that throughout World War II (1939–45), the woman's silhouette was "frozen"—everything was trim, tailored, and tedious. The corollary holds that Christian Dior launched an entirely New Look in 1947. Not so! In Paris before the occupation and in the United States from 1939 until 1942, designers offered definite hints of an emerging fashionable figure with cinched waist, long full skirts, and narrowed shoulders. Until wartime restrictions went into effect, clear hints of a change were in the air. Chic matrons wore bouffant skirts, and college students sported dirndl skirts with trim sweaters tucked into them. Nothing in this silhouette required a major change in brassieres; the full-breasted look with varied degrees of pointiness persisted. Before the guns cooled, in fall 1945 and spring 1946 long, full skirts, high heels, and rounded hips appeared on fashion runways on both sides of the Atlantic.

An ensemble that maintained the GIs' morale was sported by the ever-present Sweater Girl, the less-censorable form of pinup. This icon of American femininity epitomized the achievements of brassiere makers. Brassiere advertisements aimed high, but the sweater promotions and features countenanced only modest swelling of the mammae (Figure 28).

Between fall 1942 and fall 1945, the War Production Board required outerwear clothing manufacturers to exercise restraint in the amount of fabric used in designs, according to the L-85 regulations. For women, this meant daytime dresses had skirts that reached just below the knee and were cut with hardly any fullness. The rules proscribed extravagant sleeves, collars, and self-fabric trim. The WPB intended to reserve productive capacity for uniforms, while not imposing outright rationing of clothing, as befell both Great Britain and the Commonwealth countries. Homemade apparel remained exempt from stylistic restrictions, so dirndls continued to appear among cotton housedresses and sport styles. When out of uniform or work duds, women indulged in pretty cotton or rayon dresses, adaptable suits, and long, slim evening gowns. Add-on accessories—notably collars, waistline peplums, and small jackets—jazzed up basic ensembles but used only small amounts of material.

Brassiere and girdle makers turned the L-85 rules to their advantage, stat-

Figure 28. Model wearing Lovable brassiere with sweater girl pose popular with GIs. *Corset and Underwear Review*, March 1940. Sara Lee Corporation, reproduced with permission.

ing (in a neat combination of virtue and profit) that "L-85 dresses require a more perfect silhouette."[68] Women had to have good shapes under dresses that molded closely to the body and lacked the distraction of extensive trimmings. Brassieres provided trim midriff control and fashionable uplift.

Making do and making over, the shameful badge of poverty in the 1930s, gained patriotic social cachet in the 1940s. Women made suits for themselves from men's civilian attire, sported two-tone dresses, unraveled outworn sweaters to make caps, and patched everything.[69] The Consumer's Victory Pledge included in a booklet from the Spool Cotton Company stated:

> As a consumer, in the total defense of democracy, I will do my part to make my home, my community, my country ready, efficient, strong. I will buy carefully—and I will not buy anything above the ceiling price, no matter how much I want it. I will take good care of the things I have—and I will not buy anything made from vital war materials, which I can get along without. I will waste nothing—and I will take care to salvage everything needed to win the war.[70]

Retailers trimmed their sails and sales in wartime, too. They cut down on fancy fashion shows, curtailed home deliveries, and did what they could to curb returns, especially by close attention to fitting brassieres and corsets. At the end of 1939, *Corset and Underwear Review* writers perceived the renewed importance of fitting, a function that no "fly-by-nighter" or "$20 a week clerk" could perform.[71] Instead, a woman steeped in knowledge of anatomy and customer psychology was required. Throughout the 1940s, fitters enjoyed a heyday.[72] According to the *Corset and Underwear Review* editor, "All the efforts of a retail store are directed to one end: to bring the customer to the department, face to face with the fitter. From that point on, it is up to her."[73]

Fitters trained new help and worked minor miracles of shaping with comfort, compensating as much as possible for the loss of almost all elastic in corset and brassiere designs. They helped women look their best in uniforms and suits that relentlessly revealed figure flaws. Like girdles, 1940s brassieres needed fitting, not only in relation to the chest circumference and breast volume but also to accommodate different styles of bra and the subtleties of shape that differentiated manufacturers. Some customers needed coaching on better techniques of putting on a brassiere: they had to be shown how to "fall into" the cups instead of manually pressing the breasts into place, a potentially harmful technique. While providing these services, the fitter could also clinch multiple sales, showing her customer several styles that would harmonize with tailored, dressy, and sporty clothes in her wardrobe.

Yet factory jobs and other war work drew women into more lucrative fields than clerking or fitting. With little time for classroom training, bra companies prepared self-study materials, and *Corset and Underwear Review* ran articles to assist would-be fitters. Manufacturers also responded to staff shortages by designing self-service packaging and innovative displays.[74] Such expedients started a trend that continued into postwar retailing of foundations, gradually reducing and ultimately supplanting the functions of the fitter.

Technical innovation in brassieres flourished in somewhat muted form during the early 1940s. Nylon fiber had entered the fabric market just as hostilities erupted in Europe. Hosiery makers seized immediately upon nylon, promptly followed by brassiere companies. Bali, Carter, Formfit, Lovable, Vassarette, Warner, and Edith Lances all advertised nylon bras made of marquisette, taffeta, and power net. These brassieres were offered for sale in 1941 and throughout the summer of 1942, then (in theory) withdrawn to conserve the fiber for use in cordage and other necessities of war. However, as shown by a 1943 Bali advertisement (Figure 29), remaining stocks of nylon were being made up into brassieres. The Minnesota Historical Society's Munsingwear Collection of 735 brassieres includes one dated 1943 by the manufacturer and made of peach-toned nylon net. By late 1945, nylon marquisette again became available to manufacturers, according to the October 1945 *Maiden Form Mirror*.[75]

Women went wild for nylon apparel, partly because it was cleverly marketed as a high-fashion fiber from the beginning. Du Pont, unwilling to allow its late 1930s innovation to be saddled with the low-class image that had dogged rayon, went all out to associate nylon fiber with fine-quality clothes.[76] Nylon had real advantages, however, not just a glamour conferred by hyperbolic advertising. Nylon outshone all competitors in tenacity and strength. Unlike the cellulosic fibers, rayon and acetate, nylon stood up well to long use. It was lightweight, washed and dried easily and quickly, and in some weaves did not require ironing. In fact, ironing without sensitive thermostatic controls was likely to scorch or melt this thermoplastic material. From today's perspective, ironing a brassiere seems ludicrous, but both cotton and woven rayon bras usually emerged wrinkled from washing and needed a touch-up with the iron if the wearer wanted a smooth contour beneath her clothes. Women shoppers were urged to extinguish their cigarettes before going into the foundations department, because one stray ash could melt a hole in the nylon.[77] Shape retention proved excellent, despite the apparent sheerness of nylon fabrics. Several advertisements for nylon brassieres touted their coolness in hot weather—a claim refuted by the experience of wearing one. In reality, nylon cloth felt as clammy as a bathing cap.[78]

Although underwire or overwire brassieres were offered by elite producers such as Vonny and André as early as 1934, this feature became com-

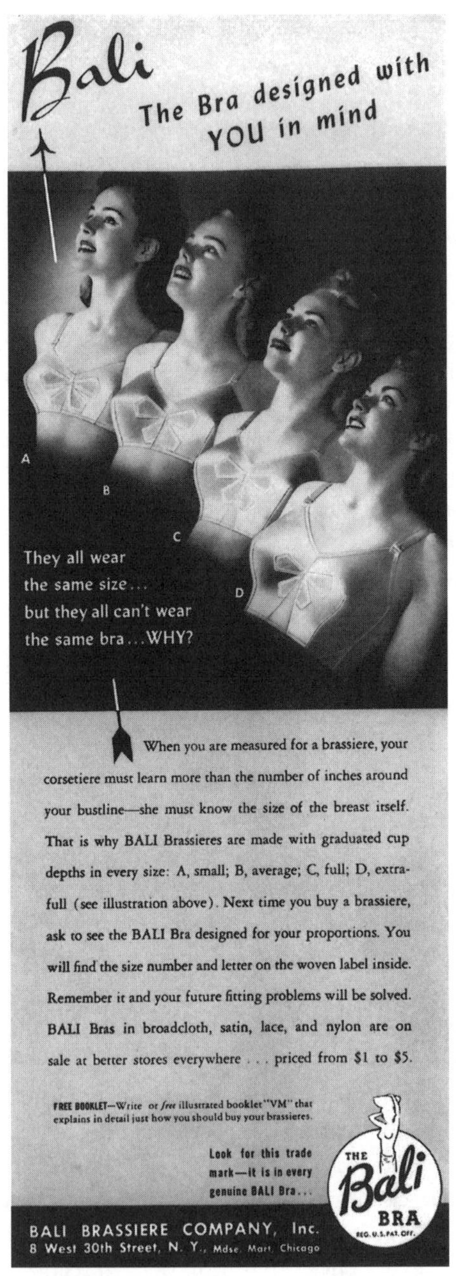

Figure 29. Advertisement for Bali brassieres showing cup sizes A-D indicating graduated proportion. *Vogue*, May 1943. Bali Company/ Sara Lee, reproduced with permission.

mon only after World War II. The War Production Board severely restricted the use of chromium-plated wire for civilian-use products. Brassiere manufacturers improvised fasteners, but renounced wiring. Besides, glamour was not what brassieres were about in 1941–45. Posture, health, fitness, and readiness for action constituted the only acceptable raisons d'être for undergarments-at-war, dubbed "Dutiful Brassieres" by the H & W Company.[79]

Despite present-day complaints about underwires, they were not an inconsiderate feat of engineering foisted on women by a male designer. Cup wires were patented by Madeleine Gabeau in 1911, and the first commercially produced style of underwire was devised by Helene Pons in 1931 and assigned to Van Raalte (Figure 30).[80] Pons envisioned an element that would be comfortable, fitting various wearers and improving the "natural" appearance of the breast. Overwires appeared in a strapless brassiere in 1934.[81] By summer of 1945, Ruth Merzon, a custom producer of exclusive brassieres, was offering "Firm, uplifted bosom with permanent separation achieved by RUTH MERZON's wired brassieres, $20 up." Those prices, about twenty times the cost of an ordinary brassiere, would have attracted few purchasers.[82] Wiring was an up-and-coming thing by 1946. Overwires that encircled the tops of the breast and stabilized the cleavage were patented by Joseph R. Bowen for Hollywood-Maxwell in 1948 and by Harry Gluckin for the Gluckin Company's Alene line in 1949. *Life* magazine featured wired bras in a 1946 story. Jack Glick, designer and patentee for the Alene line, demonstrated how wired styles were designed. Working on a live model, he traced the wire placement superimposed on a conventional brassiere with straps.[83]

One technical innovation that did not succeed in brassieres was the zipper. Invented in 1893, and only much later called the zipper, this slide-fastener was sufficiently reliable by the 1920s to appear in purses and waterproof overshoes.[84] By the late 1930s, designers including Elsa Schiaparelli were putting plastic zippers into their dresses. One venturesome physician, Bernard Notes, patented a Lastex maternity brassiere fastened at center front with a zipper.[85] Apparently this idea did not catch on. It probably caught all right—in all the wrong places! Occasionally long-line brassieres had zippers, but generally the slider technology influenced corsets and corselettes much more than it did brassieres.

An all-latex brassiere loomed on the horizon, with the patent granted to Charles E. Zimmerman and John F. Skold in 1944.[86] For obvious reasons of scarcity, this project was put on hold until the war was over. In fact, the Playtex brassiere did not reach consumers for almost a decade, appearing first in 1954.

War's survivors included most of the brassiere companies. A few small companies may have expired, as was all too common in wartime, but the

March 31, 1931. H. PONS 1,798,274

BRASSIÈRE

Filed July 5, 1929 2 Sheets-Sheet 1

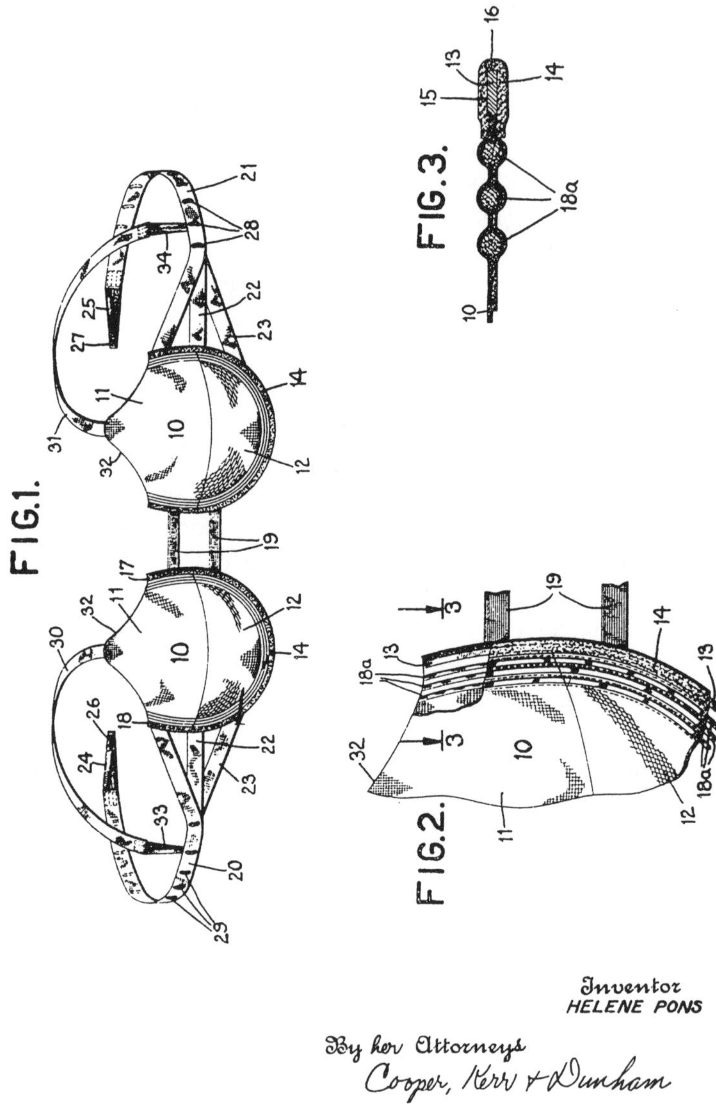

Figure 30. Illustration of an early underwire brassiere with distinctly separated cups, patented by Helene Pons.

larger established manufacturers remained intact. Gabrielle Poix Yerkes went to brassiere heaven in August 1941,[87] but her company continued to make bras through 1949, eventually disappearing into one of its girdle-making affiliates. Nature's Rival had merged with Venus Foundations (Chicago), which produced the College Girl line of brassieres in the 1940s. Munsingwear continued to offer the Foundettes line. Other knitwear brassiere companies, including Carter and Van Raalte, became a more limited presence in the trade. The heavier brassiere structure preferred by women during the war probably could not be achieved with knitting machinery, and the fine rayon-silk yarns requisite for knitting became practically extinct.

One of the challenges faced by the brassiere industry was providing for the many who started their families during the war. A clutch of new firms was born, rather like the baby boomers. Most of the newcomers arrived between 1940 and 1945, but no matter: statistics demonstrate that the baby boom actually began in 1940. More babies were born in 1943 than in any previous year of the twentieth century—offering irresistible opportunities for manufacture of maternity and nursing bras.[88] During the 1930s, New York corset and panty maker Henry Plehn launched the Peter Pan line of brassieres. Plehn, known as a genial host of lavish parties for the foundations trade, patented a less rigid method of creating brassiere cups from stitched cloth.[89] This less expensive and purportedly more comfortable bra sold under the style name Merry-Go-Round, sidestepping Hollywood-Maxwell's Whirlpool trademark.[90]

Tre-Zur, one of the Los Angeles companies, firmed up with the impetus from Max Witkower, who managed to combine allure and function in his many patents for Tre-Zur's brassieres.[91] Ingeniously designed cups and strap arrangements in various Tre-Zur styles offered convenience for nursing mothers, support for large breasts, or a crisscrossed system of uplift in which each side could be adjusted independently—appealing to the many women with unequal-sized breasts.

With many babies on the way or in the cradle, Tre-Zur and the established companies (Venus, Maiden Form) gained competitors for the patronage of those millions of pregnant and nursing women. Lov-é of Hollywood offered both maternity and special-sized brassieres. Shrewdly, the owner, Madame Des Lauriers, chose to advertise in the *American Journal of Nursing*, where she would reach the women who influenced their many patients. Beautee-Fit, also based in Los Angeles, served both maternity clients and women who required decisive uplift. As had the Bali Company, Beautee-Fit took its name from a successful brand. Western Corset Company, as the firm was known in the early 1930s, ill represented a manufacturer who was selling far more bras than corsets. A. Soundel Becker and his son Victor achieved eleven brassiere patents between 1943 and 1958.[92]

Facing a declining demand for his skills in the 1930s, Cleveland tailor Frank Farino went to work for a small custom brassiere company.[93] He bought the business in 1939 and began to search for a way to develop his clientele. The corset buyer for the May Company asked, "Why don't you do maternity bras? No one's making them." By 1940, Leading Lady was launched. Farino devised and patented a brassiere that adapted to pregnancy but could be used when the wearer was no longer pregnant.[94] Leading Lady was sold first in the Cleveland area, but its market soon spread, for example, under J. C. Penney's private label Adonna. Leading Lady continued to serve primarily the maternity market, but also made mastectomy bras and styles adapted to women with large breasts.[95]

Wonder Bra was produced by d'Amour Foundations, with offices in Montreal, Boston, and New York. In the 1940s, Wonder Bra's claim to patented fame was an inverted-V-shaped slit in the top of the cup, just below the strap. This provided adjustability that made movement easier and accommodated cyclical enlargement of the breasts. Lilyette, another newcomer with long-term potential, flourished in New York. Cue-T-Bra, the first style launched by Lilyette, spurned heavy stitching, maintaining the chest-forward silhouette via darts, gathers, and center insets.

Not surprisingly, one refugee story figures among the war-time anecdotes of new companies. Olga and Jan (John) Erteszek fled from Poland, barely ahead of Hitler's armies in 1939. Making their way through Russia by way of China, they took two years to reach the United States, settling in California. By 1944 they had a daughter and a girdle company; brassieres followed in 1947.[96]

A few other brands came on the market in late 1945 and 1946. An uncomfortable-looking U-shaped wire between the cups constituted the Alene brand's special feature. Alene represented the most prominent line developed by Harry Gluckin and his associates. Generally noted for private label merchandise, the Gluckin Corporation banked on patented styles of under- or overwires to win entrance to the fashionable market.[97] Jack Glick, who was principal designer for Gluckin Corporation for about ten years, had a hand in producing the wire shapes. These were intended to offer the degree of breast separation expected from "a good, custom-made bra." At $7.50, the Alene styles cost about half the going rate for custom versions. Between 1944 and 1946, Gluckin and Glick also patented various X-shaped cup-plus-strap adjusting features, but these did not appear in Alene advertisements.

Lillian Hunau, another talented designer, helped to launch Exquisite Form in New York in about 1945. She, too, had a patent for a special wiring feature, which duly showed up in 1946, as war era restrictions on metal eased.[98] Exquisite Form was one of the earliest major brassiere companies to advertise in *Ebony*, a magazine of fashion and social features for African Americans first published in 1945. Identical copy, featuring white models, was used in *Ebony* and other consumer magazines until the late 1960s.

French fashions began to trickle back into the United States after the Liberation in summer 1944. Joseph Berlei, a European brassiere maker, marketed his unconstructed-looking J. Berlé delineators at $16.50 each. Individual fitting and design details helped account for the high price. Playing on the enthusiasm for all things French, Raymond and Suzanne Redares, a couple with French heritage, launched the Mam'zelle brassiere line. Raymond held a patent for an early form of cross-your-heart styling, but the inspiration was probably Suzanne's, because she had experience working in a California brassiere company, whereas Raymond had been a corset salesman.[99]

An almost audible sigh of relief rose from the pages of *Corset and Underwear Review* when peace was declared. Gone were the stern calls to duty, replaced by blandishments to look beautiful. Brassieres sported sexy plunges, embroidery and lace, and lots of color. The V-for-victory motifs, touted somewhat tongue-in-cheek in the bras made by Poix, Eddy-Form, and Renée of Hollywood yielded to U's of wire, specially positioned to separate the breasts and accentuate the cleavage.[100] Strapless designs gained a beachhead in fashion, with further incursions in the late 1940s and 1950s. An Edith Lances number of Alençon lace, with deep U-décolleté, fetched $22.50 at retail. Color blossomed. Red, yellow, aqua, gold, and tropical prints blazed in matching panties and brassiere.[101]

Outerwear fashion bloomed with billowing ballerina-length skirts, draped bodices, and fancy trims. Designers in Paris and New York indulged in furs and elegant fabrics in vivid colors. The California style came into the spotlight, featuring lively sportswear and a casual flavor. Enthusiasm for such stars as Katherine Hepburn, Dorothy Lamour, Betty Grable, and Jane Russell added luster to anything in apparel coming out of Hollywood and its environs.

While the American populace was celebrating peacetime, brassiere and corset makers were suffering hangovers. The vexatious Office of Price Administration remained active almost to the end of 1946, forcing producers to maintain steady prices while their input costs skyrocketed. Labor had grown accustomed to war-production wages, leading both apparel and textile workers to demand higher pay. Cotton fiber was also more expensive than in 1940. Even shortages continued to dog the manufacturers; government restrictions were not easily thrown off, and conversion from making uniforms to making civilian apparel took time. Nylon, being exempt from price restrictions, became a lifeline to many a brassiere maker. Du Pont developed Nyralon, a blend of nylon and rayon, to stretch the supplies of the much-desired synthetic.[102]

Production may have been a headache, but marketing was going very well. Casual flirtation blossomed into passionate courtship, as brassiere companies wooed teenagers for their allowance money, which added up to millions of discretionary dollars annually. Added to that sum was the cash parents were prepared to spend on their daughters' wardrobes. Special fashion fairs, youthful saleswomen, "hep" fitters, teen advisory boards, and displays of inexpensive styles that suited young budgets and bodies—nothing was too much. Companies' advertisements glorified the charms of pigtailed bobby-soxers (Figure 31)—promising them improved self-confidence and protection of their maturing bodies.[103]

Following the 1934 success of *Mademoiselle*, teen magazines proliferated. *Calling All Girls* led the way in 1942, with *Seventeen*, *Miss America*, *Junior Bazaar*, and *Deb* appearing between 1944 and 1946. Teentimer, a wholesale supplier, ran an eponymous Saturday morning radio show that featured popular bands, other entertainment, and well-targeted advertisements for those local stores that bought merchandise through Teentimer.[104]

Fear lurked behind the fanfare. What if this postwar generation chose to toss out their corsets and opt for simple binders in lieu of brassieres, as did the flappers of 1918? That debacle held off for more than a decade. On the contrary, May 1946 brassiere and corset sales showed an increase of 20 percent over the same period in 1945.[105] Outerwear fashions became ever more curvaceous and décolleté, and the teens' taste for bras was confirmed.

Brassieres were no longer commonly sewn at home from commercial patterns. They had become too complex and time-consuming for women juggling household duties and wartime work. The single exception related to those outerwear bras for use in sportswear or casual ensembles that were called play suits. In these cases, the cost differential between homemade and commercial bra-tops may have justified the sewing time involved. Commercially produced bra-tops were very prevalent in fashion magazines: a typical ensemble included the bra, a short skirt or pair of shorts, and sometimes a type of shirt-jacket for coverage when needed for social decorum. The corollary of this was building brassieres into clothing, especially swimwear, which began in the second half of the 1920s and emphatically reshaped swimsuits. Examples of the impact of this trend are the patent for a bra-top secured by Rose Marie Reid and the emergence of Jantzen, an established swimwear maker, into the underfashion industry.

Catalog sales maintained their strength throughout the war. They were convenient for wartime employees who worked long hours. Strict gasoline

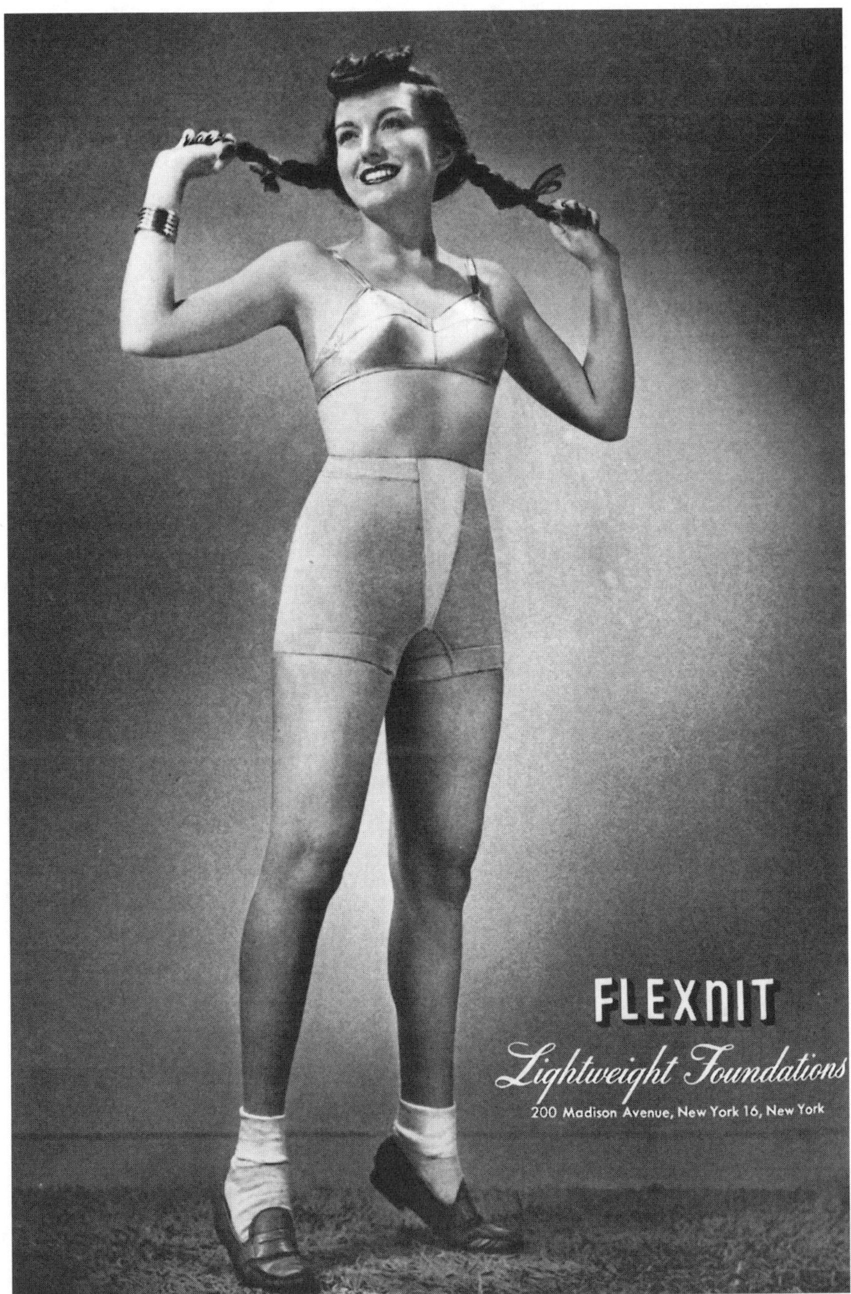

Figure 31. Youthful model with bobby-soxer image wearing Flexnit brassiere. *Vogue*, August 15, 1946.

rationing discouraged needless shopping forays. Only limited styles were offered, at controlled prices. Door-to-door sales, which had languished during the war, staged a slight comeback.

Consumer gripes pushed manufacturers to devise improvements in brassieres. As soon as a greater range of textiles and fasteners became available, better models came on the market. By 1946, brassiere styling had embraced various features for greater support, less binding, some accommodation for expansion in the cup, and other devices that offered adjustability. Straps were made to "give" more and yet stay in place. Marquisette offered coolness, its open structure compensating for the potential stickiness of nylon. Colors and printed patterns introduced a lively note. Basic types of brassieres included the bandeau, long-line, corselette, strapless, and a rudimentary minimizer. Numerous companies accommodated the maternity customer, and prosthetic brassieres were starting to be marketed.

Most regions in the United States had at least one major producer by 1946. California had become a rival to New York and Chicago. Southern firms were planted in Georgia and Texas. In fact, even companies with coastal home offices scattered their manufacturing facilities. Hollywood-Maxwell launched production in Minden, Louisiana. Of the sixty-three companies we tracked, none went out of business in the early 1940s, in strong contrast to other industries. Many smaller producers of hard goods who could not obtain government contracts simply had to close their doors. They lacked sufficient supplies and access to transportation to meet the needs of civilian customers.

Major challenges remained for the industry. Manufacturers needed to construct cups that would retain their shape through constant laundering. Another persistent problem was how to make straps comfortable and stable in position. Also unmet was the need for better prostheses and brassiere-prosthesis combinations. Cancer became Enemy Number One, once Hitler was out of the way.

The more prescient members of the foundations industry saw what was required for improved business in the domestic market: knowledge of which customers subscribed to specific media, so that advertising could be better targeted. In this respect, marketing to teens provided a test pattern. A few business people perceived that knowing where customers lived and what they earned would permit careful design of advertising.[106] Serious marketing research began to guide product development and presentation. Most foresighted of all were producers who recognized that export of brassieres and girdles outside of the United States held the key to solid and expanding postwar prosperity.[107] The U.S. economy boomed between 1947 and 1959, as would the economies of Europe and Japan.

Middle-class American families had money to spend on luxuries: travel, commercial entertainment, socializing, and the glad rags to complement their social lives. Willingly or reluctantly, many women who had been in the workforce returned to full-time homemaking and child rearing. Maternity wear blossomed like the abdomen at eight months. Women wanted and needed easier care in all apparel, including undergarments. All of these trends drove the shape of brassieres to come.

6 Boom and Busts

President Harry Truman pledged prosperity would come with peace at the war's end. Hope was high, but many Americans were unnerved by fear of communism both at home and abroad, as witnessed by the short-term celebrity of Senator Joseph McCarthy in his hunt for Communists.[1] Russia faced off with the Western Allies in what Winston Churchill famously dubbed the cold war, but it was anything but cold, considering the competition to produce a thermonuclear bomb. Fallout shelters proliferated.[2]

Soldiers returning to civilian life and jobs were anxious to start families. The GI Bill provided financial support for education that would be the springboard to the American Dream they had been promised. Thousands of servicemen crowded the nation's campuses; women flocked to new educational opportunities, too, though fewer were eligible for government funding. Often the dream pursued by students included a suburban tract house, such as those built by the tens of thousands by Bill Levitt.[3] New housing created demand for a full array of appliances, all intended to save work. Ironically, these conveniences produced higher expectations of neatness and hygiene: "More work for mother," as Ruth Schwartz Cowan phrased it.[4] Easy-care finishes and fiber blends, plus casual styling, offered some relief from the tedium of laundry. Nylon tricot lingerie featured permanently pleated frills, a touch of luxe for Mrs. Suburbanite.

America's population had increased from 122 million in 1929 to 162 million by 1954, and buying power had outstripped the population growth. In the prosperity that followed 1940, quality was the first demand. People wanted value for their dollar, but they also wanted more luxuries. Once materials became available, intimate wear makers were in the catbird seat. Formfit-Rogers, Olga, Maidenform, and Bali grew rapidly during the 1950s.

With metals released to consumer industries, the American public renewed its love affair with the automobile, styled in the 1950s with a plethora of chrome and tail fins. Vacation trips became easier because of the development of a superhighway system funded by a federal bill that allocated $76 billion in 1956.[5] Forays across the country were eased by cheap gasoline and by the growth of motel chains, a trend led by Kemmons Wilson's Holiday Inns. Clothes designed especially for travel utilized nylon (and later polyester) knits; drip-dry wovens expedited away-from-home care.

Traffic was not the only thing that was accelerating. Restaurant drive-up service became available, and true fast food appeared with the advent of McDonald's hamburger restaurants and Kentucky Fried Chicken emporiums in the 1950s. When the family chose to stay home, a variety of convenience foods—TV dinners and other frozen products—shortened the interval between homecoming and dinner. Women needed all the convenience they could get, because contrary to the 1950s image of homemakers, many American women contributed to family income with paid employment.

* * *

Migration of black Americans from the South to the West, Northeast, and Upper Midwest that had begun in the early twentieth century accelerated during World War II and continued with the arrival of peace. Economic improvement stirred African Americans' aspirations to participate fully in American life through the civil rights movement. Bloody confrontations characterized efforts to integrate both the schools and public transportation systems in the North and South. The legal battle of *Brown v. Board of Education* started in 1954 but did not produce integration of schools until the mid-1960s. Civil rights of all citizens gained a place in the national consciousness. Businesses began to see a new market among black Americans.

The brief but fierce Korean Conflict created shortages, driving up prices on many goods. Intimate wear makers suffered another short-term crunch on materials and metal components, but struggled to cope. Women held more military positions in Korea than in previous wars. Brassieres were issued as part of their uniforms, but women veterans we interviewed wore their own garments due to intense brand loyalty.

The displaced women of the World War II civilian workforce had exchanged their overalls for maternity clothes. The baby boom that accelerated in the United States following World War II brought with it several challenges and opportunities for brassiere manufacturers.[6] Demand for maternity wear exceeded supply by a wide margin. Those producers able to provide buyers with a reliable supply succeeded where their less organized competitors failed. Nationwide, maternity and nursing customers often had to search for retailers carrying designs that met their needs. Leading Lady and Fancee Free enjoyed regional success with their specialized lines. Several of the styles of the 1940s and 1950s were rather awkward and stodgy looking, usually offered only in white and devoid of embellishments.[7] A Fancee Free style (Figure 32) was patented by a registered nurse, Herma Wiedle Dozier, known by her colleagues for her assertive enthusiasm for her products, including maternity garter belts, brassieres, and lightweight girdles. Gradually maternity bras were made with front closures, drop-cup designs, leak-proof pad pockets, flannel liners, and zippered cups. With the adoption of national advertising campaigns, Anne Alt, Venus, Lane Bryant, Leading Lady, and Fancee Free, became leaders in the field.[8] Only the largest retailers carried a variety of products for the maternity customer. Women often turned to mail-order firms like Montgomery Ward, J. C. Penney, and Sears, Roebuck to fulfill their requirements, although catalog selection was usually limited to one or two styles. Despite the burgeoning population, demand for nursing bras was reduced because general practitioners and pediatricians now recommended bottle feeding. It was thought to be more easily regulated and sanitary.

More reliable and expansive than the maternity market was that for high-fashion goods. Christian Dior and other Paris fashion designers were again the style arbiters, and America's fashion industry often followed their lead. Italian high fashion began to make inroads in the U.S. market, beginning in the early 1950s.[9] Couturiers were emphasizing the tiny waist and high, well-defined bosoms between 1947 and 1955. Pauline Gordon, head of an exclusive brassiere company, wrote about "working partnerships" between Paris designers and American apparel makers. Added to the complication was a breakdown in the distinction between outer and inner wear. Gordon predicted the improvement in long-line brassiere design based on French principles.[10] With fabric shortages and price controls abolished by the end of 1946, companies were poised to respond to demand. By 1947 Maiden Form was importing silk and Irish linen with which to make dainty and alluring styles.

Achieving the feminine ideal of the 1950s entailed constant effort. Everything needed to be coordinated in an ensemble, including accessories and underpinnings. In 1948 *Vogue* illustrated twenty-two brassiere styles for different types of outfit.[11] This degree of specificity continued to the end of the 1950s. Ready-to-wear designer Anne Fogarty urged women: "Be certain you have the right bra contour for every dress and silhouette."[12] Advertisers featured slim models, diet advice, and exercise themes.[13] Almost every woman's magazine regularly ran articles with the latest diets. Even pregnant women were urged to restrict their weight gain in order to quickly recapture their pre-

at last . . .

the perfect pair for maternity wear by Fancee Free

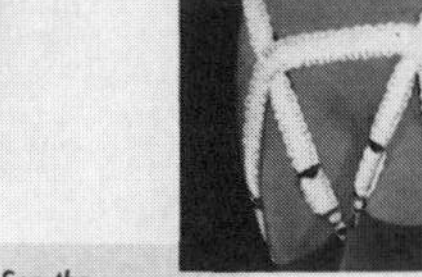

See the
FANCEE FREE line
Hotel Vanderbilt
November 17-22

You'll find the doctors are happy to recommend the FANCEE FREE Bra just as they have the FANCEE FREE Garter Belt. The FANCEE FREE Bra will be shown along with the FANCEE FREE Garter Belt at two medical conventions during the month of December.

the sensational maternity and nursing bra
it's new . . . it's expandable . . . it's adjustable

Two for the money—that's what your customers get when they buy the new FANCEE FREE Maternity and Nursing Bra. For it gives extraordinary support during the late months of pregnancy . . . carries over as a perfect nursing bra. Made of finest broadcloth, the FANCEE FREE Maternity and Nursing Bra is *completely adjustable.* Cups are adjustable by means of a drawstring. Double bands that cross under cups adjust with Parva buckle on each side. Disposable pads available.

White Broadcloth Style #711 . . sizes 34 to 40, B, C and D cups. (Pat. Pend.)
Price $21.00 per dozen, 8/10 EOM, suggested retail $3.00 (FOB Store)

Fancee Free ® MANUFACTURING COMPANY
5467 Delmar • St. Louis 12, Mo.
Herma Wiedle, R. N., President

24

CORSET & UNDERWEAR REVIEW for November, 1952

Figure 32. First maternity bra for her Fancee Free Company, patented by Herma Wiedle Dozier. Note the front drawstring for shaping. *Corset and Underwear Review*, November 1952. Reproduced with permission.

natal figures. Dieting and exercise demanded discipline, but complete allure required a relaxation of restraint.

Movie stars provided glamorous examples of idealized figures. Audrey Hepburn typified elfin grace for the petite woman, Grace Kelly and Lauren Bacall exemplified long-lined elegance, and Marilyn Monroe and Jayne Mansfield set the pace for women who aspired to voluptuous curves. Whatever a woman's physical proportions, she tried to make her curves look well edited in sheath dresses, pencil-slim skirts, and cinch belts. The more worldly and sophisticated women took their cue from the Duchess of Windsor, who was dressed by the expatriate Chicagoan Mainbocher. Unlike periods before and after the 1950s, sportswomen did not set fashions.

Sexuality was openly espoused in the late 1940s and 1950s. Alfred Kinsey's 1953 *Sexual Behavior in the Human Female* created an even greater bombshell than his earlier research on American men's sexual practices.[14] *Peyton Place* became both a best-seller in 1956 and a catchphrase in the American popular lexicon, connoting the seamy sexuality of small-town America.[15] Movie stars of the 1950s also exuded erotic power: from Marilyn Monroe's kittenish poses to the churlish scowls of Marlon Brando and James Dean. Elvis Presley's writhing set the example for rock and roll performers. No wonder brassiere makers, like Model, joined in the erotic fun. Its Illusion design created a daring effect with completely transparent cup sections and firm satin underlift.

The renewed emphasis on feminine sexuality produced brassiere designs to harmonize with body-revealing décolleté styles: plunging necklines, bare midriffs, halters, backless models, and strapless dresses. These were featured by almost all makers. Several styles were made to be worn out-of-doors as play tops, halters, or sun wear; many had detachable straps (Figure 33). The 1950 Shutter Bra was designed to be partially visible in the neckline of the gown, with flaps or lace cuffs at the top of the cups. In the same season, Lady Marlene introduced a boned bra bodice in black velvet for evening wear and a similar design in white piqué for sports and day wear. With the two-piece bathing suit becoming more popular, it was hard to tell whether a mode was meant for the beach or the ballroom. Strapless brassiere patents outnumbered other styles during the 1950s. Without exception they included some form of wire or metal framing, in conjunction with elastic panels. Whether short or long-line, the emphasis was on the curvaceous, hourglass silhouette.

Multicolored or printed brassieres appeared in advertisements with themes taken from Egypt or the South Pacific. Exotic and romantic names abounded, like Nephretiri, Cleopatra, candlelight, and cinnamon-desert. Copywriters waxed enthusiastic, describing products in purple prose. Stores

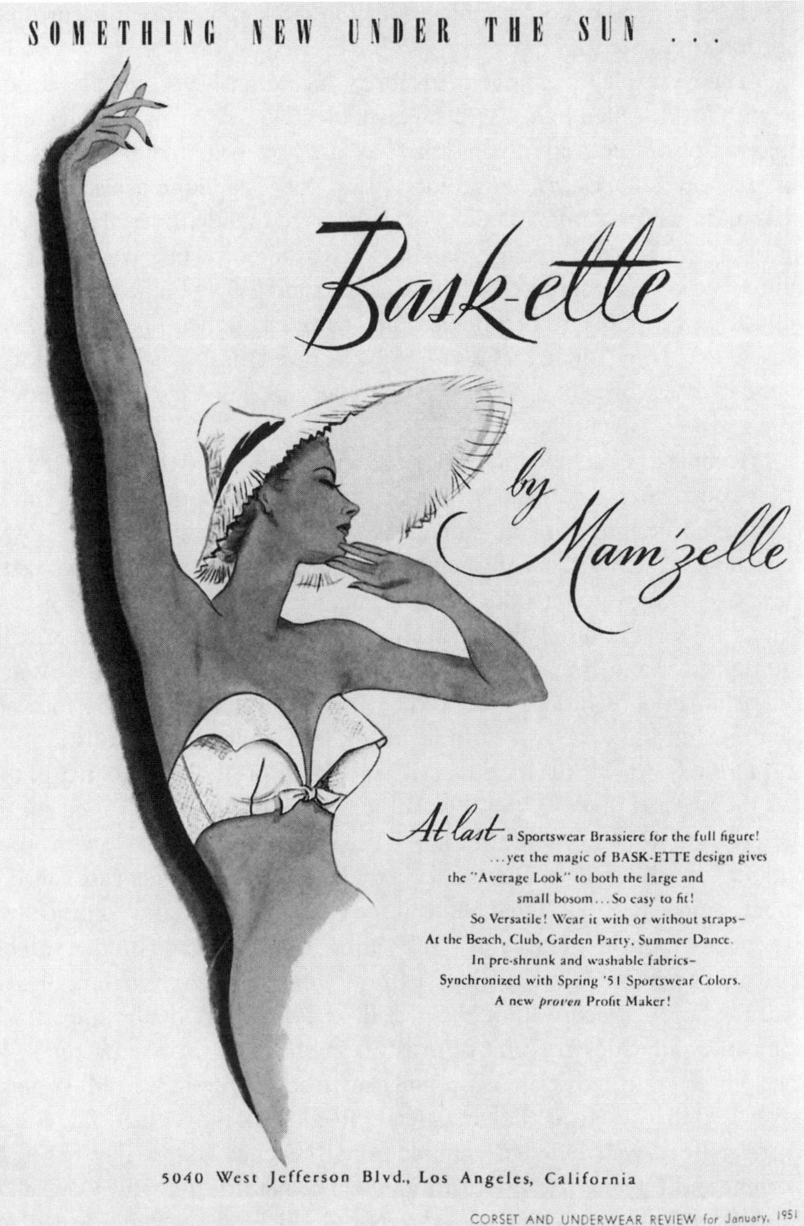

Figure 33. Trade advertisement for strapless sportswear brassiere by Mam'zelle intended for sunbathing. *Corset and Underwear Review*, January 1951.

were hard-pressed to keep popular models in stock for enthusiastic customers. The industry rose to the challenge with increased production.

There was plenty of novelty in fabrics, including eyelet, which was popular with Model, Bien Jolie, Maiden Form, Flexees, and Perma-lift. Nylon marquisette, power net, and rayon satin were used by many manufacturers. Gossard had several lines with embroidery; Lily Daché appliquéd daisies on strapless bandeaux for Nemo. Maiden Form marketed their leftover Mexican plaids and ginghams to the teenage market (see Figure 26), while Warner featured dotted Swiss, and lace was the favorite of Olga and Lily of France. Women were inundated with dots, ruffles, flowers, and patterns on their underwear. An exclusive 1947 New York City fashion show featured fur brassieres in ocelot and white or black broadtail. They had asymmetrical designs with one shoulder bare and were tied in the back.[16]

Technical details and interesting fabrics distinguished the bras of the postwar period. Special stitching of the cup sections was popular. Peter Pan had forty-seven designs with its patented Merry-Go-Round stitching; Lovable sold the Action Bra. This, incidentally, featured one of the earliest cross-the-chest or X designs, reintroduced by Playtex with the "Cross Your Heart" slogan in 1954.[17] Exquisite Form called its versions with Circloform stitching the Equalizer and #225, Flexees made the Roundweave, and Miss America Bra Company of Chicago produced the Roundabout. Maiden Form, Kabo-Nemo, Munsingwear, and Formfit introduced undersection stitching only, and Hollywood–Maxwell claimed that its Whirlpool Bra, patented in 1935, was the original that everyone else copied. Several companies varied the idea with vertical stitching, while Marja of Texas created the Hi-A style with "round and out" stitching. Peter Pan offered a trademarked Elasto-net rim, called the honeycomb ("bee free") that allowed the cups to expand and contract "with every body motion" (Figure 34). In addition to patented and unique stitching patterns to reinforce the cup shape, extra attention was given to the straps that held the cup in place. Although specialized contractors made straps for bra companies, strap designs came primarily from the brassiere manufacturers, and the split or branched strap was popular with several designers. Most makers advertised this design as allowing greater freedom of movement. The original Wonder Bra[18] was the main example using branched straps (Figure 35), but Formfit and Lilyette had popular models. The Naturflex Cradle Cup offered "divided strap action" that earned it the Good Housekeeping Seal of Approval.[19] The Circloform brassiere from Exquisite Form was offered with and without "Floating Action," defined as a "revolutionary new design principle introducing tangent straps."[20]

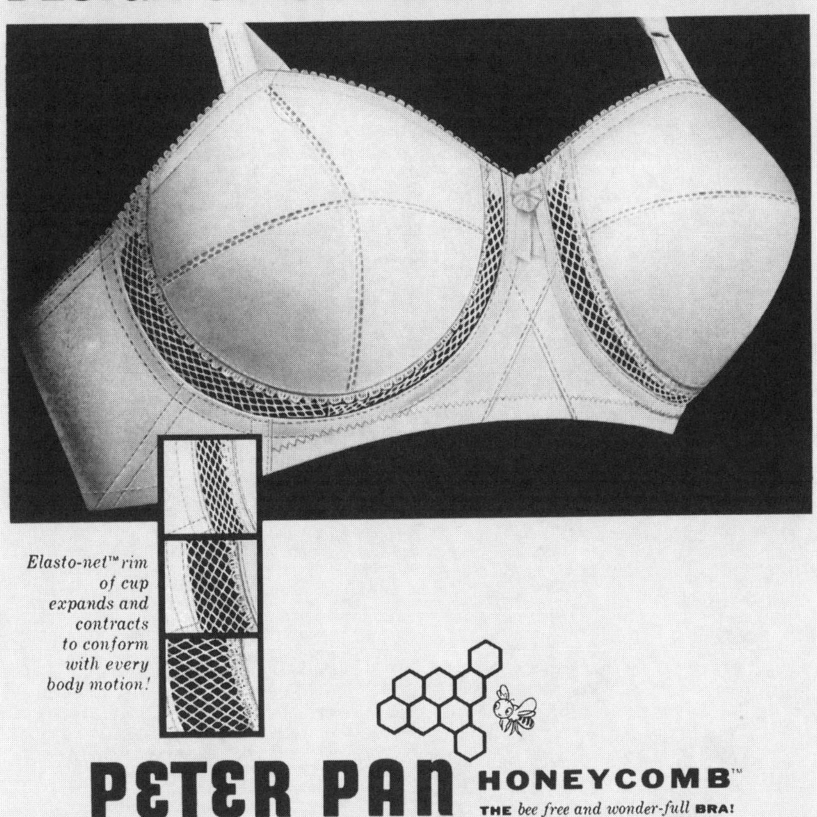

FIRST MAJOR ADVANCE IN BRA DESIGN SINCE HIDDEN TREASURE*
Elasto-net™ rim of cup expands and contracts to conform with every body motion!
PETER PAN HONEYCOMB™
THE bee free and wonder-full BRA!
Everyone will be buzzing with excitement! Your department will be a beehive of activity! All because of this new concept in bra design! World-favored Hidden Treasure cups keep fullness, uplift, and contours constant, while the circle of Elasto-net gives bust a freedom found only in this honey of a bra! Nothing – and only nothing – is so cool, so comfortable. In white Wamsutta Lustercale. A, B, C cups. 27.00 doz. – retail, 3.95 • Peter Pan Honeycomb will be widely advertised, promoted, and publicized. Be sure that Honeycomb shoppers make a beeline to your store!
no body is perfect . . . every body needs Peter Pan
Peter Pan Foundations, Inc., 389 Fifth Avenue, New York 16 · Montreal
CORSET & UNDERWEAR REVIEW for July, 1958
7

Figure 34. Trade advertisement for Peter Pan brassiere featuring expandable cup design with Honeycomb inserts. *Corset and Underwear Review*, July 1958.

Figure 35. Early advertisement for original Wonder Bra styles featuring the branched strap. *Corset and Underwear Review*, January 1952. Sara Lee, reproduced with permission.

Some women required more from a brassiere than stitches and straps, as this limerick shows:

There was a young lady of Skye
With a Shape like a capital I;
She said, "It's too bad!
But then, I can pad."
Which shows you that figures can lie.[21]

Padding was all the rage again. Various methods of faking an ample bosom had been employed from time immemorial, but the 1950s offered high-tech ploys. Foam rubber became the augmenter of choice for most makers; however, Kyle of California used eiderdown in its Konturettes brassiere.[22] Peter Pan employed felt for its "falsies."[23] Some like Maiden Form and Jantzen had removable pads inserted into special pockets, but many were built into the cups. Names like True Form, Secret Charm, Radiant Security, Curves 2-U, and Complement coaxed buyers to purchase these enhancers.[24] The Très Secrète developed and produced by La Resista Company of Bridgeport, Connecticut, made an inflatable brassiere with a little plastic straw for blowing it up to the desired size (Figure 36).[25] Padding was not the only thing added to brassieres: Kabo offered the Bou-K-Bra, which contained a removable "Scent-Petal" secret pocket where a personal cologne or perfume could be cached to add a touch of fragrance.[26] Gem-Dandy offered the Mon-e-Bra, with zippered front section between the cups to hold money or jewelry (Figure 37).

Not all innovations related to style; some were matters of life and health. Breast cancer diagnosis increased following World War II. In 1951 public health statistics indicated that one in five Americans would suffer from cancer in his or her lifetime, with breast cancer the most prevalent type among women.[27] Strong scientific studies were yet to be completed, and some physicians still blamed the breast binding of the 1920s for breast cancer.[28] The awareness of breast cancer was very high within the industry, and the trade publications fostered informational campaigns to encourage breast self-examination as early as 1952.[29] Retailers showed short films about breast cancer in their lingerie departments as a public service to customers and staff. In 1952 Terese Lasser founded Reach-to-Recovery, a program by which former patients could offer moral support and information to other women with breast cancer.

The mastectomy patient presented a complicated task for designers. Creating a brassiere that would contain a balanced and natural-feeling prosthesis while at the same time supporting the remaining breast in a comfortable way was only part of the puzzle. Many clients for these special brassieres were

ıdemoiselle for November 1951
47

"Wrapture"

Très Secrète*
(VERY SECRET)
INFLATABLE BRA
MAKES ALL OTHER WAYS TO A LOVELY NATURAL BUSTLINE OLD-FASHIONED!

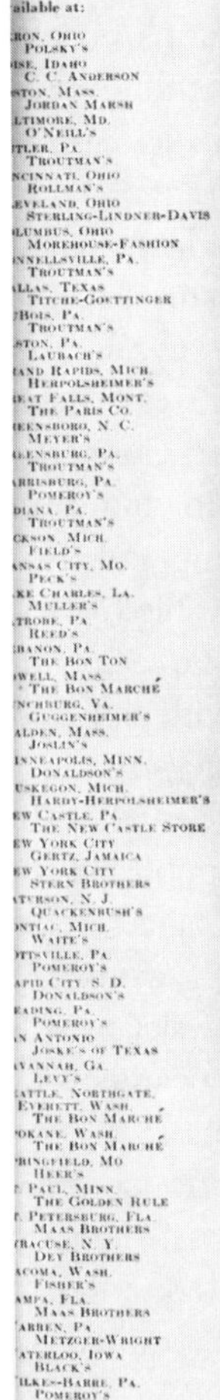

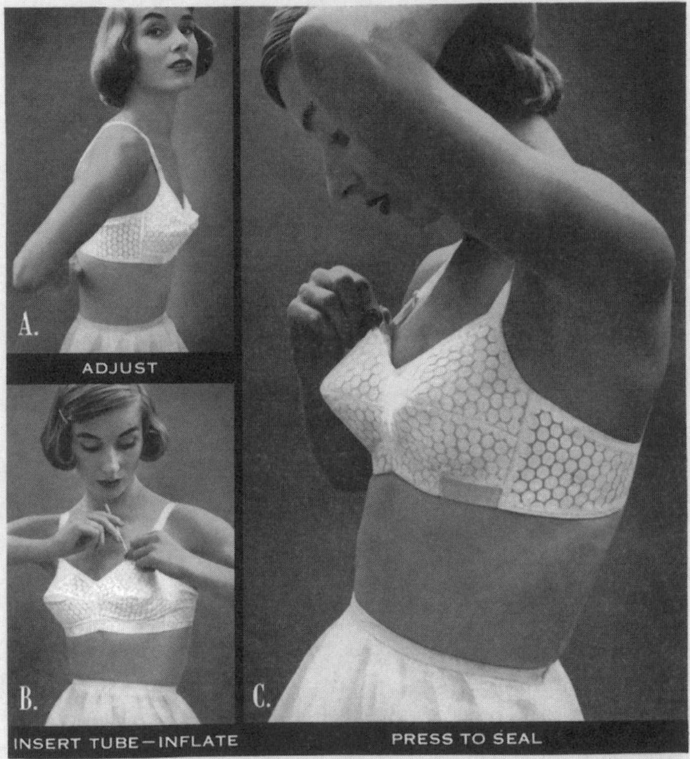
A.
ADJUST
B.
C.
INSERT TUBE—INFLATE
PRESS TO SEAL
Patented and Pat. Pending in U.S.A. and Foreign Countries.
*Reg. U.S. Pat. Off.
It's Perfection without Detection
It's new! It's revolutionary! Très Secrète is the only bra ever made that gives you the desired bust-line! No heavy pads or rubber cups—just weight-less air for that lovely figure you've always wanted. Très Secrète, with two removable plastic, adjustable in-flatables, is made of long-lasting figured nylon. (Quick-drying, needs no ironing!) You don't even need a try-on—just come in and buy one! In white—sizes 32, 34, 36 A and B cup. $5.00
LA RESISTA CORSET COMPANY
45 Park Avenue, New York City, N.Y. • Bridgeport, Conn.
Mail to the listed store nearest you, or to:
Dept. LR, Allied Stores Corporation
401 Fifth Avenue, New York 16, New York
Please send me a Très Secrète Bra advertised at $5.00 plus 25¢ for postage and handling. Enclosed is check ☐ or money order ☐ for $......
Size .... Cup .... Quantity ....
Name ....
Address ....
City .... Zone .... State ....
(Include local taxes, if any)

Figure 36. Model wearing a Très Secrète brassiere, which the wearer could inflate to desired size by blowing into a straw. *Mademoiselle*, November 1951.

Figure 37. Trade advertisement for Mon-e-Bra, with zippered center pocket to hold valuables against loss. *Corset and Underwear Review*, April 1951.

psychologically as well as physically scarred from radical mastectomy, the treatment of choice for almost all patients with breast cancer during the 1940s and 1950s. Weighted and balanced breast forms for the mastectomy patient were designed with natural shapes by companies like Identical Form, Miriam Gates, and Lov-é (Figure 38).[30] Patents awarded to medically trained designers were no more successful than those grounded in the fashion industry. Companies like Leading Lady prepared certified fitters with special training to assist these customers. The sensitivity training of fitters as well as the choice of well-made brassieres helped to restore patients' sense of their own femininity and beauty.

New materials made their way into the manufacture of brassieres. Drip-dry fabrics like Orlon acrylic (mid-1940s) and Dacron polyester (1951) were quickly adopted by the industry, though not always with satisfactory results.[31] Synthetic rubbers had been used widely in wartime applications and were the first transfer technologies used in the foundation garment business. The foam rubbers used in padding and synthetic rubber used in elastic proved to be worthy substitutes. Metal sundries were threatened immediately following the war because the steel industry was halted by successive coal strikes. Nylon had been restricted during the war but had never completely disappeared from the intimate wear market; its popularity with designers and buyers rested mainly on its translucency in the form of marquisette. Incredibly, many advertisements featuring nylon brassieres touted its coolness. In fact, in marquisette and other open weaves nylon may have been acceptably cool. Rayon was the fiber in shortest supply immediately after the war, and prices trended upward as a result. Cotton supplies were also uncomfortably tight. A loss of about 10 percent of cotton spinners and looms compounded the effect of poor crops in 1946 and 1947.[32] Other industries siphoned off the best workers with offers of higher wages. Maiden Form and other producers experimented with several fabrics, including woven silks and linens and rayon bengaline. However, a survey indicated that American women were not particularly fiber-conscious when it came to purchasing brassieres.[33] Penney's reported rayon satin as the favorite for brassieres in 1948, but by 1955 cotton broadcloth was the preferred fabric.[34]

As Americans bought more automatic washing machines and dryers, fiber content of all clothing became more of an issue. In 1948, the Model Company advertised their new Bias-Cup Bra, which they claimed "could not be washed out of shape."[35] Anne Fogarty chimed in with laundry advice: "Wash bras after each wearing; most are made of miracle fabrics and dry in a matter of hours . . . [therefore] Bras probably need more replenishing than other underwear items. However firm their original construction, constant washing must take its toll.

more and more top stores **STOCK**– more and more physicians **RECOMMEND**– more and more customers **WEAR** the wonderful new LOV-É "TWIN"® with exclusive patented weight control for PERFECT BALANCE.

write for details

"TWIN" REGULAR
For average mastectomy case. Sizes 32 thru 39. Supplied with lace-edged removable cover.

Retail:	$12.50 ea.
Your List	75.00 doz.
Your List	6.25 ea.

"TWIN" T
Regular "Twin" with added point for muscle amputation above breast. (Specify left or right.)

Retail:	$13.95 ea.
Your List	90.00 doz.
Your List	7.50 ea.

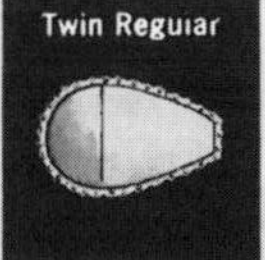

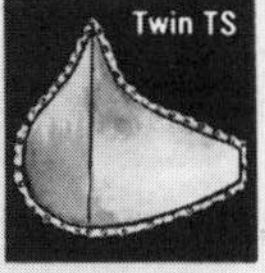

28 SIZES · 4 BASIC SHAPES

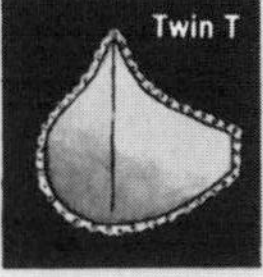

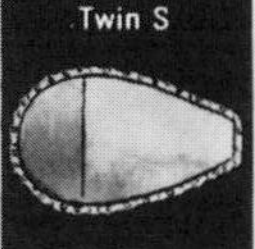

"TWIN" S
Regular "Twin" with added length for muscle amputation under arm.

Retail:	$13.95 ea.
Your List	90.00 doz.
Your List	7.50 ea.

"TWIN" TS
Regular "Twin" with added point and added length for muscle amputation above breast and under arm. (Specify right or left.)

Retail:	$16.50 ea.
Your List	105.00 doz.
Your list	8.75 ea.

BRASSIERE COMPANY
7494 SANTA MONICA BLVD., HOLLYWOOD 46, CALIF

38 CORSET & UNDERWEAR REVIEW for November, 1958

Figure 38. Trade advertisement for postmastectomy breast prostheses offered by Lov-é brassiere company. *Corset and Underwear Review*, November 1958.

Even if the rubber or straps do not yet show signs of wear, they will, to coin a phrase, 'lose their hold' with time."[36]

An item available from Hollywood-Maxwell as an "impulse buy" for lingerie counter sales was the patented bra presser.[37] The freshly washed bra would press itself as it dried while held over two plastic molds by stretchable rubber rings. We found no information on its success as a moneymaker or laundry aid.

Advice for improving brassiere wear included the ideal method for putting one on. Bess Oerke, a home economist, advised this:

> Slip both arms through the straps. Bend over from the hips so that the breasts fall forward and rest comfortably in the cups. While bending over, hook the garment behind your back as far down your back as you can reach. Stand erect again, place both forefingers inside the bottom of the brassiere, and run your fingers around the garment. As you do this, pull the garment down in the front and in the back.[38]

Plastics and treated rubber were used in several brassiere applications. U.S. Rubber produced Playtex all-rubber brassieres, but these found limited acceptance because they trapped perspiration. Front-closing brassieres appeared in the 1950s, when Warner advertised its Good News model, which featured a zipper. Sacony Rubber Company produced its Locket Bra, similar to that patented in 1949 by Sydne Cousins.[39] Between 1951 and 1957, Flexees brought out the Avant and the Figurama,[40] and Hollywood-V-ette featured Petal Skills with a front plastic closure. Charmfit showed its MagiClose Bra with "the revolutionary new Velcro fastener" in wrap-around bands across the front.[41] American women in general did not adapt to these new designs, and their popularity was limited to those with restricted flexibility. The first brassiere marketed to be worn while sleeping was seen in 1958.[42] Thankfully it did not include the very popular underwire construction in its design.

Wire became an essential component in the brassiere industry. With the war over, chromium plated wire was again available, and manufacturers promoted the efficacy of flexible spiral, flat, and round wires. An emphasis on rigidity hit a new peak with advertising of 1950s underwire brassieres. These were marketed primarily to large-breasted customers at first, but were soon discovered to thrust and uplift smaller bosoms to new heights. The numerous configurations of heavy wire separating the breasts, spiral wire under the breasts, flexible wire over the breasts, branching, and circular wires used by designers in every company were a torturer's tour de force. As the fashion focused on the pinched waist, the corsetlike Merry Widow (Figure 39) by Warner led the way. Manufacturers tried to outdo each other with metal reinforcements. Breasts were not only encapsulated with wire encircling cups; they were sepa-

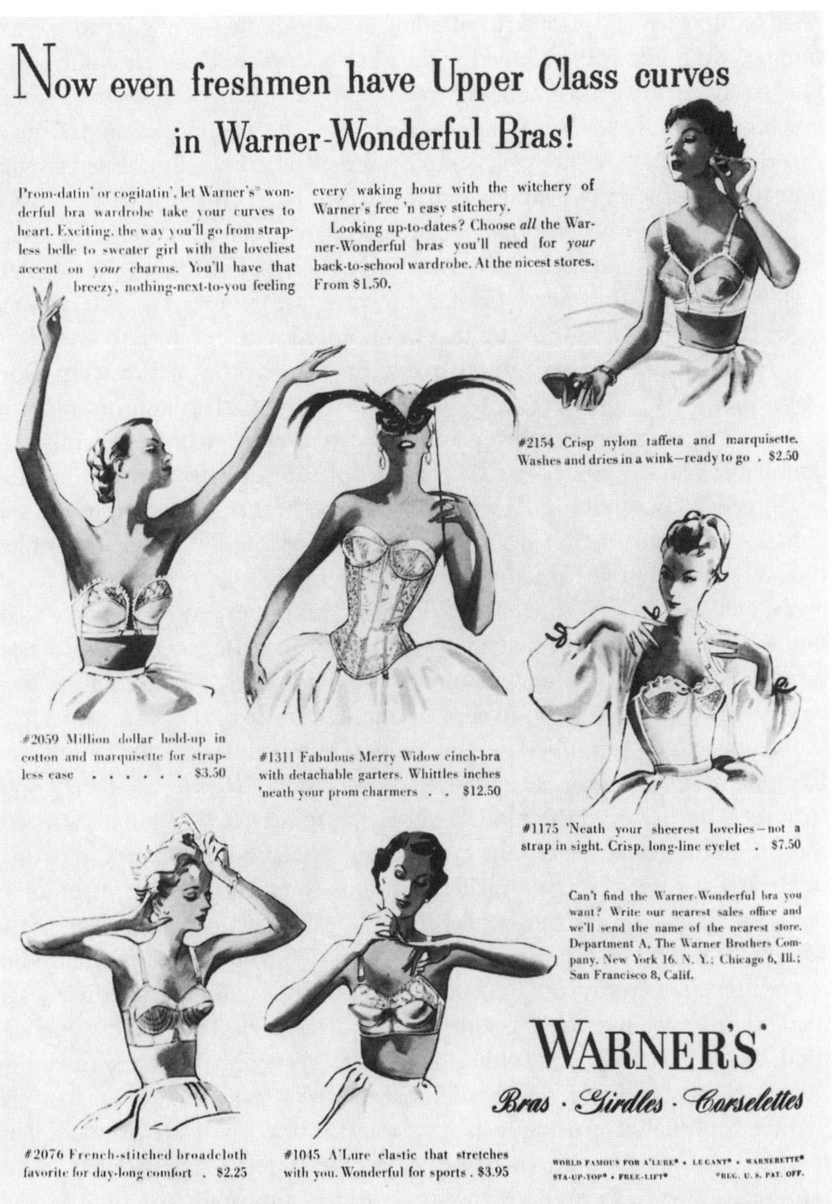

Now even freshmen have Upper Class curves in Warner-Wonderful Bras!
Prom-datin' or cogitatin', let Warner's* wonderful bra wardrobe take your curves to heart. Exciting, the way you'll go from strapless belle to sweater girl with the loveliest accent on your charms. You'll have that breezy, nothing-next-to-you feeling every waking hour with the witchery of Warner's free 'n easy stitchery.
Looking up-to-dates? Choose all the Warner-Wonderful bras you'll need for your back-to-school wardrobe. At the nicest stores. From $1.50.
#2154 Crisp nylon taffeta and marquisette. Washes and dries in a wink—ready to go . $2.50
#2059 Million dollar hold-up in cotton and marquisette for strapless ease $3.50
#1311 Fabulous Merry Widow cinch-bra with detachable garters. Whittles inches 'neath your prom charmers . . $12.50
#1175 'Neath your sheerest lovelies—not a strap in sight. Crisp, long-line eyelet . $7.50
Can't find the Warner-Wonderful bra you want? Write our nearest sales office and we'll send the name of the nearest store. Department A, The Warner Brothers Company, New York 16, N. Y.; Chicago 6, Ill.; San Francisco 8, Calif.
WARNER'S*
Bras · Girdles · Corselettes
#2076 French-stitched broadcloth favorite for day-long comfort . $2.25
#1045 A'Lure elastic that stretches with you. Wonderful for sports . $3.95
WORLD FAMOUS FOR A'LURE* · LE GANT* · WARNERETTE* STA-UP-TOP* · FREE-LIFT*
*REG. U. S. PAT. OFF.

Figure 39. Consumer advertisement illustrating Warner's Merry Widow and other popular silhouettes of the 1950s. *Mademoiselle*, August 1952. Reproduced with permission. All trademarks and copyrights are owned by Warnaco, Inc.

rated or otherwise positioned in anatomically astounding configurations. Steel boning and semiflexible braided wires were encased in channels along seamlines to create brassieres that held breasts high and firm in both short and longline versions. Perhaps the ultimate in wired brassiere was the patented Maurice Lobel design that was not only strapless but also backless. It claimed to support the breast with "a yielding arcuate-shaped band" that partially encircled the torso, leaving the back bare.[43] Any maker who did not follow the strapless trend soon found itself with stock on the shelves. Essentially, the brassiere was not necessary for healthy breasts; however, the fashion-conscious woman required the brassiere silhouette that harmonized with her outerwear.

Some of the best recognized name brands across America were those of brassieres. Manufacturers coordinated packaging with sales promotions in newspapers, magazines, subway and bus cards, radio, television, and store counter displays. Radio was a critical part of the advertising world because nearly every household in America tuned in to hear soap operas, music and comedy programs.[44] Slogans like Hollywood-Maxwell's phrase describing their V-ette design as "America's most asked-for brassiere" were repeated in every medium. The Wonder Bra Company not only used advertising techniques on their customers but had a special film made to indoctrinate their sales personnel.[45]Television programs of increasing popularity, such as *I Love Lucy*, were beamed into living rooms across America. The high cost of national television advertising put it beyond the budgets of all but the largest companies. Regional television time was purchased by Lovable to advertise their popular lines. They featured live models displaying brassieres. The public accepted these seminude models until the early sixties, when body-stockings were used to cover the torsos. To gain cachet and fame for their products, promoters used rising film stars and minor celebrities. Lovable Company had a Girl of the Month, for example, Jean Brown in May 1950. Companies that specialized in maternity, mastectomy, and nursing styles frequently concentrated their ads in medical, nursing, and public health journals. Before television advertising was used, many bra companies sold in regional markets only but were forced by the popularity of television to go national and be prepared to supply a national market. National advertising agencies reaped the rewards of an expanded clientele from this trend. Some companies succumbed under the pressure to deliver goods nationwide. Long-lived, highly respected companies including Model, Venus, Madame Adrienne, and Stein and Company (Perma-Lift) expired during the 1950s.

Maidenform began its still-famous "I Dreamed" campaign in 1949, continuing until 1969. The campaign was quite possibly inspired by the Joseph Magnin department store ad with the caption "Last night I dreamed I had nothing on but my black Gossard." Since this slogan was reported in the January 1946 issue of *Corset and Underwear Review*, it might well have prompted the design of the Maidenform dream campaign. Whatever the source of inspiration, the campaign was created by Kitty D'Alessio at the Weintraub Agency, which had assumed the accounts for Maidenform after World War II. Note that simultaneous with the hugely successful advertisements came an elision of the company name to one word.[46] Each "dream" ad showed a photograph of a single brassiere-clad female model in a "dream" role: traveling, shopping, working, engaging in sports, and enjoying fantasy activities. Several of these were on the cutting edge for the time, such as "I Dreamed I Won the Election" (Figure 40). The design of the ad leaves no doubt that she was running for some important office. These consumer ads were coordinated with an equally brilliant series of cartooned ads in the trade magazines. The contrast between the consumer and trade focus was acute, with the former accentuating the allure of the fantasy and the latter emphasizing a lightly humorous but genuine business realism.[47] Even the television ads were coordinated with the Dream theme. Conversely, much mid-1950s print advertising copy was lifted straight from the script pages of popular television programs. Munsingwear appropriated the phrase "What they want are the facts, ma'am!" from *Dragnet*.[48]

The customers to whom this advertising blitz was directed were very carefully chosen by the industry. Companies like Sarong, Peter Pan, and Jantzen focused seriously on the youth market. This was based on the belief that a customer once sold a name brand would remain loyal throughout her lifetime. Fitters were coached in measuring and fitting the teenage buyer with professional courtesy, free of condescension and motherly advice. Each adolescent was to receive private attention, free from mother's input. Articles in the trade magazine *Corset and Underwear Review* regularly instructed retailers in the subtleties of selling to high school and college students. Ads that lured the mothers of adolescent girls promoted purchases of preteen training brassieres as a rite of passage. These were garments with minimal shape, often softly padded to provide the first curves on a prepubescent body, but meant to assure mother and daughter of their common bond (see Figure 48). A 1955 advertisement for the Formaid Slip-On Bra stated, "Look, ma . . . no hooks!" which assured young wearers of freedom to slip into the brassiere "like it was a sweater" (Figure 41). J. C. Penney stores carried slip-on styles in the mid-1950s.[49] In 1958 Hollywood V-ette Vassarette sponsored a study by syndicated columnist Eugene Gilbert, a respected authority on the fast-growing, fast-spending youth market.[50] In 1956 *Scholastic* magazine's Institute of Student Opinion found that 13 million teenagers averaged $10.55 per week of discretionary spending money earned from after-school jobs like babysitting, retail selling, and waitressing.[51]

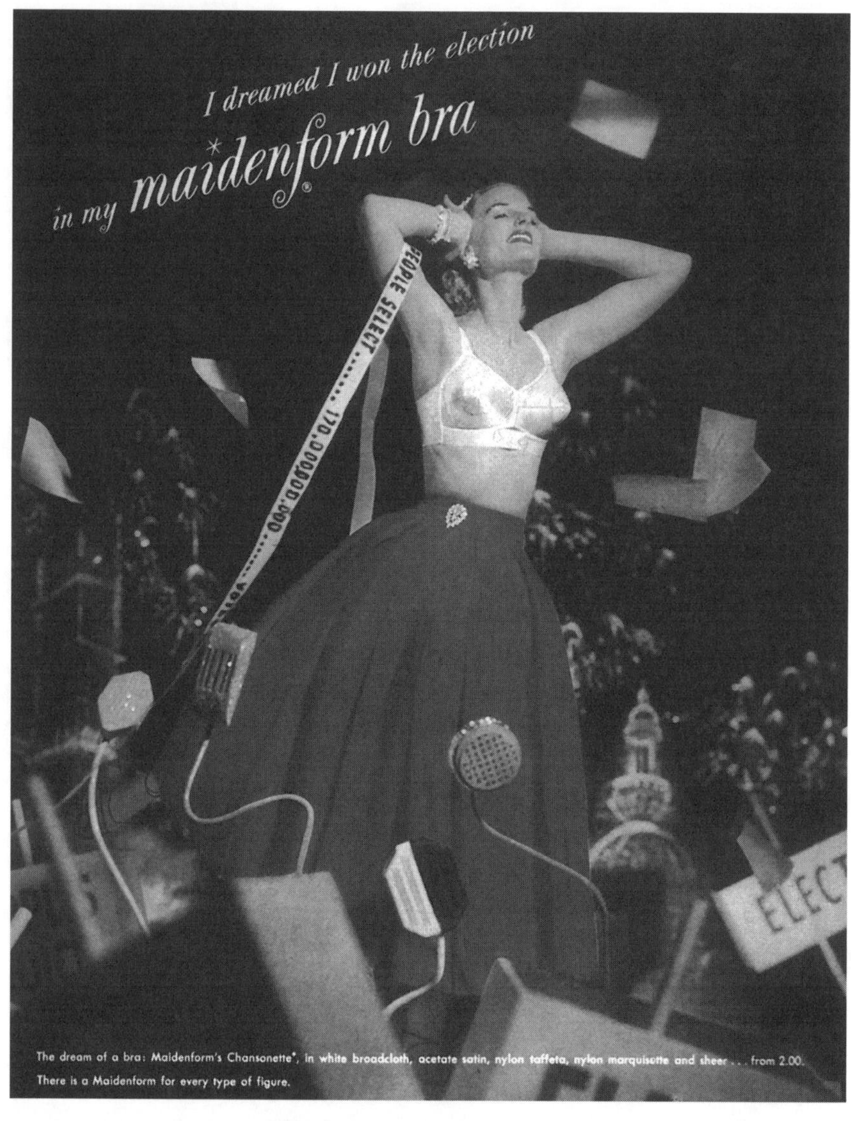
I dreamed I won the election
in my maidenform bra
PEOPLE SELECT ...... 170,000,000 ......
ELECT
The dream of a bra: Maidenform's Chansonette*, in white broadcloth, acetate satin, nylon taffeta, nylon marquisette and sheer . . . from 2.00.
There is a Maidenform for every type of figure.

Figure 40. An example of Maidenform's "Dream" campaign designed for the Weintraub agency by Mary Fillius in 1952. Reproduced with permission.

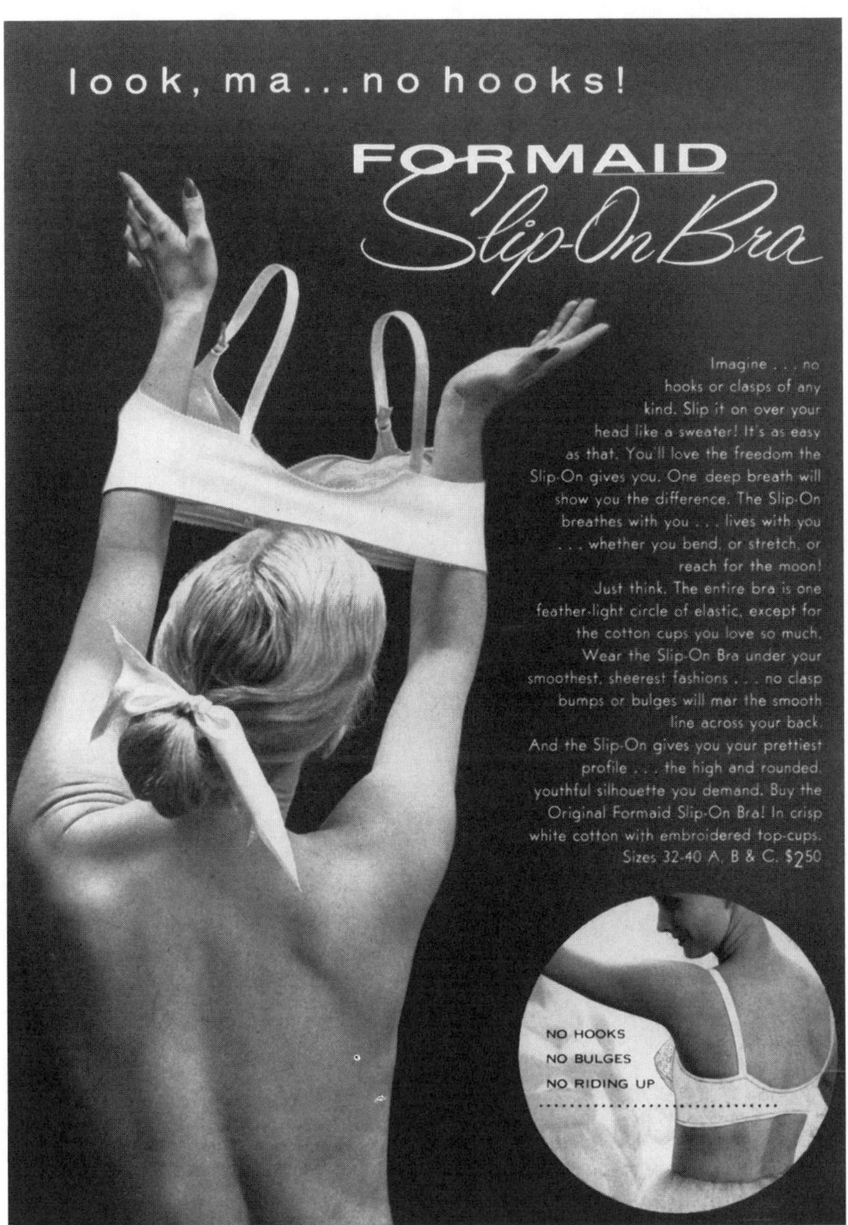

Figure 41. Model demonstrating the elasticized Formaid Slip-On Bra with hook-free design and cotton cups. *Mademoiselle*, August 1955.

Retailers were urged to create separate departments for their junior customers and to employ the word *junior* as a size, not an age, in early 1952. Olga advertised a contest asking, "What's the good word?" to substitute for *junior* because "Junior has nothing to do with an age. It's a size, a style, a figure, a proportion!"[52]

Fitters remained an important part of the retail scene in the 1950s (Figure 42). Mary Suzuki, a columnist who seemed knowledgeable about bra and girdle styles, answered questions and gave advice to readers in a *Mademoiselle* occasional feature called "The Fitting Room." *Seventeen* counseled its young readers on the etiquette of fitting rooms, and even *Farm Journal* exhorted its readers to be fitted for their bras, rather than buying them "over the counter."[53] Part of the responsibility of sales representatives included training local retail fitters in the nuances of fitting their line of bras. Over-the-counter purchases became an increasing temptation in the later 1950s, as some bra companies began to push self-service—so much less costly than training fitters. Maidenform and Playtex were early leaders in providing retailers with fixtures for self-service display.

Fitters often worked with older women, who were not forgotten in the advertising. Campaigns directed toward this customer stressed the need to substitute the modern brassiere and girdle combination for the old-fashioned corselette foundation, which many of them still wore. As evidenced by the number of corselettes and full foundation garments available in catalogs throughout the 1950s, compared with the offerings of brassieres, a good proportion of the larger and older women continued to purchase familiar, old-fashioned styles.[54] Education of these customers was considered a challenge for the brassiere department sales staff. Brassiere makers promoted special clinics and training sessions to assist matrons in making the transition to modern foundations.

Catalog sales remained steady, particularly as prices began to climb with rescinding of wartime price controls. Several styles sold by catalog companies were produced by prominent makers but sold under proprietary labels like Sears's Charmode, Montgomery Ward's Joan Browne, and Penney's Adonna brands.[55] Many of these brassieres sold for less than $1, although more expensive lines were available, with the average catalog brassiere priced around $2.50 in the 1950s. Certain large companies like Even-Pul (Glamorise), Maidenform, and Model negotiated to supply particular styles that could be sold via catalog with their name brand, but the majority of styles seen were no-name designs.

By 1954, the working wife was a major contributor to family incomes, according to *Corset and Underwear Review* research director Melvin Marden.[56] He pointed out that 20 percent of families in the lowest income bracket had

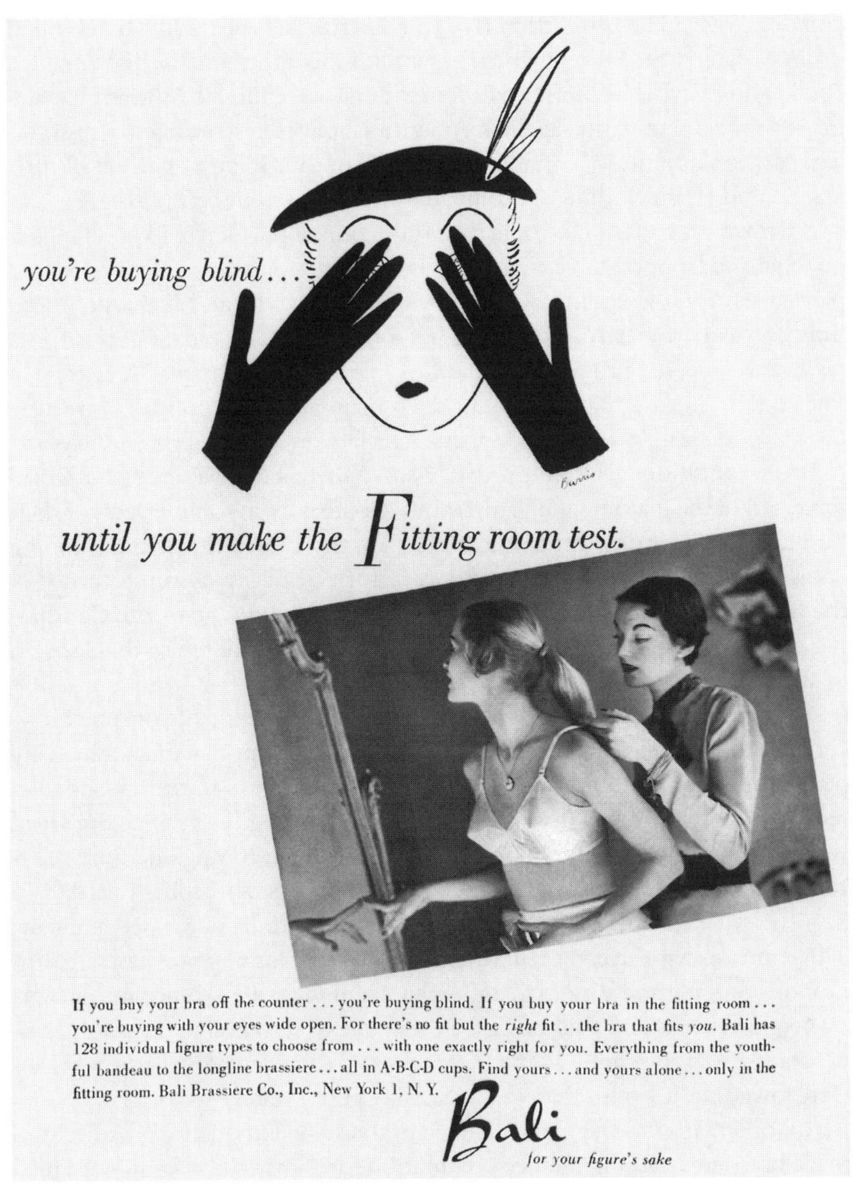

Figure 42. Model demonstration of being professionally fitted for a brassiere. *Harper's Bazaar*, May 1950. Sara Lee/Bali. Reproduced with permission.

working wives. The proportion rose to 40 percent in the middle bracket and dropped again to 20 percent when the families' income was in the higher range. Radio and television commercials for clothing were directed toward females as the primary purchasing agent in America's families. According to a 1956 college textbook on dress, a middle-class family of four spent 15 percent of their annual budget on clothing, as compared with 20 percent on housing.[57]

Cost was a constant factor in the production of brassieres. To offset higher material and labor costs, makers turned to facilities outside the United States, particularly for sewing. Initially the Caribbean and Central America produced intimate wear. Later Mexico, the Philippines, Taiwan, and Southeast Asia became venues for production. The Lovable Company opened a factory in Puerto Rico in 1952, taking great pride in maintaining its policies of treating their workers with a paternal kindness.[58] Its factory was the first on the island to be air-conditioned, a comfort that ensured them a reliable and stable workforce. All of the major manufacturers moved offshore in some aspects of their business, often cutting out garment pieces in the United States and shipping components to be sewn by their offshore factories. Bulk items were returned to the United States for packaging and distribution around the world. Continuing postwar strength of labor unions in America contributed to the decision of some makers to establish extraterritorial factories.

Pricing was a technical art and required a knowledge of consumer psychology to produce the ideal result.[59] Cost was not the primary factor in many purchasers' choice of a brassiere. Display positions, fabric aesthetics, and sales techniques often proved decisive. Garments of varying prices were displayed within each size grouping, in order to tempt women to upgrade their selections. In 1952–53, brassieres recommended for college wardrobes varied from $2.30 to $3.60 each. Three was the average number to be purchased annually. This contrasts with an earlier survey of housewives' clothing purchases in Minneapolis/St. Paul and Birmingham, Alabama, in 1948–49. Women in Alabama owned fewer bras and paid more for them ($4.59 each average) than in Minnesota ($2.64). Southern women were doubly disadvantaged because wages were lower in the South than in the North Central states.[60]

Women around the globe demanded the style and quality of American-made brassieres. Despite France's reputation for dainty and couture-designed intimate wear, the durability and quality of America's goods quickly gained a respectable and reliable foothold in the international feminine undergarment market. Direct exports and licensing agreements for local production were held by makers in countries as far-flung as Australia, Canada, Denmark, Great Britain, Japan, Malaysia, Mexico, New Zealand, Norway, Sweden, and South Africa.[61] Advertising campaigns designed for America were frequently repeated verbatim, leaving interpretation to the locals, sometimes with curious results. Maidenform's "I Dreamed I Was a Matador" alienated potential customers in Spanish-speaking countries, which regarded the bullfighting as the exclusive province of men. There were inroads into the United States bra market, particularly by Canadian firms like Exquisite Form and Gossard as well as by Japanese makers. Brassiere imports from Japan soared from a mere $322 to $850,000 between 1953 and 1956.[62]

The proliferation of American brassiere makers continued. One estimate stated there were more than 175 companies, while another inflated the figure to 500. California was a beehive of brassiere production. Long established companies like Tre-Zur and Hollywood-Maxwell shared the spotlights with Anne Alt, Beautee-Fit, Charmfit, Elaine, Pauline Gordon, Heléne, Renée, and the quintessential Olga. Growing up as the daughter of a fashionable Warsaw dressmaker, Olga Erteszek, assisted by her husband, Jan, soon set up shop producing foundation garments that caught on with Hollywood's denizens. Her first brassiere was introduced in June 1948 and gained immediate acceptance partly due to inspired ads promising that "Behind every Olga, there really is an Olga." This statement encouraged purchasers' confidence in the personal touch.[63]

California was also the adopted home of New York entrepreneur Frederick Mellinger, who began to sell Los Angelenos intimate wear in 1947 at his Frederick's of Hollywood stores. He expanded his specialized customer base by mail order.[64] Initially Frederick was a retailer, but by the late 1950s he had absorbed manufacturers like Tre-Zur. His large ads were routinely placed in the romance and movie magazines featuring racy commentary and saucy drawings of buxom beauties, but he purchased small spaces in fashion publications like *Vogue*, *Seventeen*, *Good Housekeeping*, *Mademoiselle*, *Ladies' Home Journal* and other decorous publications. Frederick's catalog sales reached millions of customers with merchandise intended to titillate both female and male customers nationwide and internationally. His Peek-a-Boo brassiere was not the first such design, but it exceeded its predecessors in notoriety (Figure 43).[65] He also sold the half-moon stick-on brassiere called Bleumette, patented by Mrs. Lea Williams in 1955 (Figure 44).[66] This was a variation on the theme of half-bras designed by Marja[67] and Maas-Cot[68] for the plunging neckline fashions that debuted in 1948. The only direct competitor to Bleumette was the stick-on Poses (pronounced "posies"), sold exclusively by mail order from 1949 through 1954.[69] Poses purportedly held up to "rough treatment . . . active sports, and with special care . . . water bathing."

Marketing assumed a primary role in the brassiere industry in the postwar period. With radio, television, billboards, and print media advertising clamor-

Figure 43. Advertisement for brassiere from Frederick's of Hollywood, including mail-order catalog information. *Mademoiselle*, May 1963. Reproduced with permission.

The New Improved*

BLEUMETTE BRA

A SENSATIONAL MAIL-ORDER SUCCESS
NOW AVAILABLE FOR RETAIL STORES

★ No Bones, No Wires

TERRIFIC SUMMER PROFIT-MAKER

The only adjustable half-way bra ever created . . . specially developed by a top New York bra designer . . . for strapless and low-cut dresses and play clothes. Offers complete freedom of movement and heavenly comfort. Enables a woman to achieve today's glamorous high lines with no embarrassing straps or back bands. Made of pliable yet sturdy material. This bra is a necessary part of every woman's wardrobe. *One pair can be worn as many times as desired.

Sizes:	A cup, B cup, C cup
Color:	Flesh
Retail Price:	Pkg. of 2 pr.—$2.98
Trade Discount:	$20.00 per dozen
F.O.B.	New York City

FREE COUNTER STAND
(sample on request)

Pat. No. 2,728,079

Nationally Advertised In Vogue, Harper's Bazaar, Mademoiselle, Charm, Glamour, N. Y. Times Magazine, Cosmopolitan, Redbook

BLEUETTE DISTRIBUTING CO., INC.
2700 Broadway, Dept. 420, New York 25, N. Y.

Figure 44. Trade advertisement from Bleuette Distributing Company for the stick-on, backless Bleumette Bra. *Corset and Underwear Review*, June 1957.

ing for the attention of the public in a free and booming economy, America was fascinated by consumer goods that exhibited fashionable change. Everyone wanted a piece of the action, to wear the latest style, to live the good life, and to move into the future. Changes in the retail marketplace like self-service were beginning to appear; packaging and product displays evolved to reduce retailers' overhead and control prices. The brassiere fitter was no longer found in every intimate wear department by the end of the 1950s. Her services were now concentrated on the client with special needs or the customer of elite stores. To the brassiere manufacturer of 1959, the future looked rosy, but the glow on the horizon proved to be a conflagration.

7 Ban the Bra?

Brassieres were riding high in the 1950s, only to face potential extinction in the 1960s. Resurgent feminism brought with it hostility toward traditional feminine trappings; chief among these were brassieres. Some women ceremoniously tossed their brassieres into a trash can, never to retrieve them. Others went braless from time to time. But the vast majority of the U.S. female population continued to wear bras.

Although reports of the demise of brassieres were greatly exaggerated, the books and magazines from that decade strongly suggest that women had become impatient with the obtrusiveness and discomfort of this foundation garment. A Bali representative commented with a touch of irony, "Some women are resigned to the fact that their feet hurt. But in bras they still demand comfort."[1] Women's disdain for bras-as-usual drove designers and manufacturers to make their products less conspicuous and more flexible or, alternatively, to create vividly colored companions to outerwear. Girdles slipped into oblivion as the majority of women seized eagerly upon panty hose in the late 1960s, but no comparable substitute emerged to support the breasts. Marketed as part of "underfashions," brassieres survived.

Too much can be made of feminism as the sole cause of woe for brassiere companies. Many other problems beset them as the 1960s unfolded. An industry panel discussion, reported in the January 1960 *Corset and Underwear Review*, deliberated the issues of imports from low-wage countries, professional fitting versus self-service, and the effort to control prices despite general inflation.[2] That panel failed to mention (and probably to anticipate) the computer's transformation of manufacturing, the influx of women of all ages into paid work, a halt to the baby boom after 1964, and the damage that branch retailing would wreak on center-city stores. Overwhelmingly male—thirty men and four women—the panel could not guess at the coming revolutions, some of them indirectly fed by the women's movement.

Feminism percolated to the surface of American life again in the late 1950s, after decades in obscurity. In 1958 Betty Friedan began the research that formed the basis of her 1963 book, *The Feminine Mystique*. In it she articulated the dissatisfaction of highly educated women who had set aside careers for homemaking and child rearing at the end of World War II.[3] This manifesto touched a nerve and provoked an explosion of feminist activism and authorship.

The National Organization for Women traced its beginnings to 1966, with Ms. Friedan serving as its first president. In the first few years, NOW endeavored to work alongside men to gain equal rights for women.[4] By 1968, the movement had become more radical. Other bastions of feminism came on the scene. Gloria Steinem founded *Ms.* magazine in 1971, thereby giving a voice to radical feminist writers. This provoked widespread debate concerning the status of women. In time, even the more conventional women's magazines, such as *Ladies' Home Journal*, began to publish articles and editorial comment on women's careers and rights.[5]

Women entered politics in unprecedented numbers, both on the national level and in state and local offices. Bella Abzug and Geraldine Ferraro were two who succeeded in their own right, not as widows or relatives of famous male politicians. Indeed, Lurleen Wallace was taunted as a catspaw for her husband when she campaigned in 1966 for the governorship of Alabama. Hecklers held up signs that read "I Dreamed I Was Elected Governor in My Maidenform Bra."[6] Still, she won 64 percent of the vote. Tragically, Governor Wallace succumbed to breast cancer in May 1968, after just seventeen months in office. Other women had happier outcomes, and by 1975, 604 women held offices in state legislatures and 19 had become members of Congress.[7]

Beginning in the 1960s, women agitated for access to a wide variety of careers that had traditionally been reserved to men. Some wanted to drive trucks, others to anchor television news programs, while others aspired to careers as surgeons. No longer were they content with primary-school teaching, social work, low-paid service positions, or factory work on soft goods. By the end of the 1960s, women had begun to move into lines of work previously closed to them. By 1967, 26,895,000 women were employed, 56.8 percent of them in white-collar occupations. Across all categories of age and marital status, one-third of American women engaged in paid work.[8]

Earlier generations of feminists had often opted for careers instead of marriage and family, but many 1960s women wanted both. They expected their husbands to share child-rearing and homemaking responsibilities so that this dual option would work. Progress in the home arena proved slow among men who had, in many cases, grown up in the 1940s and early 1950s and never anticipated changing a diaper or flourishing a dish towel.

Of all the revolutions affecting women, the sexual revolution had the greatest implications. Access to reliable contraceptives from the mid-1960s gave women greater control over their reproductive functions. Birthrates declined gradually, with wider spacing of children. This trend further stimulated work outside of the home, helping to keep the economy buoyant. Freed from the fear of accidental pregnancy, some women expressed their sexuality more openly, wearing provocative apparel and "underfashions." Bali and Hollywood Vassarette showcased lacy brassieres that maximized cleavage and made "sure you're seen in all the right places."[9]

Eroticism took a backseat to health matters in some instances. By the late 1960s, treatment options for breast cancer were being reconsidered. Surgeons performed fewer radical mastectomies, substituting lumpectomies and less drastic procedures.[10] Physicians increased the use of chemotherapy and radiation as adjunctive therapies, thus improving survival rates. Activists succeeded in pressuring federal granting agencies to increase funding for breast cancer research more than fivefold in the late 1980s.[11]

One of the central targets of committed feminists was the image of women as sex objects. The most ferocious activists tackled this problem head-on by rejecting conventional feminine appearance. No more shaved legs, makeup, elaborate coiffures, or form-fitting clothing, and definitely no more bras or girdles. News reporters publicized several incidents of women publicly discarding feminine trappings, giving rise to the misleading expression "bra burnings." (Actually, the only burning incident was a staged one, held in Atlantic City.)[12] While this tactic dramatized the women's movement, it alienated a segment of the potential audience—women who aspired to fuller lives but who began to stereotype feminists as unkempt, drab, and shapeless. Some women chose homemaking as their career, finding fulfillment in caring for a family.[13] The most vocal feminists rejected this choice as incompatible with their vision of women's equality.

Ferment in society arose not only from the women's movement, but also from the intensifying demand by black Americans for full civil rights. Students and other youth staged violent protests of U.S. participation in the war in Southeast Asia. The Kennedy and King assassinations exacerbated societal alarm and a sense of serious national decay. Periodic rioting tore up or scarred the centers of U.S. cities, small and large, in all geographic regions. A special report in *Corset and Underwear Review* listed ten practical steps for minimizing damage during riots and keeping in touch with customers.[14] With the gutting of several city centers, retailers fled to suburban shopping malls, posing new challenges to distribution and marketing alike.

Despite the turmoil, the 1960s were largely a prosperous time, based in part on still-cheap energy, a fool's paradise lost with the Arab oil embargo of 1973. The baby boom swelled the cohorts of teens and twenty-year-olds, with overwhelming impact on music and fashion. A succession of youthful subcultures—surfers, rock fans, and hippies—dominated the headlines. The parental generation took fright at their children's consumption of incomprehensible music, frenetic dancing, and recreational drugs. Yet there was little the "over-thirty" crowd could do to halt the youth-quake. Music rocked ferociously. Sixties dances involved the whole body, not just the feet. A rubber spine, loose clothing, and freedom from confining underwear were mandatory to performing the twist, watusi, locomotion, and hully gully.[15] Who needed a bra or girdle, anyway, if her figure approximated the stalklike silhouette of the British model Twiggy?

In fashion, elegance and understatement yielded to riotous colors, bold shapes, and delight in synthetic materials, despite the tentative stirrings of environmentalism. Clothing for the young and not-so-young glowed in hues of candy pink, chrome yellow, tangerine, and purple, which often mingled in a single print. The pervasive petrochemical industry marketed its low-cost polyesters and nylons, not least to the foundation makers. These fibers' easy care offered Americans a huge boon, one which extended to brassieres as well as to outer apparel. Machine washability and freedom from wrinkling made brassieres truly wash-and-wear items. Durable press, popularly called "permanent press," required the finish to be baked into the fabric. Beginning with cotton and polyester, treatments of this kind were attractive to consumers, but they caused problems. Treated garments discolored with chlorine bleach and had to be washed and dried at low temperatures. Formaldehyde, used in the curing process, came under suspicion as a carcinogen, and durable press was eventually replaced by synthetic blends, such as cotton and polyester.

Nonetheless, consumers continued to expect "miracle fibers." Mylar, a polyester-coated foil, helped designers create metallic looks without weight or stiffness.[16] Space-age styles, evoked by such NASA exploits as the 1969 moon landing, caught America's imagination with clean-lined, shiny shapes.

Whereas metallic effects enjoyed only a brief heyday, Spandex came to stay. Introduced by Du Pont in 1958, this new elastomer acquired the Lycra trade name in 1960. Vyrene, trademarked by U.S. Rubber Company, became available in 1961.[17] The brassiere industry quickly recognized the potential of this new stretch fiber and incorporated it into their products. Power nets and lace of spandex resisted sunlight, body oil, and perspiration and offered firm control with minimal bulk and weight.

Not everyone succumbed to the charms of synthetics. Hippie eclecticism offered dramatic contrast to both space-age looks and preppie conservatism. In the mid-1960s, thrift-shop chic took hold, spiced by ethnic influences from several continents. This period was succeeded by extensive reliance on white fabrics and Indian togs—guru chic. Finally, back-to-nature inspired hand-crafted, earth-toned duds and Native American trappings. Bare-breasted "chicks" decorated post–Haight-Ashbury communes.[18] Through the various phases of hippie fashion, calico prints and soft cotton crepes provided alternatives to the structured shapes made of polyester double knits.

Standards of grooming, like clothing styles, split the generations. Of the four-letter words that riled the elders, H-A-I-R may have been the most potent. How much, where it grew, how often washed, what color or degree of curl: these were the stuff of never-ending skirmishes in many families, schools, and communities.

Ultra-short skirts spelled doom for thigh-length stockings among the mainstream fashion-followers, starting about 1966.[19] Panty hose covered millions of legs by 1969. Full-length stockings were nothing new; tights had been worn for sport, theater, or casual occasions, particularly during World War II when nylon largely disappeared from consumer products. Being sheer, panty hose were dressy enough to go everywhere, sometimes accompanied by panty girdles but often providing the only figure shaping below the waist.

The sexual revolution paved the way for acceptance of nudity and the nearly nude look of see-through clothes. If a man could bare his chest, so could a woman. Sheer garments, peek-a-boo effects, and cling were "in." To make this fashion work, youth and firmness were mandatory. By 1969, the ideal figure aped the contours of barely pubescent girls. Legs were "in" and breasts were "out."[20] The mini-shift skimmed over mini-breasts, raised to the level of the armpit. (Twiggy looked almost concave.) Great gams drew the wolf whistles for those whose liberation coexisted uneasily with acceptance of masculine admiration.

By the end of the 1960s, some legs had gone undercover as women sported pants for all occasions and in all places. Dressy pantsuits generated as many social confrontations as unconventional hairstyles and barbering, because bifurcated garments defied traditions of dress-up attire for women. Pants also offered an option to consumers loath to wear calf-length midi skirts after savoring the free leg movement made possible by miniskirts. Although longer lengths succeeded in less extreme and softer versions in the early 1970s, nothing displaced pants. Unisex outfits featured his-and-her pants, accompanied by shirts and other accessories that challenged gender categorization.

If pants for women proved controversial, blue jeans for all-purpose wear were more so. Those who embraced some level of hippiedom or collegiate proletarianism wore tattered jeans, held together with the approved types of patches and inexpert embroidery. T-shirts, used informally even in the late 1930s, became a mainstay of youthful wardrobes, usually emblazoned with the wearer's favorite slogan or visual "statement."

Meanwhile, back in the couture atelier, Yves Saint Laurent, successor to the deceased Christian Dior, dressed affluent ladies in body-skimming shifts that aped optical paintings, tuxedo pant suits, and peek-a-boo confections of beads and macramé.[21] He shared the headlines with André Courrèges, whose white minis and board-stiff pantsuits generated the witty headline "But Monsieur Courrèges, What About Mrs. Bottomly?" That was Paris. London rivaled its wartime ally, but at lower price points. Mary Quant set the youth market abuzz with inexpensive high style, garments priced to sell to wage-earning youth, not just the gilded children of America's upper middle class. Italian designer Emilio Pucci dressed ladies who wanted easy-packing silk prints in ebullient colors. Other Italian couture houses supplied their wealthy customers with high-fashion leathers, knits, and tailored ensembles.[22]

In the United States, the 1960s opened with the crisp looks favored by First Lady Jacqueline Kennedy. Her style rested on the creations of Oleg Cassini, but other women of her set bought chic suits and lavish evening gowns from James Galanos, Norman Norell, and Bill Blass. At a slightly lower cost, Bonnie Cashin crafted leather, suede, and tweed into fetching looks. Cashin popularized a layered effect that has continued to echo through the decades. Waistlines were still in evidence in the early 1960s, and hems skimmed the kneecap as late as 1965, but between 1966 and 1969 waists went undercover and thighs came into the spotlight. With such tumult in fashion, what were bra makers to do?

At first, they did pretty much what they had been doing in the 1950s: making pointy-cupped bras with low backs, low fronts, or no straps. Maidenform introduced a star-flower style that reshaped the breasts into rocket nosecones. Padding augmented natural cleavage in newer materials, notably the polyester fiberfill that supplanted rigid cups and rubbery linings. Fiberfill overcame the annoying tendency of foam rubber to become dry, hard, and powdery from repeated washing. Frederick's of Hollywood and Bleumette continued to market aggressive uplift. However, the torpedo's long reign over high fashion ended in the mid-1960s, as brassieres took on rounded contours and words like *minimizing* crept into advertising copy. Peter Pan, Warner, and Hollywood Vassarette promoted curvaceous shapes.

Plunging necklines, both for evening and for daytime wear, hit the fashion scene in fall 1963 and spring 1964. Aggressive eighteenth-century cleavage, on exhibit in the hit movie *Tom Jones*, allegedly augmented the trend. Warner, Gossard, Formfit, and Bali marketed brassieres that glorified the wearer's breasts.

This market had depth, or breadth, depending on whether the styling department engineered a model to plummet to the navel or bare the shoulders with just a peek-a-bosom.[23]

Just as important as specific cup shapes were cup textures. These became seamlessly smooth (Figure 45) to fit unobtrusively under sweaters, double knit dresses, and even T-shirts. Molded cups held their shapes, and by implication the wearer's shape, through many machine laundering cycles. Heat-shapable "thermoplastic" polyester and nylon, along with spandex, became the mainstays of bra making.

Unchanging shape and size were not acceptable to every wearer. Some women gladly bought one of the many brassieres cleverly contrived to expand and contract with the daily or monthly changes in breast volume of the wearer. All sorts of mesh inserts, cup borders, and entire brassieres accommodated size fluctuations—not to mention the needs of women sized B on one side and C on the other. Stretch straps attempted the neat trick of yielding with movement but not giving way so much that the breasts sagged. Recall that in the 1940s American women had rated straps as the sorest point in brassiere design.

Americans seemed satisfied with the bras available on the home market in the early 1960s. They bought an average of seven bras per year, in contrast to European women who purchased three *soutien gorges* annually, holding out for quality and good fit over quantity.[24] In contrast to Americans, Europeans liked nylon bras because they dried quickly after hand washing, a typical Continental practice at that time.

American women expected their brassieres to stand up to machine washing, so in 1965 *Consumer Bulletin* published a wear study of twenty-eight brassieres from twenty-two U.S. companies. After a minimum of 150 hours of wearing, with washing at low temperature after each day of wearing, a dozen bras rated a "recommended" status. Those were Bali Bow-Bra 498, Bestform Cosmopolitan, Exquisite Form P589, Formfit Romance 566, Maidenform Arabesque 7730, Perma-lift Self Fitting Bra 52, Peter Pan Soft Treasure 60–1, Playtex Living Stretch 159, Sears Charmode (18–52503), Vanity Fair 71–8, Warner's Stretchbra 1059, and Youthcraft Americana Rise "N" Stretch 845. Ten other bras received "intermediate" ratings, and six were "not recommended." Excessive shrinkage in laundering, as much as 14 percent, contributed heavily to a negative rating, and some bra straps began to separate into their component layers. *Consumer Bulletin* writers warned against drying padded bras in the dryer, because high heat could ignite the foam liner. Ironing also proved problematic for some bras, especially cotton bras with nylon trim.[25]

Customer complaints found their way into consumer journals, including the lament of a woman whose skin peeled away when she removed her adhe-

Lovable Seam-Free*
sweater bra
SHAPES UP THE MOST SPECTACULAR FIGURES FOR AUGUST AND SEPTEMBER! LOVABLE'S PATENTED BEST-SELLER TAKES OFF FOR FALL . . . GREAT FOR BACK-TO-SCHOOL BUSINESS . . . BRILLIANTLY ADVERTISED IN AUGUST SEVENTEEN AND OTHER LEADING PUBLICATIONS. BUY IT NOW, IT'S S-M-O-O-T-H!
The world's leading producer of popular priced bra fashions.
THE LOVABLE BRASSIERE COMPANY, 180 MADISON AVENUE, NEW YORK
West Coast: Los Angeles 16. Factory: 2400 Piedmont Rd., Atlanta, Ga.
*U. S. PATENT NO. 2857916

Figure 45. Trade advertisement for the Lovable Seam-Free brassiere for a smooth look under knits for schoolgirls. *Corset and Underwear Review*, July 1960. Sara Lee Corporation, reproduced with permission.

sive Bleumette bra (see Figure 44). *Consumer Report* staff alerted women to painful pulling on the skin, much like removing adhesive plaster, and warned them against removing the protective shield inside the cup. Reapplication of adhesive for a second wearing was even more likely to hurt the skin.[26]

Bleumette was not the only way to achieve the bare look wanted in the mid-1960s. Conventional brassieres began to lose the stiffness lingering from 1950s aesthetics. Those who wanted "less" for their money got it, most famously in the "No-Bra" patented by Rudi Gernreich for Exquisite Form in 1967 (Figure 46).[27] This sheer, elastic-meshed brassiere had a single dart for shaping. An improved model eliminated all darts by exploiting stretchy thermoplastic fabric. Anyone wearing this style in flesh tone could easily fake the braless look. Gernreich and Exquisite Form had exercised much art to simulate "natural" beauty. Further art was required to design publishable advertising images for what Gernreich had wrought. The *New York Times* printed a wispy bra spread diagonally across a background nude woman of maximum vagueness, but *Vogue* showed the new bra in use on a classically posed model who avoided any salacious demeanor.[28]

Transparency in brassieres was not wholly new, because as early as 1950, Olga had manufactured a teen bra that was both very skimpy and see-through.[29] Poirette sold a lacy Promise Bra, Maidenform's Sea Dreams displayed near transparency, and Warner answered the challenge with the Body Bra.[30] Oleg Cassini designed the provocative Room at the Top Bra in nylon and Lycra spandex for Peter Pan.[31]

The industry board advisory to *Corset and Underwear Review* met periodically to discuss problems and review trends. In January 1965, this team of buyers and manufacturers discussed the influence of the "nude look on future foundation designing and the foundation industry" overall. Many board members recognized that the trend to no-bra, no-girdle looks constituted a major shift in fashion toward comfort and freedom of movement. How to achieve that while providing the functions of a brassiere was the big challenge. Myles Friedman, representing Bien Jolie, articulated the task for bra makers: "Many present day bras have an unnecessary abundance of coverage in fabric and elastic, in size and appearance of shoulder straps, and back elastics, in an over-degree of adjustability of buckles and hookings. Much of this can be, and is being, eliminated through ingenuity of design and fitting."[32]

Clearly, modern women wanted foundations that could be worn without uncomfortable reminders of their presence. "Not all that bra" said one advertisement. This attitude represented a clear break with the past, when women accepted restraint and moderate discomfort in order to achieve the fashionably polished look. As Mrs. M. Powell, buyer for Woodward & Lothrop, a

Aug. 29, 1967 R. GERNREICH **3,338,242**

BRASSIERE

Filed June 4, 1965

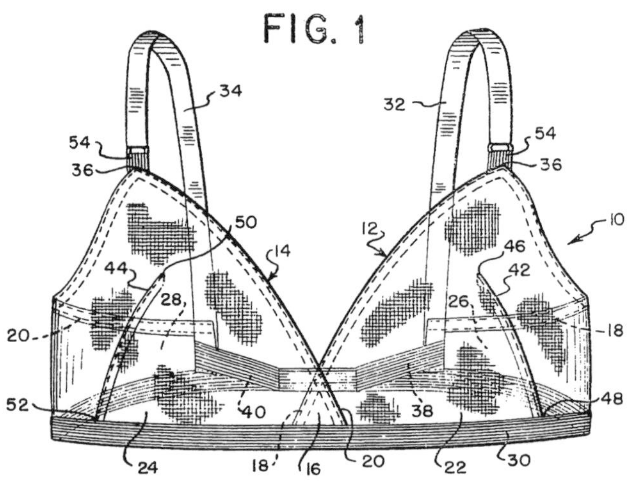

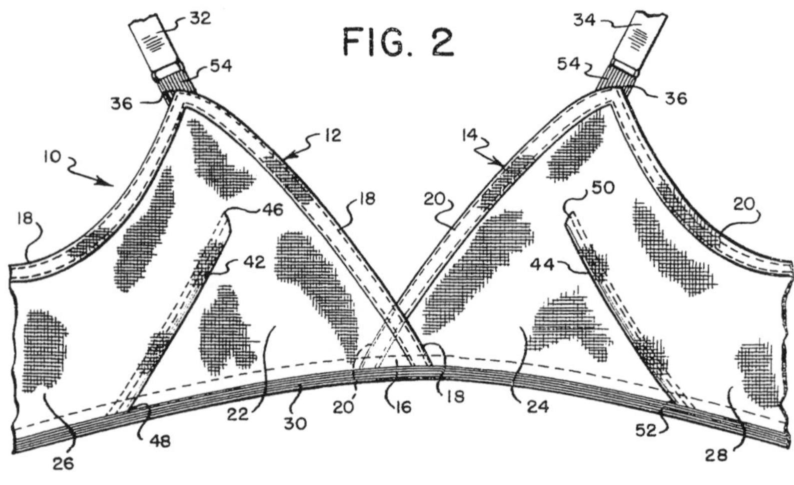

INVENTOR
Rudi Gernreich
BY
ATTORNEY

Figure 46. Patent illustration for the first "No-Bra," constructed of nylon tricot or other soft, transparent fabric by Rudi Gernreich. Later versions had no dart.

classy Washington, D.C., department store, put it: "The grandparents of this generation wanted comfortable foundations but did not have the nerve of today's youngsters to demand it."[33] Two years later, Fran Rothenberg adduced Twiggy's celebrity as one reason girls could be content with "their non-figures" and willing to wear a "little nothing" bra. These teens bought looks and disdained the functional aspects of foundations.[34] Despite this trend in youthful taste, padded bras did not suddenly drop out of sight. In fact, contour styles with thin padding continued to sell reasonably well even in the late 1960s when other categories suffered falling sales.

At the opposite end of the spectrum from braless teens, some pregnant women and other adult customers felt the need for brassiere support around the clock. Despite his association with the no-bra look, in 1966 Gernreich also designed the "snoozable" Exquisite Form brassiere for sleeping. Once more, Gernreich could not really claim a "first," because Maidenform had offered its own Sweet Dreams bra in 1960. Likewise, Tru Balance made a Private Life brassiere of textured nylon "Helanca" lace in the early 1960s, presenting it as an option for lounging or for wear with the "new fashion silhouette."[35]

Long before health and fitness sparked nationwide zeal for athletics and workouts, 1955 brassiere styles foretold the coming of the sports bra.[36] Henson Kickernick advertised its Step-In Bra, and Hollywood Vassarette showed a "stay there" pullover bra whose knitted contours eliminated the need for hooks.[37] This company took their concept further, patenting the equivalent of a sports bra in 1969.[38] The Jantzen no-hook represented another pullover style.[39] Brassieres of this type were advertised preponderantly in magazines with a young readership, such as *Mademoiselle* and *Seventeen*. Evidently, brassiere companies did not trust anyone over thirty to accept the pullover bra concept.

* * *

The 1960s tripped out on color, so it is no surprise that intense colors and kaleidoscopic prints became popular in underfashions. Coordination of underwear with outer ensembles constituted a fad. Panties, slips, pettipants, and, of course, bras and panty girdles came in matching colors or prints. Reversible underpinnings converted from lilac to deep pink at the flick of a wrist. Single-colored foundations of pastels, black, and red shared the spotlight with electric pink, acid green, purple, wine, and chrome yellow. Clouds of color announced the location of the "slimwear" or "contour" department. Prints ran the gamut—navy and white bias plaid, Monet-inspired whirlpools, Japanese nature motifs, Hawaiian flowers, and paisleys. Jantzen advertised a printed brassiere coordinated with a sleeveless tent dress that purposely showed off the bra straps.[40]

Despite the fanfare, printed designs accounted for just 5 percent of coordinated lingerie sales, against 29 percent each for brown-beige tones and blues. Pinks drew 16 percent of color sales, reds 15 percent, and greens 6 percent. Department stores found it tricky to orchestrate coordination between foundation and lingerie departments, and they struggled with a high proportion of markdowns, but color coordinates proved worth the effort, accounting as they did for 5 to 10 percent of store business in intimate apparel. Career women, fashion devotees, and gift buyers purchased more than three-quarters of the coordinates sold in 1963.[41]

Luxury at an affordable price was embodied in the lacy materials favored by practically every brassiere manufacturer during the 1960s. Throughout the 1950s, lace had been limited to occasional trim on the styles of a few manufacturers. With the arrival of spandex, lace could be made stretchy, enlarging its possibilities. Kathy Johnson, a designer employed by Munsingwear, recalled that she had made annual pilgrimages to lace-making centers in France and Italy to study antique patterns for adaptation in Hollywood Vassarette brassiere lines.[42] Advertising copy played up the themes of glamour and extravagance, a sybaritic love of beautiful textures next to the skin. Jantzen wrote of its Curvallure bra, "The feel on the body is angelic," and Formfit enthused over "lustrous Satin-Glo nylon tricot. . . . Exquisitely soft, yet styled for firmest lift."[43] In response to this demand for elegance on a budget, J. C. Penney began to publish a catalog in 1963 that included many styles of brassieres.

Designers of casual brassieres renounced elegant fabrics, borrowing instead the practical interlock cotton and blended fabrics used in underwear and T-shirts. Advertisements showed a man with a chunk cut from his polo shirt, by implication for use in his woman companion's Youthcraft/Charmfit brassiere.[44] Fruit of the Loom, known primarily as a supplier of knit underwear for men, presented an abbreviated bra top ambiguously hinting at underwear/outerwear usage.[45]

Perhaps because pregnancy was often a chosen condition in an era of contraceptives, maternity wear became more glamorous and better adapted to women in the workforce. Instead of hiding away, pregnant women stayed on the job up to and beyond the seventh month. Women were also marrying young—32 percent under twenty years in 1960—and did not shed their youthful tastes with incipient maternity.[46] Companies specializing in maternity bras, such as Fancee Free, Anne Alt, Charma, and Leading Lady, updated their styles by streamlining the shapes, adding attractive trims, and expanding available designs to include décolletage and sensuous features. Contrast the 1967 style

(Figure 47) with the dowdy first effort by Herma Wiedle Dozier, the owner of Fancee Free (see Figure 32).

Maternity buyers trained their staff to entice pregnant women to buy comfortably sized, lightweight maternity bras. Sales pitches to physicians and nurses reportedly emphasized how foundations could benefit all customers, not just those with medical complications.[47] Retailers were advised to place maternity foundations with related outerwear, a time-tested ploy for making associated sales.[48] While maternity wear reached for a new level of allure, the La Leche League successfully promulgated breast-feeding, which encouraged an Earth Mother imagery—a different vision of womanly sexuality.[49] Toward the end of the decade, falling birthrates betokened declining business in maternity and nursing bras.

Maternity clientele could not begin to compete in numbers with the millions of teenyboppers and preteens frantically chased by brassiere manufacturers. Up through the early 1960s, producers had aimed to attract the thirteen-to-nineteen set, which in 1964 totaled 11,923,000 and spent $85 million on brassieres. During the late 1960s, companies targeted girls ten to twelve. Labels such as Teenform, Teencharm, Heaventeen by Jantzen, and Holly Bra catered to this group almost exclusively. Mercy Dobell commented that "the bra has joined the lipstick and 'heels' in becoming one of the beloved symbols of growing up."[50]

Some teen companies used advertisements that bordered on the exploitative, showing mere children in bras only in waist-up shots; other firms added a demure petticoat and pictured the child in a mother-daughter pose that connoted wholesomeness and trust (Figure 48).[51] Dismaying as it seems in retrospect, the statistics supported these sales pitches: "Girls are growing older, younger all the time. It's sophisticated thirteen before it's sweet sixteen, because it's wedding bells at eighteen."[52]

A survey of girls aged fourteen to seventeen was conducted for *Seventeen*. Sixty-one percent of respondents bought bras for back-to-school, acquiring an average of 1.7 and paying an average $2.99 per bra.[53] Note that price ranges for most producers were $1.50 at the low end to between $10 and $15 at the upper level. Bien Jolie and Warner's offered outliers priced $25 and $29.50.

College freshmen continued to be ready customers for brassieres; 96.3 percent of this group bought bras as part of the back-to-school wardrobes. By 1967, this proportion had slipped to 85 percent, but still exceeded the loyalty of high school girls, of whom only 77.1 percent bought bras.[54] To the extent that bralessness became a trend in the late 1960s, it may well have been strongest among the high school set. If that was the case, bra manufacturers had lost not only sales but customers for at least a few years of their lives.

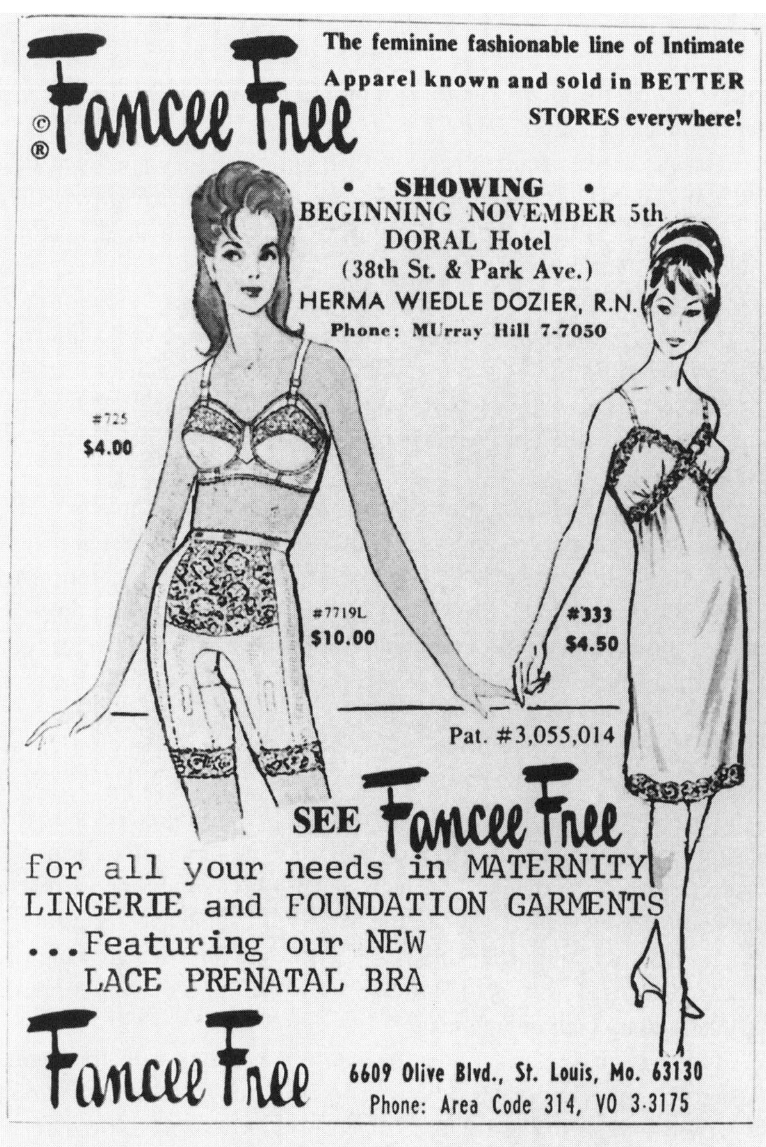

Figure 47. Trade advertisement illustrating updated version of Fancee Free maternity brassiere. Note that the drawstring is gone. *Corset and Underwear Review*, November 1967. Reproduced with permission.

Around the world, in any language, teenagers and their mothers have Teenform on the tip of their tongues! With good reason, too, since Teenform has been the outstanding leader, and innovator in the field of intimate apparel for girls from 9 to 16. For over 13 years Teenform's worldwide reputation for quality has been built on its high standards and solid experience in creating bras, panties, girdles and garter belts for the teenage market. It makes a business of knowing what teenagers want and need—and sees that they get
it; it keeps an understanding eye on teenage problems in growing up, with informative booklets prepared under the guidance of the Child Study Association. Teenform knows the tremendous impact of advertising and backs up its products with a national advertising campaign in leading teenage magazines such as Seventeen, Ingenue, Teen and American Girl, as well as full-color ads in McCall's, the world's largest circulation women's magazine. It has established a dynamic in-store promotion program in the finest
CORSET & UNDERWEAR REVIEW for April, 1963

Figure 48. Teenform trade advertisement emphasizing mother-daughter bond in choice of first brassiere. *Corset and Underwear Review*, April 1963.

The fashion for seminude looks may have been only one factor in this decline. Department stores, hard up for reliable and competent help and struggling to provide training to their staffs, resorted more and more to prepackaged bras, in display units provided by the manufacturers.[55] Although the boxes listed size information, described features, and pictured the bras on live models, no package could replace a fitter's guidance in selecting a bra. Before the decade was over, Warner and other companies were sending their bras with a rack for unboxed display. Even the package information was gone. Teenagers who had an unsuccessful first experience in buying a bra might well have decided to chuck the whole thing and go natural.

Perhaps Warner had the right idea for long-term success. Other companies, including Maidenform, jumped on this bandwagon. Open display of bras, previously limited to a few items on lighted forms, might entice women to examine and try on something uplifting. Self-service may also have appealed to women's growing sense of autonomy and demand for choice. There were costs, naturally, particularly in the difficulty of keeping merchandise in order and the increased danger of shoplifting.

Preteens were not the only newly important customer group. In an era of Black Power, brassiere makers finally recognized the purchasing clout of this formerly taken-for-granted group of consumers. Frank Seymour, a Detroit consultant, outlined the situation in 1966 in a report for *Corset and Underwear Review*. Demographic projections to 1972 showed black Americans constituting 13 percent of the total population, but one-fourth to one-sixth of the populations of Baltimore, Washington, D.C., Philadelphia, Cleveland, Detroit, Chicago, Atlanta, Houston, New York, Miami, and St. Louis. Educational gaps were narrowing in the mid-1960s, compared with 1950 statistics. Along with rising numbers and education came increased militancy in demanding equal treatment as prospective customers and as potential employees. Seymour emphasized the diversity within this population, across economic level, religious affiliation, and age group.[56]

Some brassiere companies were beginning to heed the changes in the black population. Lovable and Exquisite Form had led the way in placing ads in so-called Negro publications. Bestform, Delightform, Glamorise, Lilyette, Formfit Rogers, and Gossard followed, advertising regularly in *Ebony*, a standard-bearer of Afro-American high fashion (Figure 49). Dark-skinned models were used routinely in photos in *Ebony*, a definite advance over the practice in the 1940s and 1950s. Mainstream newspapers and magazines also began to show African-American models by the late 1960s. Even the products were becoming more appealing to these women. As noted above, varied shades

Gossard Keeps America Beautiful

...in Lycra®

Turn corners into natural curves. With Answerette. A mere wisp of a girdle. Makes you round where a woman should be round, firm all over. Sheer nylon and "Lycra" spandex smoothes you. Exclusive criss-cross innerbands hold in your tummy and curve your upper hip, then reach down in back to round your derriere. Naturally.

Your Answerette bra is a natural too. Light, easy-going roundness that moves right with you, but still holds its place. And your shape.

Be an American Beauty in Answerette. It's your duty.

Answerette by **Gossard**

Answerette Brief, #400-1, $8. Long-leg, #490-1, $12. Regular Pantie, #450, $10. Girdle, #410, $9. White, deb blue, black, naturelle, frosted yellow. Answerette Bra, #2120, $3. Contoured, #2720, $4. White, frosted yellow, naturelle. *Foundations in nylon and Lycra* spandex; bras in cotton, nylon and Lycra* spandex. *DuPont registered trademark.* / The H. W. Gossard Co., 111 North Canal Street, Chicago 60606

Figure 49. Gossard advertisement as seen in *Ebony*, November 1966. Sara Lee Corporation. Reproduced with permission.

of browns and tans competed with blues nationally in sales of fashionable brassieres. Fashion colors, prints, and black likewise attracted sales across ethnic groups. More conservative women continued to wear white bras, often ordering them by mail when area department stores did not provide their preferred styles.[57]

New styles of merchandising kept pace with the new styles of products among brassiere companies and "new" audiences. Cooperative advertising, shared by producer and retailer, was not new, but executing the ad in three dimensions, via store displays, was innovative. Having been promoted on color television, a mainly visual medium, bras had to be offered in a visually compelling manner.[58] The high cost of television advertisements deterred some brassiere makers, so they resorted to print media and to radio spots, using the latter particularly to reach young customers who were glued to their radios as many as twenty hours a week, grooving on rock music. Unlike previous eras, movie stars did not shrink from promoting brassieres. Brigitte Bardot lent her name to a line of foundations and "sun bras and bikinis" produced by Lovable, starting in 1960. Bardot was regarded as a "fashion pace setter in France, [the rest of] Europe, and America."[59] The styles were presented on anonymous models' figures, not La Bardot's famous form.

During the 1960s, the hours of department store shopping expanded dramatically. As early as the mid-1950s, a few downtown stores began to stay open one or two nights per week, but suburban branch stores typically remained open six nights by the end of the 1960s. A large proportion of sales were made between 6 P.M. and closing (9 or 10 P.M.), undoubtedly due to the rising proportion of women who held daytime jobs. Across all ages, by 1965, 38 percent of women worked. In age groups 18–24 and 40–59, the percentages ranged from 47.1 to 57.1.[60]

Astute advertising could not ward off all problems. In autumn 1968 a major scare swept the bra companies. Yves Saint Laurent, arbiter of French fashion, made a throwaway comment that "lingerie is finished" with the arrival of see-through clothes, not incidentally those featured in his latest couture collection. Manufacturers were in a snit. Mercy Dobell, then editor of *Corset and Underwear Review*, had to soothe readers' nerves. She cautioned retail buyers about how small the demand would be for genuinely bare breasts and exhorted them instead to choose soft bras in flesh tones at the upcoming market week.[61] In 1969, Dobell reiterated calming words, in the face of continuing "no-bra publicity." Remaining fashion-conscious and keeping visible were the best things bra-carrying departments could do to refute the doomsayers. Her contacts "with buyers from coast to coast" showed that bra sales were "running ahead of last year." Nonetheless, foundations departments no longer racked up the highest percentage of profits storewide. They were under pressure to change or be blended into departments with related lines.

From the producer viewpoint, there was a real crunch. Developing products became ever more costly. Warner reportedly spent almost $1 million to develop its stretch strap. Companies began to merge to survive. Formfit and Rogers (a lingerie maker) had led the curve, linking up in 1956. Hollywood Vassarette emerged the following year from a combination of Vassar Underwear Company and Hollywood-Maxwell, purchased by Munsingwear in 1951 and 1957, respectively. Lovable bought the long-independent Kops Brothers in September 1968. Gossard merged in 1962 with Artemis, a lingerie firm, and linked up with Wayne Knitting Mills in 1967 to become Wayne Gossard.[62] Strength from runaway sales of panty hose made hosiery companies an attractive mate to hard-up brassiere manufacturers. Luckless Treo, finding no partner, succumbed in 1966. Bali forestalled outright merger, but by 1969 Hanes, another hosiery maker, held 42 percent of Bali's stock. Mike Stein referred to "obvious merchandising synergisms" in describing the arrangement. The list of manufacturers (see appendix) illustrates these and many other changes. This spate of 1960s consolidations foreshadowed the megacorporations created by 1980s and 1990s combinations.

Even if they did not merge, brassiere makers could bolster their bottom lines by venturing into production of swimwear, as Maidenform did, or by expanding collections to include fashionable loungewear. Note that caftans and hostess culottes enjoyed popularity in the late 1960s and early 1970s.

Changing tastes represented only one challenge to brassiere firms. Sometimes a company got into trouble when the third generation members of the controlling family lacked the talent for or interest in the business to which grandparents and parents had devoted their lives. Other manufacturers succumbed by failing to expand overseas or to adopt the computer technology that was beginning to transform all aspects of their business.

Bali, a firm whose beginnings dated to 1927, heartily embraced the computer and wisely used it to maximize their efficiency. In a report for *Corset and Underwear Review*, Bali stated it was "one of the few apparel companies to have joined the computer revolution."[63] The Bali Stock Inventory Control program entailed working with each retailer to formulate a sales goal for Bali products. Both parties determined how much inventory was required to reach that goal, with detailed plans of styles, cups, band sizes, and colors. Fed into the computer, these highly specific data allowed managers to provide just what the retailer needed at each point in a selling season. Bali benefited by being able to plan the workflow in its factories and adjust its lines to maximize availability of fast-moving items. Retailers enjoyed an above-average number of stock turns, avoided being out of highly salable styles (stock-outs), and minimized their investment risk.[64] Much of the guesswork was removed from production, making possible the optimal use of plant, materials, and personnel.

Mike Stein, son of founding couple Sam and Sara Stein, took over leadership of Bali at the crucial moment. Harvard educated, he had the knowledge and youthful energy to build on his parents' business acumen by harnessing the efficiency of computerization to limit the damage from price inflation and consumer fickleness.[65] Product development did not come cheaply: Bali required a full year to develop a new style. Stein also helped to expand overseas sales—the lifeblood of several brassiere companies in the 1960s.

Young American women may have been passing up brassieres in the 1960s, but women overseas were just beginning to explore the novelty and relative comfort of American bras. Healthy sales figures from Europe, the Americas, or Asia undoubtedly helped to offset flat or declining numbers in the U.S. market. Sol Rubinstein of Maidenform offered his perception that U.S. brassieres' popularity "has something to do with the fact that the brassiere is considered essentially an American development."[66]

In 1964, when more than forty-six bra companies were actively exporting, an article in *Corset and Underwear Review* campaigned for expanded presence of American companies overseas. This article, adapted from a New York Department of Commerce pamphlet, promoted export as the best chance of expanding despite a saturated U.S. market. Another benefit included stabilization of production schedules, due to inverted seasons south of the Equator. Large orders, typical of importers, reduced the unit cost of manufacture. Credit risk tended to be lower than with domestic retailers. Finally, exporting companies found they could keep styles in production longer if they were working with the more conservative overseas markets. It was sometimes more economical for coastal companies to develop markets across an ocean than across the country. To do well as an exporter, an American bra maker needed a good product, with widespread appeal, reasonable pricing, steady output, organization for good delivery, and a generous measure of patience. The writer cautioned readers that the reputation of all American firms could be compromised by the sharp practices or obnoxious behavior of a single company.[67]

Just about every producer of brassieres did some exporting, either directly, through overseas retailers, or via manufacturers' representatives or importers. Many operated joint ventures in a host country, finding that this gave them a more accurate idea of the tastes and sizing needs of women there. Wacoal, a Japanese firm that currently sells higher priced brassieres in the United States, began as a maker of bras for the Japanese woman and also as a representative of Peter Pan's product lines.

American bras reached scores of nations, including most countries of Europe. Even France accepted imports from nine U.S. companies, to judge from the reports filed in the trade press. Women could buy American-made bras in Great Britain, Ireland, Australia, New Zealand, the Caribbean, southern Africa, islands of the South Pacific, the Middle East and Western Asia, Japan, Hong Kong, China, India, the Philippines, and Malaysia. Wherever Western fashions penetrated, so did American bras. Amusingly, one exporting company listed Hawai'i, admitted to statehood in the 1950s, as an "export" destination.

Products had to be adjusted to the requirements of international consumers. It made sense to have employees who knew the host country and its women very well. Size ranges and tastes varied widely, not least in Europe. Women in France were usually petite, while most Italians were curvaceous and most Germans and Scandinavians were statuesque. In some places high fashion sold best, whereas others more readily accepted staple designs. Surgical bras and breast forms also had a market abroad.

This demand did not make the pickings easy. Peter Pan delineated the scope of its effort to set up plants in Europe; Sweden was described as one example. Beginning with a plan for the factory, Peter Pan staff worked with their overseas partners to choose and engineer styles, adjust sizing, develop specifications, provide swatches of requisite materials, train and supervise staff, oversee quality control, help with advertising, and in general maintain constant liaison with European business partners.[68] Yet Peter Pan was not discouraged with this effort, and in 1964 it had thirty-two licensees with plants in fifty-six countries.

American import of bras reached $10 million in 1965, approximately equaling the value of U.S. exports. Under pressure from domestic companies, the U.S. government placed quotas on finished goods from Japan. This effectively hit one company, Wacoal, which was virtually the only Nipponese bra maker.[69] For the time being, Japan remained a distant fourth to the major sources for foreign-made bras; the Philippines, Hong Kong, and Jamaica produced the vast majority of such products in the United States.

Despite the implied threat to domestic producers embodied in quotas, overseas producers posed far less threat to U.S. companies than did domestic private-label merchandise, such as Sears Charmode lines. One industry representative claimed this brand had as much recognition as any producer branded brassieres. By various technical and marketing strategies, scores of brassiere companies survived the stormy 1960s to face new perils and adventures in the last three decades of the twentieth century.

Soaring energy costs in the early 1970s forced bra makers to substitute more cotton for petrochemical polyester and to generally improve manufacturing efficiencies. Fashion veered wildly from snug shirt-dresses to voluminous, blousy styles that obscured the breast. Midi fashion dominated in one season, hot pants and halters in another. Women began to break into executive levels and wanted "success"-oriented clothes, not frills. Only the most nimble of companies could hope to remain attuned to their customers and survive as independent firms.

8 Wondering About Bras

On the centennial of the patent for the first modern breast supporter in 1963, no celebration was held, no awards were presented, and no articles of historic revelation appeared. Indeed the anniversary passed without notice. The article of clothing most identified with women rated not a mention of its historical status either in mainstream media or scholarly journals. Even the brassiere manufacturers failed to celebrate this milestone.

The thirty-plus years following the centennial of the brassiere's inception saw more change in the social order and the corporate structure of the industry than in the products themselves. Mergers and acquisitions shaped the brassiere most powerfully, but feminism and equal rights exerted almost as pervasive an influence. We will delineate these forces broadly. The changes in the foundations industry, which parallel the metamorphosis of American apparel producers, deserve a comprehensive and meticulous treatment that would fill another book.

Just as in decades past, the ups and downs of the American economy affected the brassiere industry as they did other manufacturing in the United States. Because brassieres may be composed of as many as forty to sixty separate parts, assembling one is labor intensive. Increasing labor costs at home drove more and more companies into third-world venues, particularly for piece sewing.

Design techniques and production methods changed, too. In the mid-1960s, gestation of a new style took as long as that of a human infant before the resulting product was ready to go to the factory.[1] That period was shortened by the introduction of computer-aided design. Further automation expedited cutting, assembly, and packaging. Many of the tasks formerly carried out by the parent company were contracted to outside sources, both domestic and foreign. The family atmosphere that dominated the industry faded as cutting edge technologies and specialized jobbers with an eye on the bottom line assumed importance.

Upheaval was also evident outside the industry. The street demonstrations of the 1960s stopped with the end of the Vietnam War, but the war's effect on the American public continued in posttraumatic stress syndrome, movies, and public debates. The Equal Rights Amendment passed Congress in 1971, yet despite rallies and lobbying efforts it failed to succeed with the thirty-seven states required to ratify it. Women continued to earn less for the same work in many industries and were having trouble climbing the hierarchical corporate ladders. Business writers began to describe a "glass ceiling"—a barrier that had not existed in the brassiere trades before 1970.[2]

Some brassiere companies continued to be headed by women who served as designers, business managers, accountants, advertising executives, and often presidents in family-dominated firms. As megacorporations began takeovers, however, those high-profile positions largely disappeared for women.

American women made strides in many fields of employment in the 1970s, with black women gaining more than whites in several areas.[3] Professional and technical work percentages rose from 10.8 to 14.3 for black women while white women gained 1.1 percent. Clerical work jumped 6 percent for black women, whereas white women saw a decrease of 1 percent. These successes increased in the 1980s and 1990s. Women in the workforce wanted particular advice about grooming, and the "Dress for Success" writers established a cottage industry.[4] These authors' focus was on outerwear; brassieres received mention only in sections about minimizing the prominence of the breasts.

The brassiere, as a garment, received some bad press in connection with the so-called bra burning staged near the 1968 Miss America pageant in Atlantic City. The furor caught the brassiere industry off guard at a time when companies were grappling with problems in production, financing, international trade, and labor.

Fashion and women's magazines with varied readership had frequent articles debating the necessity of brassieres in American women's wardrobes. While *Ms.* magazine gave feminists a voice in 1971 and contained no advertisements for brassieres, neither did *Ms.* editorialize or campaign against them. The politics of dress was discussed in a 1979 article for example, in which working women were advised to wear tailored suits and avoid frills or items such as dangling earrings that might be deemed too feminine for the workplace. But brassieres were not specifically mentioned.[5]

The intimate wear industry was reactive rather than proactive. Complacency seemed to have replaced competency just at the time when corporate raiders were looking for targets. In the span of thirty years, many brassiere makers fell under the control of corporations, which swallowed them whole and then spat back only those names with national and international recognition, like Lovable, Bali, Playtex, and Wonderbra. Beginning with the Canadian company that eventually became Sara Lee, followed by Warnaco (formerly Warner), Vanity Fair, and Intimate Brands, more than 90 percent of all the independent makers were subsumed. We have outlined some of the changes in a chart of selected makers.

Large and vigorous family companies with international markets, such as Garson's Lovable, surrendered their names to Sara Lee. Despite the continuation of popular brand names, the integrity of design-to-production that once typified those labels has disappeared. A few survivors like Leading Lady and Camp Healthcare persevered in niche markets and hung on to their loyal followers, the former making bras for maternity and large sizes, the latter serving mastectomy patients. As Al Corrado, chairman of the board of Leading Lady, explained "few family-owned companies survive into the third generation."[6]

Examination of particulars in one company may shed some light on general trends. The Maidenform Company redirected their advertising away from the Dream campaign in 1969, and that seemed to signal a loss of focus. Throughout the 1970s it produced softer, unstructured styles and marketed them under such labels as Sweet Nothings and Precious Little. In the 1980s, Maidenform ads on television and in print featured male celebrities "addressing women and their lingerie" yet focused on feminist-based themes. The ultimate in this continuing campaign came in the 1990s series of ads with four photographs not depicting their products but with captions like this one: "Perhaps this ad will eliminate any confusion between women and various unrelated objects. . . . . Cute Chick. Doll. Real Tomato. Fox. While Images used to describe women are simple and obvious, women themselves rarely are. Just something we like to keep in mind when designing our lingerie."[7] Maidenform attempted to convince American women that it "address[ed] women's issues, positioning itself as the company that understands and supports women" (to quote its website). Maidenform lost market share steadily through the 1970s and 1980s. After a number of changes in leadership, the company rose from bankruptcy reorganization in 1997, to continue under a nonfamily management team. Fairchild listed Maidenform as seventh in its top ten lingerie companies for 1999, outranked by four Sara Lee brands, Victoria's Secret, and Jockey for Her.[8] Whether it will regain its former glory, only time will tell.

By the 1970s, the rush was on to move overseas for production of bras. Offshore factories now produce virtually all intimate wear, which may have a label or a small component part attached in the United States, allowing the "Made in USA" mark. Brassieres sold in malls and discount stores are made in

Honduras, Mexico, Dominican Republic, the Philippines, Hong Kong, Indonesia, and other sites outside of the United States. Jobs have gone abroad along with brand names, and the primary reason for this is money. Subsistence wages in the third world allow American women to purchase inexpensive items of intimate wear. Moving the manufacture to countries with cheaper labor did not guarantee manufacturers' success. Several companies came to grief in the maquiladoras (assembly plants) of Mexico and in Central America. For example, the Mexican-made Olga label, owned by Warnaco was having labor problems in 1997.

Hard-hit members of the International Ladies' Garment Workers' Union merged with the Amalgamated Clothing and Textile Workers in 1995 to form a new union but this did not bring their jobs back.[9] The import markets picked up as the value of the dollar remained strong against the yen and European currencies. Japanese companies made inroads into the high-end brassiere market with the Natori and Wacoal brands, which carried Japanese labels but were made in the Philippines or Indonesia.[10] Canadian, British, and French brassieres have been briskly marketed to customers in the United States.

Innovation by American brassiere manufacturers did not stop. Some patents represented fresh ideas, but others were just quirky. They ranged from a brassiere with a fur lining to a style engineered with an electric heating system to relieve breast pain. Of special interest was a brassiere for postoperative heart surgery patients. More generally useful was the bra-sizing calculator, patented by Lynn Sehres in 1982. This device encompassed a "circular slide-rule of imposed disks" composed of measurements of the chest, overbust, and underbust; when set to the clients' specifications, it could predict appropriate bandsize and cup depth for brassiere customers. Some fitters and retail merchandisers found it helpful, but the general public did not. The Leading Lady Company, in line with its mission to provide for special clients, licensed a brassiere patented in Canada in 1999. In 2000 the Arthritis Association recommended this design for a front-closing brassiere with adaptations for women with restricted hand movement. The wearer's left hand anchors the left side of the bra by a ribbon loop, while the right hand slips into a ribbon strap at the right front and guides Velcro fasteners into place.

Brassieres in the 1970s gradually abandoned exotic and vibrant colors seen in of the 1960s and retreated into pastels, beiges, and browns. This may have represented a reaction to the greater variation in their customers' skin tones, but it also reflected a middle-of-the-road philosophy. Rigidity was passé; contours and softness were the name of the game. Customers were leading busier lives and demanded easy-care clothing and gentler fashions, preferably in earth tones. Easy-care fibers suffered a short-term setback when their prices rose with petroleum prices in the early 1970s. The brassiere industry responded by re-emphasizing natural fibers, to which science added finishes for easy care.

Body-hugging styles of dresses and sweaters enjoyed popularity in the early 1970s, but were soon replaced by softly draped cuts. In the 1980s roominess evolved gradually into big-shouldered silhouettes that overwhelmed the torso. Breasts were inconspicuous, as perhaps suited the wishes of women breaking into upper management positions in American business. Brassieres emphasized the natural look with minimal construction and deft use of spandex. By the late 1980s the form-fitted fashions again took hold. In the 1990s a lean look cut close to the body prevailed for those customers with bodies to match. Breasts were once again outlined, making the timing right for push-up brassieres, and where better to market the hottest fashion than in California, home of Frederick's of Hollywood and Victoria's Secret?

Two styles, nearly opposite in composition and intent, dominated the period: the sports bra and the push-up specials. Nike and Champion, a division of Sara Lee, dominated sportswear, and the push-up caused a struggle among the "Big Four" manufacturers. In several ways these models typified the dichotomy between the energetic and the erotic. The sports enthusiast was not expected to be the beauty contestant, nor was the fashionista anticipated to win the 400-meter hurdles. Girls and women were expected to wear bras from one group or the other. But as the century neared its close, lines began to blur.

Precursors of the sports-bra have been worn for a hundred years,[11] as have pullover, step-into, and knitted brassieres. As elasticized fabrics have improved, joggers, soccer players, and other athletes have experimented with each new design. A consensus has not yet been reached, but Brandi Chastain doffing her shirt to expose a sports bra following the victory of the U.S. women's soccer team in the Women's World Cup went a long way toward promoting the Nike brand. Other makers have their enthusiasts. The national craze for aerobics throughout the 1980s and 1990s provided sports bra makers with a large market.

Our discussions with participants in aerobics classes revealed that many women with bosoms larger than a B-cup frequently wear two sports bras simultaneously to increase comfort by decreasing breast bounce. Jockey International (formerly Cooper's Inc., makers of men's briefs) benefited from the energized market for sports bras and used that as a springboard into producing a wider range of intimate wear. In 1981 it licensed with Yves Saint Laurent, in 1994 it purchased Formfit from I. Appell, and in 2000 it established an exclusive licensing arrangement with Liz Claiborne. In addition, Jockey for Her was selling three different cuts of fashion brassieres in 1999 (Figure 50).

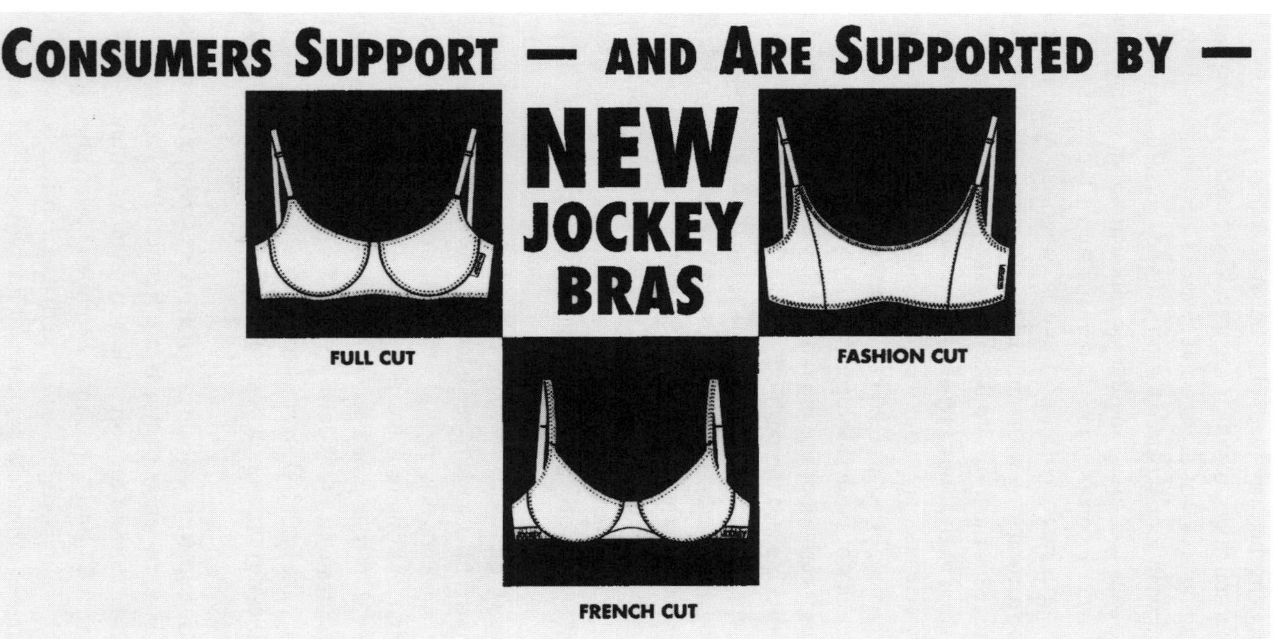

Figure 50. Three designs for fashion styled brassieres by Jockey for Her in soft knit fabrics. Courtesy of *The Jockey Briefs*, July-August 1999. Reproduced with permission. © 1999 Jockey International, Inc. World Rights Reserved.

In a related trend, Playtex has marketed the Eighteen-Hour Bra since 1970 with great success. Jane Russell, known for her curvaceous figure, endorsed this style on television and in print media. Comfort sold well to women with full curves and busy schedules.

At the other end of the spectrum of comfort and fashion, the rock star Madonna brought the brassiere and other undergarments into the spotlight. Her blatant use of brassieres and corsets as outerwear initially shocked the fashion establishment but her fans followed her lead. She played a prominent role in defusing the eroticism of burlesque strip-tease, making it almost banal.

In the same mood of eroticism, the push-up brassiere has made an impact on the intimate wear market. Louise Poirier designed her Wonderbra in 1964 and patented it in 1971 for the Canadelle Company, previously known as the Canadian Lady Corset Company.[12] This brassiere was licensed to the Gossard Company for production in the United States and the United Kingdom. Gossard had started business in Chicago in 1901, and had moved into Britain in the 1920s. A conflict arose because the British firm Courtlands acquired Canadelle in 1994 and wanted to sell the Wonderbra themselves. Gossard's license was revoked, and in response it produced the Ultra Super Boost brassiere. The war of the push-up bras was heating up. Sara Lee purchased the Wonderbra name in late 1993 and then, after a wildly successful advertising blitz to launch the product in 1994, failed to produce bras quickly enough to meet demand. They now enjoy a large market share in this specialized garment type. Intimate Brands launched its Miracle Bra in 1995 to compete with Wonderbra. Then the Bioform Bra with a glass-reinforced polypropylene "keel" and body-forming elastomer cup was introduced in October 2000 by the British lingerie company Charnos.[13] Linda Wachner, CEO of the Warnaco Group, formerly employed by Victoria's Secret, presented the Nothing But Curves in 1999 as a direct competitor.[14] Their 2001 model, the Miracle Bra, appears in Figure 51. Vanity Fair offered the X-Bra, which pushed the bosom to new heights. Despite the posturing and promoting done by each of the push-up brassiere makers, the garment has limited appeal. Most are heavily underwired, making them very stiff and uncomfortable.

Victoria's Secret began as a private company in San Francisco in the early 1970s.[15] The primarily female-run firm took the erotic and hidden from the bedroom to the television screen in less than a decade. Playing on the name Victoria, the company cultivated a pseudo-English image and gave a fictitious London address on its bags. From 1946 through the 1970s Frederick's of Hollywood had dominated the market in provocative lingerie, balancing a saucy catalog with discreet advertising in print media. That dominance was lost to

Figure 51. Victoria's Secret Miracle Bra. Reproduced with permission.

Victoria's Secret,[16] whose jewel tone push-up brassieres, panties, teddies, and sleep wear in shiny fabrics are sold in retails shops, by catalog, and on-line to customers around the world. Intimate Brands, owner of the Victoria's Secret label, was bought by the Limited in 1982 and went public in 1995. Marketing information is closely guarded, but millions see its annual fashion show worldwide on the Internet and cable television. Frederick's languished with a steadily falling market share after the 1984 death of founder Frederick Mellinger. After Frederick's filed for Chapter 11 in 1997, it was purchased by the Knightsbridge Company. The company reemerged under the leadership of Linda Lo Re. The attempt to rejuvenate the world-famous label into a modern icon, with a touch of the old trademark pink, has shown promise with 1999 sales of $140 million from catalogs and two hundred retail stores, forty-five in California. In the same year Victoria's Secret grossed $2.1 billion from catalogs and 902 stores.

The three other multinational corporations making brassieres are Warnaco, Vanity Fair, and Sara Lee. Both Warnaco and Vanity Fair have seen their market share fall considerably in the face of competition from companies like Intimate Brands. Sara Lee Company acquired name-brand brassiere makers Strouse-Adler, Playtex, Bali, and Wonderbra. All of Sara Lee's products are manufactured offshore.

As previously mentioned, we conducted an informal survey of about sixty women over the age of fifty regarding their brassiere purchases and wearing habits. Several questions were open-ended and we invited additional comments. We particularly sought out women with military experience, to glean information about government-issue brassieres. Although we made no attempt to secure a random sample of American women, respondents gave us helpful clues to their brand preferences, wearing practices, and attitudes toward bras. The octogenarians provided insights into failed attempts at homemade brassieres as well as several accounts of wearing brassieres in military service. Most respondents began to wear brassieres between ages eleven and thirteen for reasons of peer pressure, modesty, support, and fashion. About one-third had worn a sports bra and liked it; the same number had worn a strapless brassiere and didn't like it. Ten percent slept in brassieres. We were surprised that about half of the respondents preferred to be braless, which they described as "more comfortable"; 20 percent of the retired respondents had ceased to wear a bra altogether. One lady divulged that she had omitted brassieres from her wardrobe throughout most of her life. Women with a variety of breast sizes and measurements went braless, heedless of the fashionable silhouette.

In conversation with high school athletes, we learned that young women wear sports bras primarily for reasons of modesty under loose-sleeved athletic uniforms. Many prefer to go braless, regardless of breast size. This was underscored by their choice to wear no bra with their prom dresses.

About 10 percent of our older respondents had lost one or both breasts to cancer and one had undergone breast reduction. Brand preference was indicated by fewer than half of the respondents; among the brands named by more than one woman were Bali, Warner, Playtex, and Penney's Adonna. White and beige were preferred over black three to one. Over 75 percent purchased bras from department and discount stores; catalog and specialty shops accounted for most of the other sales. While more than half of the respondents had been fitted for a brassiere, most did not find the experience helpful in choosing a size or style; the exceptions were women who needed postmastectomy brassieres and prostheses fitted.

Our review of recent fashion magazines revealed a few brassiere-related items. In July 1999, *Allure* published a report of the work of Dr. Thomas Baker in Florida. Baker developed a vacuum-producing brassiere, initially meant to reestablish breast growth for postmastectomy patients without further surgery. This treatment has been shown to stimulate growth of breast tissue, providing an alternative to implants and reconstructive surgery.[17] *In Style* devoted eight pages to guidelines for choosing the right bra size and styles for different purposes.[18] Fabrics such as Cool Max were recommended for sports bra customers. *Good Housekeeping* tested 125 brassieres in August 2000 and reported its findings in a question-and-answer format with illustrations.[19] As fashions have changed to less structured shapes, brassieres have generally tended to follow softer lines.

Magazines are no longer the most prolific source of information about brassieres. The Internet and World Wide Web, which have grown simultaneously with the changes in the corporate structure of many brassiere makers, provide enormous detail about brassieres. Business websites offer extensive information, but this can be quickly outdated in this milieu of mergers and acquisitions. Many non-business sites have lewd or pornographic material under the key word "brassieres."

* * *

There was no single inventor of the undergarment we know as the brassiere. The breast supporters patented in the 1860s and 1870s were almost certainly not the first such garments to be worn, but they provided a response to fashion that continued and diversified. Outerwear styles routinely established the direction for changes in brassieres. From boyish flatness to torpedo to plunge and sportif chic—where the fashion goes, brassieres are likely to follow. Health issues drove the initial development of the brassiere, and health has never disappeared as an influence on design, though fashion has become dominant. For most women there is no medical reason to wear a brassiere. It is a matter of personal choice. There is no one brassiere for those who do feel the need for one, just as there is no one lifestyle for all women. Today, the brassiere is tied not to breast size, but to age and taste in clothes.

Both men and women have taken active roles in designing, producing, and marketing American brassieres. Companies usually begin with the ideas and drive of one or a few founders, then expand, diversify *or* find niches and specialize in particular markets. By the third generation, most brassiere producers have been absorbed into multiproduct conglomerates.

Companies that survive for several decades must respond to fashion. They adopt new materials and methods readily, and actively contribute to technical advances by patenting innovations. Computer-assisted design and manufacturing helps companies to control costs and thereby cope with inflation in the cost of staff. Successful producers respond to demands in the marketplace and conduct consumer research. Their advertising keeps current to complement up-to-date products. Despite the recent hoopla about "vision" and "strategic planning" in business, companies' often stumble onto effective practices as they strive to make a success of their enterprise.

The evolution of this woman's garment holds lessons for budding entrepreneurs. Inventors are most successful when they persevere in improving their invention *continually*. A one-off innovation cannot sustain a business.[20] Fresh ideas are always needed, or at least wanted, in fashion industries. Even concepts that appear to have been recycled are changed perceptibly from the original inspiration. Present-day brassieres have by no means solved all problems; much remains to be done in dependability of sizing, as well as in customization of size and shape. Breast tissue varies in weight from eight ounces to over ten pounds, depending on the size of the woman. Therefore, the engineering of support must adapt accordingly. Computers hold much promise for overcoming these difficulties. The American Woman is still waiting for her ideal brassiere.

Appendix A
Selected Brassiere Manufacturers

Name	*Start*	*End*	*Patentees*	*Brands/Notes*	*Extant 2000*
Pre-1900					
Warner Brothers Corset Co. (Bridgeport, Conn.)	1874 First bras 1902	Reorg. 1998	Gertrude Sepaerack Stanley H. Phillips Mary P. Jacob/ Caresse Crosby	Warner Merry Widow Invisible Valentino Intimo Calvin Klein Speedo Sports Bra	Yes
Now Warnaco					
Flynt (Boston)	1880	1895	Olivia P. Flynt		No
Kleinert (New York)	1888		Rose Kleinert	Bras through early 1950s; Dress shields	Yes
Classic	1890	1903	Louise Stitt	Classic	No
Delineator	1890	1905		Butterick Pattern Company	No
Delsarte	1890	1900		Exercise proponent	No
Kabo (Chicago)	1899	1963+	Franz Reinhardt Grace Haderlein Goldie Anderman	K-bra Bou-K-Bra	No

Name	*Start*	*End*	*Patentees*	*Brands/Notes*	*Extant 2000*
Kops (New York)	1895	1968	Daniel Kops Waldmar Kops Lily Daché Murray Zucker Frances Komar Ewen Duff Seigfried Leffman Gertrude Nickerson	Nemo Little Nemo Contessa Merged with Lovable 9/68	No
Nature's Rival (Chicago)	1900	1933	Clarence Mayer Adolph Lipman Isidor Roth	Bought by Venus (Chicago)	No
Newell	1900	1910	Caroline D. Newell		No
J. Walter (New York)	1900	1930+	Dr. Jeanne Walter Rolland Gazelle	Mostly corsets Rubber Bra	No
1901–1918					
Henry William Gossard (Chicago) Owned by Courtlands UK 2000[1]	1901[2]		Samuel S. Gossard Patricia Morehouse Pearl Steimetz Ruthada Yonts Katherine Cunningham Mary Park Martin Park Hildegard Wipperman	Acclaim, Flair Licensed Wonderbra until late 1993 Ultrabra 1994 Ultrabra Super Boost	Yes
S. H. Camp (Jackson, Mich.)	1903		Ariel LeMay	Camp Mastectomy Special Needs	Yes
DeBevoise (Newark, N. J.)	1904	1935–6	Charles DeBevoise	DeBevoise	No
G. M. Poix (New York)	1904	1951	Gabrielle Poix Yerkes	A.P. Uplift Brassiere Directoire Girlish Form	No
Treo (Jamaica, N.Y.)	1905	1966+	Samuel Metz Meyer Schloss	Cheers	No

Name	*Start*	*End*	*Patentees*	*Brands/Notes*	*Extant 2000*
Benjamin & Johnes (Newark, N.J.)	1905		Alfred Benjamin Estelle Popp Isidor Roth	Previously LaWalohn Bien Jolie	Yes
Lane Bryant (New York)	1914		Albert Malsin		SL
Boyshform	1915	1925	Mae Pruzan Walter Pruzan	Boyshform	No
Beauty	1915	1960		Beauty	No
Model (New York)	1915	1950s	Harold Rose Augusta Johnson Henry Schoebel Elvira McKeefrey	Model Illusion	
1918–1929					
Carter	1920		Harriet Redmond	Stopped bras 1947	Yes
Lily of France		1920	Sonia Berdack[3] Sophie Berdack Isabel Bernfeld William Kurland	Lily of France Enhance	VF
Munsing-wear Original start 1885 (Minneapo-lis)	1920[4]	1972	William D. Brown Theo Schaumer Ruth Kapinas	First bras 1920 Foundettes Vassarette Hollywood-Vassarette	No
Van Raalte	1920	1950s	Helene Pons		No
Even-Pul/ Glamorise (Bayonne, N.J.)	1921		Jack LoCascio Patrick J. Moran Irivng Rosner	Originally Maid-Well Even-Pul Glamorise Exclusively large size	Yes
Dorothy Bickum	1922	1961+[5]		Dorothy Bickum	No

Name	*Start*	*End*	*Patentees*	*Brands/Notes*	*Extant 2000*
Maiden Form/ Maidenform (Bayonne, NJ)	1922[6]	1997 Chpt. 11 Reorg. 1998	Wm. Rosenthal	Maidenette Maiden Form Rendevous Allo-Ette Chansonette Sweet Nothings Self Expressions	Yes
Alberts Mfg. (New York)	1925	1965	Jacob L. Alberts	Charma	No
Lovable (Atlanta, New York)	1925	1998	Arthur Garson Frank Garson Richard Buemueller	Lovable Private Labels	SL
Lov-é (Holly-wood)	1925[7]	1963+	Mdme. DesLauriers	Personal Pattern Lov-é	No
Bali Fay-Miss until 1941	1927		Sara Stein, designer[8]	Bali Bali-hi	SL
Hollywood-Maxwell (California)	1929[9]		Hattie Volk Maxwell Volk Joseph R. Bowen DDS Shirley Maxwell? Theo Schaumer	Whirlpool V-ette Nu-Vu	VF
1929–1939					
Wm. Gluckin Company (New York)	1930	1955	Edwin W. Gluckin Harry Gluckin Edward Astor Ceyl Anselmo Jack Glick Simon Grishman	Alene Brand Private Labels	No
Kestos	1930[10]	1950s	Rosamond L. Kennedy Klin	Kestos	No
Milady	1930[11]			Milady	W
Venus (Chicago)	1930[12]	1958+	Maurice Lipman George Diebold	College Girl Private Labels	No

Name	*Start*	*End*	*Patentees*	*Brands/Notes*	*Extant* 2000
Beautee-fit	1933	1960s	Victor Becker A. Soundel Becker	Original Name: Western Corset Co.	No
D'Amour (New York)	1933 [13]	1961+	Frances Pilot Israel (Hi) Pilot	D'Amour Wonder-Bra	No
Madame Adrienne (Calif.)	1934	1950s	Adrienne Hirsch [14]		No
Lilyette	1934 [15]	1968+	Max Kaufman Sarah Katz Kaufman	Rondo	No
Marja (Jacksonville Tex.)	1934	1959	Margia Childs Hamlin	Hi-A	No
Renée of Hollywood	1934 [16]			Jezebel	Yes
Vanity Fair	1911; first bras 1934			Vanity Fair It Must Be Magic Skin-to-Skin Nike Sports Bra Tommy Hilfiger lines Body Sleeks	Yes
Anne Alt (Compton, Calif.)	1930s	1960s	Anne Alt	Form-o-Uth Maternity bras Curvaceous	No
Formfit (Renssaler, Ind.)	1930s [17]		Samuel Kunstaater Sigmund Kunstaater Jerome Abelas	Life	No
Stein & Co. (Chicago)	1930s	1957+		Hickory Perma-Lift	No
Tre Zur (California)	1930s	1953 [18]	Max Witkower Lola Spare		No
Venus (NY)	1930s	1950+	Herman Schnaittacher	Maternity only	No

Name	Start	End	Patentees	Brands/Notes	Extant 2000
1939–1946					
Leading Lady (Cleveland)	1939		Frank Farino	Maternity Large Sizes Arthritis Bra	Yes
Lances	1940		Edith Lances Sydney Alberta	Edith Lances High priced Custom-fitted	Yes
Peter Pan (New York)	1940		Henry Plehn	Heaventeen Merry-Go-Round Hidden Treasure Freedom Ring	SL
Olga (Los Angeles)	1942[19] First bra 1948		Olga Erteszek	Olga Sensuous Solution	W
Glamorise	1945	1963+		Formerly Even-Pul Specialize in large sizes	Yes
U.S. Rubber/Sacony	1945	1991		Playtex Cross Your Heart Locket	SL
Frederick's of Hollywood	1946	1998[20] Chpt. 11 Reorg. 1999		Rising Sun Peek-a-Boo	Yes
Mam'zelle (Hollywood, Calif.)	1940s	1950s	Raymond Redares Suzanne Redares-design	Bask-ette Dream Bra Cross-lift	No
Miller Bra Co. Exquisite Form (New York)	1940s		Lillian Hunau Bernard Rashkin	Rondé Vu Exquisite Form Circloform	VF
1947–1959					
Fancee Free	1947		Herma Weidle Dozier, RN	Fancee Free Maternity only	Yes

Name	*Start*	*End*	*Patentees*	*Brands/Notes*	*Extant 2000*
Jantzen	1948[21]		Bernard Galitzki Samuel Smith Margaret Wittenberg Jack Michel	1st bra Jan. 1948 Jantzen	VF
Dominion Corset Co. (Canada)	1948		Pierre Amyot Marian E. Child Fernand Derochers Charles Sachs Moe Tuschman Joseph Verreault	Sarong Daisyfresh Gothic	Yes
———			———	———	
Canadelle			Louise Poirier—Canadian patent awarded in 1971	Wonderbra (1964) Licensed by Gossard for UK and USA until 1994.	SL 1991
Bleuette	1957		Mrs. Lea Williams[22]	Bleumette	No
1959 +					
Amoena (Marietta, Ga.)	1980			Denmark based Post-Mastectomy	Yes
Jockey for Her (Kenosha, Wis.)	1982			Jockey for Her Liz Claiborne Intimates	Yes
Just My Size	1994			Just My Size Specialize in Large-size	SL
Victoria's Secret (Columbus, Ohio)	1970s (late)			Miracle Bra Originated in California Owned by The Limited	I
Wacoal America (Japanese Owned)	1970s			Parfage Minimizer Donna Karan (DKNY) High end prices	Yes

Name	*Start*	*End*	*Patentees*	*Brands/Notes*	*Extant 2000*
Wonderbra	1994			Wonderbra	SL

Key
I = Intimate Brands; SL = Sara Lee; VF = Vanity Fair; W = Warnaco
+ = Indicates last known date, but company may have persisted.
? = Items have not been found in more than one source.

1. Website "About Gossard" http://.../about.asp?mscssid.

2. *CUR*, April 1957, 116. Operated in Britain under license from 1922; in 1930 the British section became independent. Merged with Artemis, 1962; with Wayne Knitting Mills in 1967; and with Berlei in 1968.

3. *CUR*, April 1949, 144.

4. Munsingwear bought Vassar Underwear Company in 1912, and sold it in 1918. After a reorganization in leadership, in 1951 Munsingwear reacquired the company now named Vassarette. The Munsingwear/Vassarrette Company merged with Hollywood-Maxwell in 1957 to form the Hollywood Vassarette label for Munsingwear. This put some end to the confusion caused by Hollywood-Maxwell when they produced a brand called Hollywood-V-ette.

5. Advertisement in *CUR*, June 1961, 177.

6. Maidenform company bought True-Form /Flexees 1992 and Lilyette (NCC) 1995.

7. *CUR*, October 1952, 128.

8. *CUR*, October 1969, 36. His son Max succeeded company founder Sam Stein in 1969. There is mention in *CUR*, October 1961, 15 that the company had been purchased by U.S. Rubber.

9. *CUR*, April 1956, 90. Gives 1931 as date, however patents are from 1929 and the likelihood is that the company had been in business by then. Hollywood-Maxwell merged with Munsingwear in 1957.

10. Mainly in Britain, although had offices in Chicago and San Francisco for years prior to World War II. An article in *Costume* 1999 gave dates into the 1950s in Great Britain, however no ads were seen in USA after 1933.

11. Merged with Fruit of the Loom in the 1950s.

12. Bought Nature's Rival in 1933.

13. CUR January 1958, 138. Several spellings are used by the company, including Wonderbra, Wonder-Bra, Wonder bra and Wonder Bra, but never Wonderbra until after the Pilots were bought out by Canadian Lady Corset Co. A Canadian patent was applied for in 1967, and awarded in 1971 to Louise Poirier, who assigned it to the Canadian Lady Corset Company, now named Daisyfresh. The Canadian Lady Corset Company licensed the Wonderbra design to Gossards of Chicago until 1993, when England-based Courtlands bought the Canadian firm. Since Courtlands wanted to sell Wonderbra, it prohibited Gossards, who also had factories and licenses in England, from selling Wonderbra, and that led directly to the competitive race in push-up bras.

14. Patent 2,072,879 filed January 6, 1934, awarded March 3, 1937 to Adrienne Hirsch, New York seems a likely match.

15. *CUR*, January 1959, 126. Merged with Maidenform in the 1970s.

16. *CUR*, April 1954, 104. Renée of Hollywood began business in 1921 as a general lingerie company, but by 1933 had moved exclusively into brassiere making. The company was founded by Sam Samuels and later run by his son Nate, and nephew Harold Samuels through the 1960s. The company may be named after Nate's wife, Renée. The name was often misspelled in advertising copy, which may explain why it was recently renamed Jezebel, after its most famous brand.

17. Merged with Rogers 1950s, was known as Formfit/Rogers, and is now held by Jockey International.

18. There is some question about Tre Zur being bought by Frederick's of Hollywood. Frederick's continued to feature the brand in advertising after the company had ceased in 1953.

19. *CUR*, April 1952, 126.

20. Frederick's was bought by Knightsbridge Capital Corp. 1997. The present management has been in charge for less than two years.

21. *CUR*, January 1948, 160.

22. *CUR*, June 1957, 138.

Appendix B
Brassiere Brands

The following list contains all the brand names of brassiere manufacturers that we found during the research for this book. Many are not named in the main text; some lasted for less than five years, while others remain in business today.

Accentuate
Adonna
Albert Mfg. (Charma)
Alene
American Lady
Angel Bra Co.
Anne Alt
Annette Fashions
Bali
Beautee-fit
Beauty
Bien Jolie
Benjamin & Johnes
Berlé, J. (Delineator)
Bestform
Best Maid Co.
Besty Ross
Beverly Vogue
Biflex
Blair Fashions
Bleuette (Bleumette)
Blue Canoe
Bonzette
Boyshform
Breathinbra
Brill Corset Co.
Brownee Bra
California Forms
California Foundations
Camp, S. H.
Canadelle
Canadian Lady Corset
Carnival
Carter
Celebrity
Champion
Chantress
Charma
Charmfit of Hollywood
Charmode
Cheers
Cherie
Clarke, B. F.
Classic
Cohama
Contessa Di Roma

Cora Nita
Corbeille Recamier
Cordé de Parie
Cordelia of Hollywood
Corona
Coronet
Crown Corset Co.
Cupid
Curtis-Eddyform
D'Amour
Damsel
Danskin
Deala of Miami
DeBevoise
Delightform
Delineator
Delsarte
Diana
Distinction
Dominion Corset Co.
Dorothy Bickum
Eddy-Form
Elaine of Hollywood
Even-Pul
Exquisite Form
Fancee Free
Fashion Form
Fashion Hour
Fay Miss
Ferris
Flexaire
Flexees
Flynt
Forever Yours
Form*aid*
Formaster
Formcraft
Formfit (Rogers)
Formost Foundations
Form-O-Uth
Fortuna
Francine of France
Frederick's of Hollywood
Fruit of the Loom
Gabeau
Gap
Glamore
Glamorise
Gluckin, William
Goddess
Gordon, Pauline
Gossard
Graceform-Camlin
Guinzberg
Half Bra Co.
Heléne of Hollywood
Henson-Kickernick
Hickory (Stein)
Holly-Bra of Calif.
Hollywood-Maxwell
Hollywood Model
Hollywood-Vassarette
Hollywood Youth
Identical Form
International Corset
Intimate Brands
Jackson
Jantzen
Jeanne Walter
Jezebel (Reneè)
Joan Browne
Jodee
Jogbra
Jubilee
Juliette
Kabo
Kayser
Kleinert
Kops
Kull

Kyle of California
Lady Marlene
Lances, Edith
La Resista
Lane Bryant
La Tosca (McLaughlin)
La Trique
Lazelle
Le Monde Corset
LeWella
Lilyette
Lily of France
Locket Bra (Sacony)
Lovable
Lov-é
Lucille of Hollywood
Maas-cot
Mabs of Hollywood
Madame Adrienne
Magicool
Maggyanne
Maiden Form/ Maidenform
Maid-Well
Maison l'Abri
Malibu
Mam'zelle
Mardi Bra
Marja
Mary Jane
Masterbilt
Materna Line
Milady
Miller Bra Co.
Miriam Gates
Model
Modern-Aire
Mold Form
Mon-e-Bra
Munsingwear
Naturflex
Nature's Rival
Nemo
Nestle Form
Newell
Not All That Bra
Novoline
Nu Eve
Nu Lift
Nu Vogue
Nu-Vu
NuZan
Olga
Ovida
Packwood
Perma-lift (Stein)
Pertform
Peter Pan
Playtex (U.S. Rubber)
Poirette
Poix, G. M.
Pretty Girl
Princess Bonnie Bra
ProSpirit
Quest-Shon Mark
Remey
Renée of Hollywood
Revelation
Romance of California
Roman Stripe
Rosette
Ruth Merzon
Sacony (Locket)
Sahlin
Saramee
Sarazin of Connecticut
Sarong
Scandele
Self Expressions
Shannon
Sho-form

Silf Skin
Slique of Hollywood
Stardust
Stein, A. & Co.
Stephanie, B.
Strouse-Adler
Surprise (Nu-Zan)
Suzan of California
Sylvia
Teencharm
Teenform
Toni Lee
Top Form
Treo
Très Secrète
TreZur
Triumph
Tru Balance
True-Form
Universal
Vanity
Vanity Fair
Van Raalte
Vassar/Vassarette
Venus (Chicago)
Venus (New York)
Vivette Foundations
Warner
W. B. Foundations
Western Corset Co.
Wilber, Ruth
Wilco Fashions
Wings
Wispese
Wonderbra
Wonder-Bra
Wonderform
Youthcraft
Youthline

Glossary

all-in-one. A name for a foundation garment combining brassiere and girdle.

backless bra. A strapless brassiere with fasteners at waist-level allowing the wearer to appear with back exposed. It is frequently worn with low cut formalwear.

bandeau. Der. Early twentieth century. French: "bandage." A simple breast covering, made without shaping or darts; frequently but not always strapless. English: Breast separator with narrow straps.

Belle Poitrine. Breast silhouette with a pointed shape, popular 1932–1940.

binder. A snug or tightly fastened chest covering, that may have multiple tails, crisscrossed, or may be a simple flat bandage. Used to prevent or reduce swelling of the breasts after childbirth or surgery.

bodice. Used since the nineteenth century to designate the upper part of a dress, from neck and shoulders to waist.

bones. See *stays*. Narrow, flexible strips of whalebone, steel, feather quills, or plastic used to stiffen and shape foundation garments.

brassiere. Der. French "a small boy's undershirt or vest." The word was first used in 1905 to designate a breast-supporting garment in America. A garment used to cover and support female breasts. Frequently consists of shaped cups, shoulder straps, and some stretchable fabric to which is attached a closure device. See soutien gorge.

breast (or bust) girdle. A term used in the late nineteenth century to describe a breast supporter.

breast supporter. A term used in the mid-late nineteenth century to designate a garment different from a boned corset that supported the female breasts from the shoulders by means of two straps.

bustier. A one-piece undergarment that combines brassiere and waist cincher; usually strapless, with boning, and garters.

Callipygian cleft. Der. Greek "buttocks." The space or fissure between the buttocks as viewed from the top.

camisette. A lightweight, unboned, brassiere and close-fitted garment reaching to hips with attached garters.

camisole. A short, sleeveless bodice or vest worn over corset or stays; a waist-length, lace-trimmed or embroidered loose bodice, worn under a sheer blouse or dress to maintain modesty. Also called a corset cover or petticoat bodice.

chemiloon. A combination corset cover and pantaloon.

chemisette. Similar to a camisole, a one-piece undergarment worn under a suit.

cloak. A loose-fitting outer garment without sleeves; a cape or mantle.

corselet/corselette. 1. A one-piece foundation garment with boning and power net or elastic side panels and a nonstretchable fabric front that encloses the waist. Frequently closed with hooks or zippers and usually has attached garters. 2. A waist-cincher belt worn over a peasant's blouse.

corset. 1. A tightly fitted, boned two-piece garment that shapes the torso; usually closed with a front busk and back lacing. 2. Since 1920s made of lightweight elasticized fabrics and called a girdle or foundation garment.

corset cover. Similar to a camisole, a soft bodice with shoulder straps, worn over the corset to protect the corset from wear.

coutil (*coutille*). A twill-weave cotton textile used to make foundation garments that require strength and resistance to tearing; used especially in the manufacture of corsets.

custom/semicustom. Garments made especially for a client; made to measure; bespoke. Or partially premade and adjusted to fit precisely as the customer chooses.

Dacron. Trademark owned by E. I. Du Pont de Nemours covering more than seventy polyester filament yarns. Originally registered in 1951. Used in combination with cottons by many brassiere manufacturers in the 1960s and 1970s.

dart. A v-shaped stitched fold made in the process of sewing a garment to aid in shaping flat fabric to the contours of the body.

décolletage. A neckline that reveals the neck, shoulders, upper back, and sometimes part of the bosom.

dolman. Der: Turkish; pertaining to a woman's outergarment with very wide armholes and narrow wristed sleeves, often one piece and looking like a cloak from behind.

D-ring. A metal component, shaped like a D, often part of the adjustable shoulder straps on brassieres.

eiderdown. The finest feathers from a goose's breast, the soft and fluffy feathers which trap air against the skin between the covering outer layer of feathers.

extrude. To press or push out; as in polyester filament.

fagoting. A method of joining two pieces of fabric with openwork stitching.

falsies. Any device which may be fitted loosely or stitched into a brassiere to augment or increase the appearance of fullness of the breasts. Used mainly as slang in the 1940–1960 period.

featherbone. Lightweight boning generally made from twisted turkey quills and used in corsets and other foundation garments to produce shaping.

fitter. A female member of the retail establishment who specialized in measuring and fitting undergarments for women. Now generally available to assist in specialty shops with mastectomy patients in choosing correct size and model of bra.

foundation garment. Evolved since 1920s, any undergarment that provides breast support and shaping of the waist and hips. Loosely applied to brassieres and girdles/corsets.

full-fashioned. A technique used in knitting to increase or decrease stitches to shape or contour a garment.

girdle. An undergarment used to shape or mold the waist and hips and sometimes the legs. Usually made of elastic fabric with or without nonstretchable panels, with or without garters.

gusset. A triangular or diamond-shaped insert placed to allow contours to be smoothly covered.

halter top. A brassiere with straps only from the front to back of the neck, allowing the upper back to remain uncovered for sunbathing, etc.

Lastex. Uniroyal trademarked yarn with elastic core. Used in stretch fabrics.

long-line. A brassiere that extends to the waist or lower; frequently with added boning to control curves, and sometimes with a very low back that can be worn with formal backless styles.

marquisette. A sheer, leno weave, transparent, net-like fabric.

mastalgia. The medical term for breast pain that may affect at regular or irregular intervals.

mastectomy. Der. Greek *mastos*: breast; *-ectomy*: incision. A surgical procedure to remove the tissues of the breast for a variety of reasons, including malignancy. Simple mastectomy involves only the mammary tissues; radical mastectomy removes all breast tissue and chest wall muscles in addition to lymph nodes in the chest and underarm areas.

mastectomy bra. A brassiere with pockets to hold one or two prosthesis for the post-surgical patient, to provide a pre-surgical bust profile.

milanese. Warp-knitted fabric with a run-resistant diagonal yarn used mainly for hosiery.

NRA. The National Recovery Administration was established by President

Franklin D. Roosevelt to assist the United States business community to regain economic stability during the Great Depression of the 1930s.

nursing bra. A brassiere designed especially for breast-feeding convenience; it may have flaps, adjustable straps, special hooks, zips, or other means to accommodate the exposure of nipples for feeding while supporting the heavy milk-laden breasts for comfort and silhouette maintenance.

paletot. A term used to name a variety of nineteenth century men's and women's coat styles, varying from an 1830s men's short jacket to an 1840s caped three-quarter length cloak and an 1880s women's full-length, long sleeved coat.

paraknit. Openwork, knitted, elastic material or fabric.

power net. A term used to describe a strong, elastic fabric used in girdles and brassieres.

prosthesis. A replica of/for an amputated or missing breast, generally weighted to conform to the feel and shape of a natural breast.

proto-brassiere. See breast supporter

push-up bra. A brassiere designed to support and emphasize the breasts in a prominent position; they frequently have padding, boning, underwires or other mechanical augmentations.

raglan. A sleeve style, which is shaped with a diagonal seamline from underarm to the neckline, both front and back.

seamless bra. A brassiere made of stretch or knitted fabric that lacks seams across the cup area, thus creating a smooth look under clothing.

soutien gorge. A French term for the garment called a brassiere in English.

spandex. A generic term for man made stretchable fabrics used in garments.

stay. A term used in sewing for application of a narrow strip of rigid material to shape a garment; commonly whalebone before 1850, then flexible steel and featherboning replaced the whalebone.

strapless bra. A brassiere held in place without shoulder straps. They frequently contain underwires, boning, elastic, or combinations of these.

strophium. A garment worn by women in ancient Rome, consisting of three bands around breasts, waist and hips supported by shoulder straps. They were made of leather, wool, or linen.

surplice closings. A diagonally overlapped or criss-crossed bodice fastening.

swami. A firmly warp-knitted fabric of rayon and cotton with wicking capacity. Usually flesh tone or apricot color.

teddy. One-piece foundation garment with minimal support.

torsolette. See *bustier*.

underwire. A U-shaped plastic or metal strip sewn into a channel under the cup of the brassiere to add support, shaping features, or rigidity to the garment. They can be removable in some styles, particularly for laundering.

Velcro. Hook and loop tape developed for astronauts. Used as closure in place of hooks and eyes, buttons, and zippers.

Vyrene. A synthetic rubber used in stretch fabric and elastics.

waist. Term for blouse or shirtwaist used from 1890 to 1920s. Sometimes referred to as corset-waist, when worn as an undergarment; similar to camisole.

Notes

Preface

1. These harmful effects were not merely speculative. Robert Latou Dickinson, a gynecologist, performed an experiment in 1887 using a small rubber bladder attached to a blood-pressure reading device; he found pressures up to eighty-five pounds per square inch under the corset. "The Corset: Questions of Pressure and Displacement," *New York Medical Journal* (1887): 507–16. In 1890, Dr. William Wilberforce-Smith demonstrated reduced lung capacities of corseted women subjects compared with those in an uncorseted control group. "On the Alleged Differences Between Male and Female Respiratory Movements," *British Medical Journal*, 11 October 1890, 843–44. These results have been confirmed in present-day replications with sophisticated equipment; reenactors who wore 1900s style corsets laced to three inches less than their normal waistline circumferences lost an average of 9 percent of lung capacity; some suffered as high as 18 percent loss. The most pervasive damage observed in corseted subjects—decline in muscular tone—happened within hours of lacing and parallels the losses experienced when an arm or leg is placed in an immobilizer or splint. Colleen Ruby Gau, "Historic Medical Perspectives of Corseting and Two Physiologic Studies with Reenactors," Ph.D. diss., Iowa State University, 1998.

2. Hilda Ericson, U.S. Patent 2,659,085, awarded 17 November 1953. Ericson claimed that her invention would retain its contour better than cloth and elastic brassieres, would produce a smooth line under clothing, and yet was of sufficient thickness to "support the breasts in youthful form." It took more than two years between patent application and award, as sometimes occurred with startlingly novel or complex inventions.

3. Heidi L. Boehlke, "Ruth M. Kapinas, Munsingwear's Forgotten 'Foundettes' Designer," *Dress* 20 (1993): 45–52.

4. Marilyn Yalom, *A History of the Breast* (New York: Alfred A. Knopf, 1997), 271–72.

5. We refer here to patented, documented breast supporters. There are hints among early 1800s undergarments of soft, shoulder-hung supports that would have been suitable to wear with thin, high-waisted dresses of ca. 1800–1820. Copp Family Textiles numbers 6691 ab, 6725, 6733 abc, 6822, and 28810, Costume Collection, National Museum of American History, Smithsonian Institution.

Chapter 1. The Birth of the Brassiere

1. Luman L. Chapman, U.S. Patent 40,907, awarded 15 December 1863.

2. Sarah Levitt, "From Mrs. Bloomer to the Bloomer: The Social Significance of the Nineteenth-Century English Dress Reform Movement," *Textile History* 24, no. 1 (1993): 27–37. Leavitt pinpoints Artistic Dress as "the first major 'alternative' fashion."

3. Most writers agree that Elizabeth Smith Miller devised the costume, probably patterning it on the attire seen in a European health spa. Louise Noun, "Amelia Bloomer, Biography: Part 1, The Lily of Seneca Falls," *Annals of Iowa* 47 (Winter 1985): 575–617. Some English women also wore this costume, as explained by Leavitt, "From Mrs. Bloomer."

4. Bloomers were resuscitated as beach attire (*Godey's Lady's Book*, July 1864) and eventually triumphed as bicycle costume in the late 1880s and 1890s.

5. Water cure or hydropathy flourished in the United States between the 1840s and the early 1860s; thereafter, it dwindled, with some facilities metamorphosing into sanitariums that stressed "hygiene, prevention, and recuperation." Hydropathy's major therapies included consumption of large quantities of water, frequent and varied baths, wrapping in wet sheets, a high-fiber vegetarian diet, and abstinence from stimulants and alcohol. Hydropathists encouraged patients to wear loose clothing so that they could breathe freely and engage in exercise. Jane B. Donegan, *Hydropathic Highway to Health: Women and Water-Cure in Antebellum America* (New York: Greenwood Press, 1986). Donegan lists persistent wearers on page 137.

6. Suspending clothing from the shoulders, rather than from the waist or hips, was central to reformism among both regular (orthodox) and water-cure physicians. Supposedly the shoulders were better able to support weight without injury, compared with organs of the abdominal cavity. Donegan, *Hydropathic Highway*, 141.

7. Foy challenged them with patent infringement. Her patents were U.S. Patent 39,910 (skirt supporter), and U.S. Patent 39,911 (corset skirt supporter) both awarded in 1863.

8. Mrs. A. Fletcher, *Illustrated Catalogue of Ladies' and Children's Underwear, Constructed on Dress Reform and Hygienic Principles*, n.p., 1900. "Strong-minded" applied to women who advocated improved opportunities and equal rights for women.

9. *Arena*, 6 (1892): B. O. Flower, "The Next Step Forward; or Thoughts on the Movement for Rational Dress," 635–44; E. M. King, "The Human Dress," 627–30; Annie Jenness Miller, "Artistic and Sensible Dress for Streetwear," 495–98; Elizabeth Smith Miller, "Reflections on Woman's Dress, and the Record of Personal Experience," 491–93; Frances W. Pomeroy, Viscountess Harberton, "How Is It We Get On No Faster?" 621–24; F. E. Russell, "Lines of Beauty," 499–503; and F. M. Steele, "Artistic Dress," 503–7.

10. Deborah Jean Warner discussed Flynt's garment as an example of reform underclothes but did not recognize that it was an early breast supporter. Warner, "Fashion, Emancipation, Reform, and the Rational Undergarment," *Dress* 4 (1978): 24–29.

11. David L. Cohn, *The Good Old Days: A History of American Morals and Manners as Seen Through the Sears, Roebuck Catalogs, 1905 to the Present* (New York: Simon and Schuster, 1940), xxi.

12. Helen Gilbert Ecob, *The Well-Dressed Woman* (New York: Fowler and Wells, 1892), 136; Frances Mary Steele and Elizabeth Livingston Steele Adams, *Beauty of Form*

and Grace of Vesture (New York: Dodd, Mead, 1892), appendix, n.p. Steele and Adams said, "Mrs. Flynt's True Corset, Boston, Mass., being made for each individual, is better worn, of course, without whalebones."

13. Mrs. O. P. Flynt, *Manual of Hygienic Modes of Underdressing for Women and Children* (Boston: C. M. A. Twitchell, 1882), 4, 27–29.

14. Mrs. M. E. Hungerford, "What It Costs to Dress a Daughter," *Harper's Bazar*, 11 March 1893, 191; U.S. Department of the Interior, Census Office, *Report on Manufacturing Industries in the United States at the Eleventh Census, 1890*, Part II: *Statistics of Cities* (Washington, D.C.: Government Printing Office, 1895), 748–49, 756–57, 796–97. The industries sampled were ironwork in New York and St. Louis; malt liquors, in New York, St. Louis, and San Francisco; and shirt manufacturing, in Brooklyn, St. Louis, and San Francisco. Women's wages for these industries and cities ranged from $10.26 to $3.58 per week. Officers and supervisory personnel earnings in these industries varied widely: from an astounding $98.14 per week (liquor, New York) to $14.51 per week (shirts, San Francisco).

15. *Dress*, July-August 1888, 41.

16. In the 1870s and 1880s, women's ready-to-wear garments were few. Manufacturers were producing most types of underwear, at-home dresses called "wrappers," and loosely shaped outer garments, including cloaks, paletots, capes, and dolmans. By the 1880s, a small selection of dresses was ready-made. Claudia B. Kidwell and Margaret C. Christman *Suiting Everyone* (Washington, D.C.: Smithsonian Institution Press, 1974), 135–37.

17. Elaine S. Abelson, *When Ladies Go A-thieving: Middle-Class Shoplifters in the Victorian Department Store* (New York: Oxford University Press, 1989), 36. A high-quality hand-sewn dress would take an experienced seamstress about one hundred hours of labor—this for a "simple" style. Machine sewing reduced the time to fewer than twenty hours.

18. For discussion of dress reform advocates in the antebellum era, see Donegan, *Hydropathic Highway*, 163–65.

19. For details on these activities, see Nancy A. Hewitt, *Women's Activism and Social Change: Rochester, New York, 1822–1872* (Ithaca, N.Y.: Cornell University Press, 1984).

20. Amelia Jenks Bloomer, *"Hear Me Patiently": The Reform Speeches of Amelia Jenks Bloomer*, Anne C. Coon, ed. (Westport, Conn.: Greenwood Press, 1994).

21. Regina Markell Morantz-Sanchez, *Sympathy and Science: Women Physicians in American Medicine* (New York: Oxford University Press, 1985), 32.

22. Norman Gevitz, ed., *Other Healers: Unorthodox Medicine in America* (Baltimore: Johns Hopkins University Press, 1988).

23. *Sectarian* in this context does not connote religious affiliation but is simply a synonym for alternative therapies.

24. Morantz-Sanchez, *Sympathy and Science*, 27, 45.

25. By 1893, women were admitted to only 37 of 105 regular schools of medicine; several of those that accepted women were obliged to provide coeducation because they were land-grant universities. Ibid., 64–65.

26. Joan Lynaugh, personal communication, 6 May 1999. See also Deborah MacLurg Jensen, *History and Trends of Professional Nursing* (St. Louis: Mosby, 1959), and National League for Nursing website: www.nln.org (17 December 2000).

27. Morantz-Sanchez, *Sympathy and Science*, 35, 58.

28. Several men also became outspoken advocates of dress reform, including James Caleb Jackson, William Andrus Alcott, Russell Trall, and Robert L. Dickinson. Some belonged to medical sects; others, such as Dickinson, were regular physicians.

Chapter 2. Brassieres Win a Niche in Fashion

1. Olivia Flynt's supporter continued to be mentioned in books offering advice about healthful dress. Frances Mary Steele and Elizabeth Livingston Steele Adams, *Beauty of Form and Grace of Vesture* (New York: Dodd, Mead, 1892), appendix; Helen Gilbert Ecob, *The Well-Dressed Woman* (New York: Fowler and Wells Company, 1892), 136. However, because Flynt died in 1897, it is unlikely that her products continued to be made after the early 1890s. "Recent Deaths, Mrs. Olivia P. Flynt, *Boston Evening Transcript*, 2 February 1897.

2. "Doing Justice to the Brassiere Department," *Corset and Underwear Review*, November 1916, 36; "The Fall Outlook for Brassieres," *Corset and Underwear Review* (hereafter abbreviated as *CUR*), July 1915, 50–51.

3. *New York Times*, 9 March 1911, 9.

4. Aesthetes were women (and a few men) whose dress reform efforts were directed toward a more artistic effect, more flowing and less constricted and decorated than mainstream fashions. "New Woman" became a catchall phrase for women who sought fuller participation in the economic, public, and intellectual life of their times.

5. *Delineator*, April 1901, 677.

6. Stitt patented her "bust girdle" on 12 December 1896. She must have been producing girdles before they appeared in such magazines as the *Delineator*. Indeed, some styles of the 1890s would have harmonized better with this supporter than would the bloused-front bodices of the early 1900s.

7. The 1908 appearance was as an unbranded product in the Sears, Roebuck catalog, 1074.

8. Featherbone, made from turkey feathers, was produced by the Warren Featherbone Company of Three Oaks, Michigan, beginning in 1883. Sally Helvenston, "From Feathers to Fashion: How the Turkey Revolutionized Women's Clothing," *Michigan History Magazine*, September-October 1996, 28–35.

9. Robert L. Dickinson, "Simple and Practical Methods in Dress Reform; with Schedules of Instructions to Patients, and Illustrations," *Transactions of the American Gynecological Society* 18 (1893): 426. Dickinson staunchly believed that women could develop their physiques so that the breasts would be self-supporting. Newell's products were accepted for advertising in Annie Jenness Miller's monthly magazine for dress reformers, called simply *Dress*. Miller continued to promote Newell's products.

10. Rose Sahlin, U.S.Patent 643,911, awarded 20 February 1900. Sahlin carried other styles of brassiere at least into the 1910s. *CUR*, November 1916, 37; advertisement in *Delineator*, April 1913, 314.

11. U.S.P. 682,426.

12. Sears, Roebuck catalog, fall 1900, no. 110, 685. Seen in facsimile: Northfield, Ill.: Digest Books, 1970.

13. For example, see *The Delineator*, May 1897, xii.

14. *Delineator*, May 1893, 436.

15. *Delineator* also sold patterns for Laura H. Johnson's patented "garment," a cropped, sleeveless camisole that tied under the breasts, giving support without stiffness. U.S.P. 644,606, awarded 6 March 1900.

16. Between 1870 and 1900, Chicago population increased by 470 percent. Boris Emmet and John E. Jeuck, *Catalogues and Counters: A History of Sears, Roebuck and Company* (Chicago: University of Chicago Press, 1950), 10, 19–20, 26–27, 37.

17. Sears, Roebuck catalogs: fall 1903, no. 113, 926; spring 1913, no. 118, 118, 245, 250–51, 253; fall 1917, 165, 232; *Hot Weather Bargains*, Bellas Hess and Company Catalog No. 78, undated, but probably 1917–18, 30.

18. Jeff Pirtle, J. C. Penney archivist, telephone interview with author, 27 April 2000.

19. Sears, Roebuck catalog, spring 1913, 250. This edition of the catalog showed sixteen models of brassiere and bust confiner, costing as much as 88 cents.

20. Claudia B. Kidwell and Margaret C. Christman, *Suiting Everyone: The Democratization of Clothing in America* (Washington, D.C.: Smithsonian Institution Press, 1974), 135.

21. Corsets were worn over the chemise, which partially protected them from soiling, whereas brassieres were worn next to the skin.

22. In factory production, each worker performs one repeated function, perfecting the skill of the worker and expediting completion of the garment.

23. New York corsetieres Mme. Meyers, Mme. Gardner, and Therese Hynds offered "bust supports" as accessories to their main lines of corsets. These did not challenge the brassiere specialists. Such advertisements appeared mostly in 1905. e.g., *Vogue* 24 August 1905, 196; *Ladies' Home Journal* April 1905, 76.

24. Michael Janes, *The Oxford French Minidictionary* (New York: Oxford University Press, 1986), 40; Marguerite Bruneau, *Histoire du costume populaire en Normandie*, 2 vols. (Rouen: Le Cercle d'action et d'études normandes, 1983–86), 25, cited in Suzanne Gousse and André Gousse, *Costume in New France from 1740 to 1760: A Visual Dictionary* (Chambly: Fleur de Lyse, 1997), 10. The French word for a breast support is *soutien gorge*. 273.

25. According to DeBevoise family history, they left France in late 1600s and lived in the Netherlands for a few generations, migrating to North America shortly after the arrival of Peter Stuyvesant. The company had started in business making underwaists and other undergarments, evidently incorporating brassieres in about 1905. Lily DeBevoise, interview with author, 11 September 2000.

Charles DeBevoise's three U.S. patents illustrate his goal of making an attractive undergarment, acceptable under the sheer dresses and blouses popular in the 1900s and 1910s. He was really producing a supporter-cum-corset-cover. U.S. patents 997,046 awarded 4 July 1911; 1,081,814, awarded 16 December 1913; and 1,106,184, awarded 4 August 1914. .

26. Karen Brown Larrimore gives several examples of early brassiere styles in "The Changing Line of the Corset, 1820–1915," Ph.D. diss. University of Wisconsin, 1984, 313–16, 543–44.

27. Valerie Steele refers to European designers such as Paul Poiret and Lucille asserting their influence in developing early twentieth-century brassieres. Steele, *Fash-*

ion and Eroticism: Ideals of Feminine Beauty from the Victorian Era to the Jazz Age (New York: Oxford University Press, 1985), 226.

28. *Vogue*, 16 August 1906, 196; Mme. Meyers advertisement, *Ladies' Home Journal*, October 1906, 70; and Anna Lent, "Braces for the Stout Woman," *Ladies' Home Journal*, February 1907, 71.

29. "What Fashion Demands of the Brassiere," *Women's and Infants' Furnisher*, August 1917, 33–34.

30. A *CUR* article in January 1917 refers to Mrs. DeBevoise as president of the company. Charles R. DeBevoise must also have been an officer during the first years of the company's existence. Mrs. DeBevoise used the occasion of a company convention to announce a 7 percent wage increase for factory operators, coupled with a shortening of the workweek from 52 to 49.5 hours. She cited the rising cost of living and the company's financial health as reasons for the timing of the raise. "Ninth Annual Convention of the Chas. R. DeBevoise Co.," 65.

31. "Mrs. Gabrielle Poix Yerkes" (obituary) *CUR*, September 1941, 57. This obituary claimed a starting date of 1906, but Gabrielle Poix had already applied for a patent for her brassiere in 1905.

32. Advertisement, *Harper's Bazar*, April 1917, 105.

33. Kops marketed under the Nemo brand and manufactured corsets as well as brassieres.

34. Advertising appeared in *CUR* as late as November 1932, 24. Venus Corporation, Chicago, purchased Nature's Rival in 1933.

35. Advertisement in *Harper's Bazar*, April 1915, 8.

36. U.S. patent 1,145,204 awarded 6 July 1915. Tom Mahoney and Leonard Sloane, *The Great Merchants: America's Foremost Retail Institutions and the People Who Made Them Great* (New York: Harper and Row, 1966), 244–58.

37. U.S. patents 1,119,296 and 1,119,298, respectively, both awarded in 1914.

38. *Vogue*, 6 December 1906, 865 and 15 August 1916, 85.

39. *Vogue*, 1 November 1913, 127. The "treco" part of the name intimates a relationship to "tricot," a fine knitted fabric with considerable elasticity.

40. U.S. Bureau of the Census, *Historical Statistics of the United States: Colonial Times to 1970*, pt. 1 (Washington, D.C.: U.S. Department of Commerce, 1976), G536.

41. Textile World Journal, compiler, *A Directory of Textile Brands and Trademarks* (New York: Bragdon, Lord and Nagle, 1918), 392–93.

42. For example, see *Vogue*, 1 May 1913, 76; 15 May 1914, 75; *Delineator*, February 1913, 106; "Indispensable Helps to Good Dressing," *Needlecraft*, 1913, 49.

43. Pearl Merwin, *The American System of Dressmaking* (Kansas City, Mo.: American College of Dressmaking, 1912), lesson 17.

44. E. B. Weiss, *How to Sell to and Through Department Stores* (New York: McGraw-Hill, 1936), 123.

45. Kabo advertisement, *Delineator*, April 1900, 573. These were both smoothly fitted styles. The shirtwaist was a tailored blouse, very popular in the 1890s and early 1900s for informal daywear and business. Tailor-made gowns employed the crisp styling associated with menswear.

46. *Vogue*, 24 August 1905, 196. Elastic swimwear first appeared in the Sears, Roebuck catalog in spring 1913, 118.

47. Marshall Field advertisement, #86, spring 1907.

48. *New York Times*, 9 March 1911, 9.

49. G. M. Poix advertisement, *Vogue*, 1 April 1912, 93.

50. DeBevoise advertisement, *Vogue*, 1 February 1913, 96.

51. DeBevoise advertisement, *Vogue*, 15 March 1914, 91.

52. Ovida advertisement, *Vogue*, 1 November 1913, 127.

53. Advertisement, *Harper's Bazar*, April 1915, 8.

54. Companies typically had between eighty and one hundred styles of brassiere, according to *CUR*, February 1917, 56.

55. Advertisement in *Vogue*, 1 June 1912, 77.

56. "Style Characteristics of the New Brassiere," *CUR*, March 1917, 37. These strategies must have been working well, because on page 43 of the same issue the columnist noted that small sizes were selling well. She wrote, "Who ever heard of a size 32 when brassieres were first worn!"

57. See, e.g., Sara M. Evans, *Born for Liberty: A History of Women in America* (New York: Free Press, 1989), 161. In late 1916 and early 1917, bandeaux were selling over brassieres in ratio of three to one. "Analyzing the Spring Style Tendencies in Brassieres," *CUR*, February 1917, 56.

58. Our research suggests that the heyday of flapperism, involving breezy behavior and attention-getting clothing, was about 1922 to 1927. In the late 1920s and early 1930s, the concept of flapper lingered among foundation salespeople as a contrast to more mature women. By 1930, the word *teen* began to replace flapper or deb for describing young women.

59. G. M. Poix advertisement, *Vogue*, 5 January 1914, 83.

60. Sears, Roebuck catalog, fall 1913, 132, 144–45.

61. Ovida advertisement, *Vogue*, 1 September 1916, 140; G. M. Poix advertisements, *Vogue*, 15 May 1913, 75 and 1 June 1913, 85.

62. Advertisement, *Harper's Bazar*, May 1917, 113.

63. "Brassiere Merchandising," 15 August 1916, 2, 16.

64. Our evidence does not directly link occupation to wearing of a brassiere. The examples are merely suggestive of circumstances that would favor more comfortable styles of underclothing.

65. U.S. Department of the Interior, Census Office, *Population of the United States at the Eleventh Census: 1890*, pt. 2 (Washington, D.C.: Government Printing Office, 1887, lxxx). Also, *Fourteenth Census of the United States Taken in the Year 1920*, vol. 4, Population 1920, Occupations, (Washington, D.C.: Government Printing Office, 1923), table 1, p. 33.

66. *Eleventh Census, 1890*, pt. 2, lxxxix.

67. *Fourteenth Census*, vol. 4, Population 1920, Occupations, table 1, p. 33.

68. Ibid., table 2, p. 34; table 4, pp. 36–42.

69. U.S. Department of Commerce, Bureau of the Census, *Historical Statistics of the United States*, part 1 (1975), Series H 751–765, p. 386.

70. *Fourteenth Census*, vol. 4, Population 1920, Occupations, table 4, pp. 36–42.

71. David Kennedy, *Over Here: The First World War and American Society* (New York: Oxford University Press, 1980), 284–86.

72. Juliana K. Albrecht, "Women's Riding Clothing in the Central United States: Ideal Fashion and Actual Practice, 1880–1930," master's thesis, Iowa State University, 1986, 155, 242.

73. Marshall Field & Co. spring catalog, no. 86, 1907, 594.

74. A description of suits worn in public baths in 1877 specified a one-piece garment, with pants that reached "about half way to the knees" and left the neck and arms bare. No skirt was mentioned. Various types of knitted and woven suits were worn in early public contests. *Chicago Tribune*, 8 July 1877, 111. Maxine Johns, "Women's Functional Swimwear, 1860–1920," Ph.D. diss. Iowa State University, 1997, 125.

75. Kate Hatch received U.S. Patent 550,171 on 19 November 1895 for a "body protector" for use while swimming. It looked like the front of a high-necked bathing suit, but stopped slightly below the waistline and was almost backless.

76. Kathy Peiss, *Cheap Amusements: Working Women and Leisure in Turn-of-the-Century New York* (Philadelphia: Temple University Press, 1986).

77. Rebecca Edwards, *Angels in the Machinery: Gender in American Party Politics from the Civil War to the Progressive Era* (New York: Oxford University Press, 1997).

78. Leading suffragists avoided wearing reform dress, not wishing to create a threatening "unwomanly" image that would endanger their cause.

79. Evans, *Born for Liberty*, 168–70.

80. Hudson D. Bishop wrote in 1904, "Every physician who does obstetrical work should give careful instruction and attention to his patient during her pregnancy. The better class of patients expect this, and a common practice is to recommend to them one of the numerous books upon this subject that are intended for the laity." Bishop, *The Obstetrical Duties of Mother and Nurse* (Cleveland: J. H. Lamb, 1904), preface.

81. Anna Broomall established an outpatient department at the Women's Hospital of the Women's Medical College, Philadelphia. "Eventually this department offered the first prenatal care in the country." Regina Markell Morantz- Sanchez, *Sympathy and Science: Women Physicians in American Medicine* (New York: Oxford University Press, 1985), 79. Even Hydropathy, in its mid-1800s heyday, had instituted care for the woman's health during pregnancy. Jane B. Donegan, *Hydropathic Highway to Health: Women and Water-Cure in Antebellum America* (New York: Greenwood Press, 1986), 90–91.

82. Admittedly, the messages about breast-feeding versus bottle or mixed-feeding were conflicting, as is documented by Rima D. Apple in *Mothers and Medicine: A Social History of Infant Feeding, 1890–1950* (Madison: University of Wisconsin Press, 1987), See especially chaps. 6 and 7.

83. Nurses Carolyn E. Gray and Mary Alberta Baker were probably the first to suggest the use of a brassiere in their revision of Joseph Brown Cooke's classic text, *A Nurses Handbook of Obstetrics*, 7th ed. (Philadelphia: Lippincott, 1915), 103. Application of a binder required the coordinated efforts of two nurses, making it almost impossible for a woman to use at home.

84. Marie Tucek, U.S.P. 494,397, filed 11 January 1893, awarded 28 March 1893. Tucek had a second patent, under the name of Mary Tucek, U.S.P. 525,241, filed 14 June 1893, awarded 28 August 1894. This second design offered more coverage than the first design. It laced in front, but was similar in strap configuration to the first design.

85. Ethel Quirk, U.S. patent 1,237,095, awarded 14 August 1917.

86. Laura Blanche Lyon, U.S. patent 818,104, awarded 17 April 1906; Jeanne Leeman, U.S. patent 1,205,758, awarded 21 November 1916; Madeleine Gabeau was a Parisienne whose patent (U.S. patent 1,009,297) was filed 21 October 1909, and conferred on

21 November 1911. This delay was not unusual; many of the most innovative designs took more than a year to patent. Gabeau's intent, according to the patent text, was to permit "adjustment of the position of the breasts without disguising their form and without danger of discomfort to the wearer." She reiterated the idea of not "detracting from the individual form," lending credence to the idea that she intended to produce separation and cleavage. Other Europeans were doing soft brassieres, too. Marianne Thesander shows a German "bustenhalter" of soft materials in *The Feminine Ideal* (London: Reaktion Books, 1997), 111.

87. Clarence Mayer, U.S. patent 1,168,732, filed 10 June 1914, awarded 18 January 1916; and Edgar Guggenheim, U.S. patent 1,167,992, filed 19 September 1914, awarded 11 January 1916. The Guggenheim patent closely resembles the contours and wrapping effect of the scultetus binder, used in hospitals.

88. Jacob claimed this in her autobiography, written under the nom de plume "Caresse Crosby," forty-one years after the fact. Crosby, *The Passionate Years* (London: Alvin Redman Limited, 1955), 20, 72–73. Her patent was dated 3 November 1914. Jacob maintained she actually had "a few hundred (units) of her design produced" for sale and that Warner bought the patent rights in 1913 and made a fortune from them (74). We have found no evidence that Warner ever produced this style. It does not appear in Warner advertisements. Jacob's prominence in the public mind may be due to her socialite status or her reputation as a fiction writer.

89. Jacob's patented design is discussed in Marilyn Yalom, *A History of the Breast* (New York: Alfred A. Knopf, 1997), 173, 176; Joan Jacobs Brumberg, *The Body Project: An Intimate History of American Girls* (New York: Random House, 1997), 109; Elizabeth Ewing, *Dress and Undress: A History of Women's Underwear* (New York: Drama Book Specialists, 1978), 115.

Chapter 3. Breasts Lost and Found

1. Dorothy M. Brown, *Setting a Course: American Women in the 1920s* (Boston: Twayne, 1987), 2.

2. Ibid., 6; Amos St. Germain, "The Flowering of Mass Society," in *Dancing Fools and Weary Blues: The Great Escape of the Twenties*, ed. Lawrence R. Broer and John D. Walther (Bowling Green, Ohio: Bowling Green State University Popular Press, 1990): 26.

3. Geoffrey Perret, *America in the Twenties: A History* (New York: Simon and Schuster, 1982), 337–38.

4. Brown, *Setting a Course*, 95–96.

5. Cecil C. Hoge, *The First Hundred Years Are the Toughest* (Berkeley, Calif.: Ten Speed Press, 1988).

6. M. Ada Beney, *Cost of Living in the United States, 1914–1936* (New York: National Industrial Conference Board, 1936), 49, 98, table 13.

7. Frances R. Donovan, *The Saleslady* (Chicago: University of Chicago Press, 1929), 203.

8. David E. Fisher and Marshall Jon Fisher, *Tube: The Invention of Television* (Washington, D.C.: Counterpoint, 1996).

9. Lynne Richards, "The Rise and Fall of It All: The Hemlines and Hiplines of the 1920s," *Clothing and Textiles Research Journal* 2 (1983–84): 42–48.

10. Even fashion illustrations do not suggest knees showing on women until the short look went out of fashion. The 4 January 1930 issue of *Vogue* contrasted "Ladies in the Winter of 1929" with "Ladies in the Winter of 1930," satirically emphasizing the plump or bony arms and knees revealed by the 1929 mode (50–51).

11. Not a thread of truth supports the persistent legend that the plummeting stock market of October 1929 brought down women's hemlines. Hemlines fell first, but that does not lead to the conclusion that falling skirts *caused* falling stock prices.

12. In the 1880s and 1910s, there had also been so-called princess styles, which fit close to the body by means of shoulder-to-hem seaming. Earlier and later princess lines did not include a horizontal waistline seam, but the 1920s example did.

13. "Here and There in the Industry: A New and Added Season," *CUR*, November 1929, 71.

14. The French comte de Chardonnet had produced a nitrocellulose fiber in 1884, but textiles woven from rayon only came into use for lingerie in the 1920s. Susannah Handley, *Nylon: The Story of a Fashion Revolution* (Baltimore: Johns Hopkins University Press, 1999), 18.

15. Sara J. Kadolph and Anna L. Langford, *Textiles*, 9th ed. (Upper Saddle River, N.J.: Merrill, 1998), 85–86.

16. Advertisement, *Vogue*, 15 June 1927, 17. The live model was contrasted to fitting on a dress form, which would decrease costs of product development but also prevent checking fit and comfort in movement.

17. According to research conducted by J. Walter Thompson in 1924–25, silk "jersey" (probably tricot) was the second most popular material for brassieres after cotton brocade and novelty weaves, specifically in Philadelphia. Office memorandum, 12 December 1924, 10, Kops Brothers' file, JWT Archives, Special Collections, Duke University. Swami was a firmly knitted fabric of yarns that blended rayon and cotton Grace G. Denny, *Fabrics*, 4th ed. (Philadelphia: Lippincott, 1936), 116–17. Milanese was a square-meshed knitted fabric of silk or rayon.

18. A patent for a brassiere, U.S. patent 1,446,928, was awarded to Harriet Lyons Redmond and assigned to the William Carter Company, 27 February 1923.

19. Joseph Mayer, *The Revolution in Merchandise* (New York: Greenberg, 1939).

20. E. B. Weiss, *How to Sell to and Through Department Stores* (New York: McGraw-Hill, 1936), 20–22.

21. Perret, *America in the Twenties*, 33.

22. *Historical Statistics*, series H 751–65, 386.

23. Lillian Eichler Watson, *Book of Etiquette*, vol. 2 (Garden City, N.Y.: Nelson Doubleday, 1923), 180–84. Woman's Institute of Domestic Arts and Sciences, *Harmony in Dress* (Scranton, Pa., 1926). Lucile Babcock, "What Should the Business Woman Wear?" *Delineator*, September 1930, 36, 48.

24. Rayon had fewer liabilities in clothing meant to be dry-cleaned.

25. Donovan, *The Saleslady*, 185.

26. Brown, *Setting a Course*, 43. We found no evidence of a woman athlete "endorsing" a brand of brassiere.

27. Perret, *America in the Twenties*, 222–23.

28. The writer of the editorial feature "Dressing on a War Income" believed that

simplified lingerie "came as a result of the war, and it is indeed interesting to notice the change that the wearing of uniforms and plain tailored clothes for war work has brought about in lingerie. It is more tailored than ever and has taken the name of athletic underwear" (*Vogue*, 1 August 1918, 50).

29. Advertisement, *Vogue*, 1 January 1923, 149. The Longerlyne was a brassiere that extended over the top of the corset for a smooth line.

30. National Industrial Conference Board, *The Cost of Living in New York City, 1926*. (New York: National Industrial Conference Board, 1926), 51.

31. "The Importance of the Corset To-day," *Vogue*, 13 September 1923, 94.

32. Margaret Elliott and Grace E. Manson, *Earnings of Women in Business and the Professions*, 3, no. 1 (Ann Arbor: University of Michigan School of Business, 1930), 178–79. Cited by Sophonisba P. Breckenridge, *Women in the Twentieth Century: A Study of Their Political, Social and Economic Activities* (New York: McGraw-Hill, 1933), 226.

33. Helen C. Hoerle and Florence B. Saltzberg, *The Girl and the Job* (New York: Henry Holt, 1919), 6–24.

34. Elliott and Manson, *Earnings of Women*, 13.

35. Donovan, *The Saleslady*, 196–97.

36. Margaret Matlack, "Budgeting the Successful Business Woman's Clothes," *Ladies' Home Journal*, April 1926, 93, 97–98, 103.

37. National Industrial Conference Board, *Cost of Living*, 79. The varied expenses related to retail information from the five boroughs of New York City.

38. J. Walter Thompson interview transcripts, New York series, interview no. 5, 24. Jill Fields documents a similar push to sell lightweight corsets and "girdles" to young girls, in "'Fighting the Corsetless Evil': Shaping Corsets and Culture 1900–1930," *Journal of Social History* 33 (1999): 375–76.

39. *Harper's Bazar*, November 1925, 167. G. M. Poix manufactured a second line of brassieres under the label Girlish Form, presumably to avoid infringing on the Maiden Form trademark.

40. "State Street," and "Demands from Young Girls Increase Sales," *CUR*, December 1929, 83.

41. J. Walter Thompson interview transcripts, New York series, no. 18, 46.

42. JWT interview transcripts, Chicago series, interview no. 8, 28.

43. The name was changed to Adonna in 1949 when the Crescent Corset Company was sold. Jeffrey Pirtle, letter to authors, 27 June 2000.

44. John Tebbel, *The Marshall Fields: A Study in Wealth* (New York: E. P. Dutton, 1947), 131. Tebbel cites Marshall Field's "commanding position" in Chicago retailing, based on a near-century of building superiority in merchandise selection and service.

45. Note that the Rosenthal design (fig. 12) includes seams to contour the cups, whereas the Pollack design relies entirely on gathering. Maiden Form's later version also included a net lining, while Pollack's used doubled fabric to create a self-lining.

46. Kenneth T. Jackson, ed., *The Encyclopedia of New York City* (New Haven: Yale University Press, 1995).

47. Others besides performers seem to have objected to binders. A DeBevoise advertisement hinted at complaints and resistance, conceding that "few figures are wholly suited to each new phase of fashion." *Vogue*, 1 June 1923, 104. A second version by Moe Rosenthal, William's brother and later general manager of the firm, explained that Enid, on a trip to Paris, noted the reemergence of curves in the French designs and accord-

ingly modified her own brassiere to form shallow cups. After returning to New York, she used the concept for customers' brassieres. The original brassiere was made of pink cotton net with silk rosebuds. History of Maidenform file, Department of Social History, Smithsonian Institution. A third account, published two decades later, states that Enid and Ida began by building uplifts into their dresses, in response to what they had seen on "trips abroad." "Maiden Form Brassiere Company Celebrates Twentieth Anniversary," *CUR*, December 1942, 90.

48. Maiden Form claimed to have introduced the uplift in 1923, in an article in *CUR*, October 1929, 15. The company implied that Paris had followed its lead in re-establishing curves in women's fashions.

49. Enid Bissett secured only one patent in her name, U.S. patent 1,874,868, filed 5 December 1930, awarded 30 August 1932. Although the Rosenthals bought out Enid's share in the business, Joseph Bissett was sales manager of Maiden Form in 1932, according to *CUR* November 1932, 82.

50. William Rosenthal, U.S. patent 1,648,464, filed 12 October 1926, awarded 8 November 1927. The patent also shows internal seaming in the cups; these are not evident in the advertising illustrations.

51. Oddly enough, "The return to feminism!" was the banner at the top of the ad, but obviously "femininity" was the intended concept (109).

52. This does not yet connote sized cups, which arrived in the 1930s.

53. U.S. patents 1,568,457, awarded 5 January 1926, and 1,615,629, awarded 25 January 1927 to Augusta S. Johnson; 1,565,808 awarded 15 December 1925 to Leo E. Levy; and 1,566,109 awarded 15 December 1925 to Elvira Campa McKeefrey. Levy's garment also had maternity use.

54. Advertisements, *Vogue*, 15 August 1918, 87; *Vogue*, 15 September 1922, 19.

55. Advertisement in *Vogue*, 15 November 1918, 28.

56. Advertisement in *Delineator*, June 1919, 70.

57. *Harper's Bazar*, December 1926, 148.

58. Poix claimed that her brassieres relieved breast pain, which she called "mammalgia." The possibility for this type of relief is supported by the April 2000 *Mayo Clinic Health Letter*, which said mastalgia, a "common but often manageable" condition, might be relieved by "wearing a supportive bra without underwires or padding during the day and a soft, cotton athletic bra at night" (6).

59. Louise Zabriskie, *Nurse's Handbook of Obstetrics*, 4th ed., rev. (Philadelphia: J. B. Lippincott, 1934).

60. Ralph W. Lobenstein, "The Development of Prenatal Care in the Borough of Manhattan, New York City," *American Journal of Obstetrics* 76 (September 1917): 381–92. Grace L. Meigs, "Maternal Mortality from Childbirth in the United States and Its Relation to Prenatal Care," *American Journal of Obstetrics* 76 (September 1917): 392–401.

61. This bipartisan bill, drafted by Senator Morris Sheppard and Representative Horace Towner in 1918, was passed in 1921 and funded once more in 1927. It expired in 1929, because a vocal segment of the medical community lobbied against it as an intrusion of government into medicine. Sheppard-Towner did not fund medical care per se, but only educational programs.

62. Frank H. Richardson, "The Nursing Mother: A Study in Lactation," *New York State Journal of Medicine* 22 (April 1922): 161–65.

63. Joseph Brown Cooke, *A Nurse's Handbook of Obstetrics*, 7th ed., revised by Carolyn E. Gray and Mary Alberta Baker (Philadelphia: Lippincott, 1915).

64. Frances Sage Bradley, "Which—A Well Baby or a Boyish Form?" *Hygeia*, June 1927, 298–99.

65. L. R. DeBuys, "Observations upon the Breasts of Mothers of the Newly Born," *Annals of Clinical Medicine* 1, (1923): 204–10; William C. Danforth, "The Care of Pregnancy," *Boston Medical and Surgical Journal* 193, 20 August 1925, 331–38. Charles R. Larkin, "Drying Up the Lactating Breasts," *Medical Journal and Record*, 20 April 1927, 527; Fred B. Smith, "The Care of the Lactating Breast," *American Journal of Obstetrics and Gynecology* 18 (November 1929): 784–89.

66. Charles H. Lewis, "An Outline of Prenatal Care," *California and Western Medicine* 30 (February 1929): 108–11.

67. Carolyn Conant Van Blarcom, *Getting Ready to Be a Mother* (New York: Macmillan, 1929), 120–21; and *Obstetrical Nursing* (New York: Macmillan, 1923); Hazel Corbin, "Suggestions for the Care of the Breasts During Pregnancy," *American Journal of Nursing* 23 (April 1923): 545–47.

68. Transcript of interviews conducted in Chicago by J. Walter Thompson Agency for Kops Brothers. Interview 5, 22. This report was dated 23 December 1924. J. Walter Thompson Archives, John W. Hartman Center, Special Collections, Duke University.

69. Advertisement in *Vogue*, 1 September 1920, 134.

70. *Harper's Bazar*, May 1929, 160.

71. In a 1932 advertisement, Lily of France claimed to have started business in the late 1890s, presumably as a corset company because this firm did not produce breast supporters. Neither did it show separate brassieres up through the mid-1930s.

72. Walter's address was Fifth Avenue, but the entry varied from 34th to 36th Streets. She occupied a suite, not a complete shop.

73. *Vogue*, 6 July 1929, 108.

74. Treo: U.S. patent 1,641,284, awarded to Samuel T. Metz, 6 September 1927.

75. The brand name does not appear in the listing of brassiere producers published in 1921. However, Mae Pruzan held a patent for a brassiere filed 15 October 1920 and awarded 28 February 1922; Walter Pruzan's patent was filed 5 May 1921 and awarded 28 October 1924. For confirmation of the emergence of the flat-chested silhouette, see *Vogue*, 15 August 1919, 66.

76. *New York Times*, 15 February 1920, n.p. Note that the Maiden Form brand came into existence to provide for women who neither had nor aspired to a boyish form as embodied in this brand.

77. *CUR*, January 1932, 111.

78. Perhaps the DeBevoises really thought of themselves as Dutch, due to their ancestors' years of living in the Netherlands. In contrast, Gabrielle Poix used her French family name for her business, even after her marriage added the name Yerkes. In her patent texts she was Gabrielle M. P. Yerkes, but in advertising copy, "Mme. Poix, famous French designer." Curiously this advertisement appeared not in a fashion magazine but in *CUR*, November 1929, 65.

79. Advertisement, *Vogue* (1 April 1922): 112. What constituted a separate "style" remained unexplained. Each different combination of fabric and trim, in the same basic cut, might well have been counted as one style.

80. *CUR*, October 1929, 72.

81. The authors have tried in vain to locate a source of *CUR* issues for 1934–36. However, *Dry Goods Merchant Trade Journal* advertising helped to pinpoint when DeBevoise advertising ended entirely. Mrs. Lily DeBevoise confirmed the fact of the company's sale but not the identity of the purchaser. Telephone interview to Jane Farrell-Beck, 8 September 2000.

82. Daniel's brother Max was also a partner in the company but not named in the patents.

83. The following information derives from an "Account History, Kops Brothers, Inc." dated 11 January 1926, held in the John W. Hartman Center for Sales, Advertising and Marketing History, Special Collections Library, Duke University, Durham, N.C.

84. Employees of JWT Agency interviewed buyers or sales personnel at twenty stores in Manhattan, the Bronx, Brooklyn, and Newark; eight stores in Philadelphia; thirteen stores in Chicago; and forty-nine stores in smaller cities in northern New York, Connecticut, Rhode Island, and Massachusetts. These data, presented later in this chapter, give a remarkable profile of consumption of brassieres and corsets in the mid-1920s. Kops had hired J. Walter Thompson to help them reposition their brand; the results persuaded the brothers to strive for products with a more youthful image.

85. The garment referred to was the corselette. One buyer interviewed by JWT candidly expressed the view that Kops needed to hire a designer. Obviously these men were not tuning in to what women wanted in foundations.

86. Kops Brothers, Inc., Account History, 11 January 1926, 4.

87. In contrast to the straight tops characteristic of early 1920s bandeaux.

88. *Trademarks, Labels, Prints to the Textile Industry*, comp. 2d ed. (New York: Bragdon, Lord and Nagle, 1921)

89. U.S. Bureau of the Census, *Fifteenth Census of the United States. Manufactures: 1929*, vol. 2, "Reports by Industries" (Washington, D.C., 1933), 386, table 3.

90. Blanche Payne, Geitel Winakor, and Jane Farrell-Beck, *The History of Costume from Ancient Mesopotamia Through the Twentieth Century*, 2d ed. (New York: HarperCollins, 1992), 544.

91. *Mobil Travel Guide: Southwest and South Central* (New York: Fodor's Travel Publications, 1995), 196.

92. St. Germain, "The Flowering of Mass Society," 28, 30.

93. John Higson Cover, *Advertising: Its Problems and Methods* (New York: D. Appleton, 1926), 115.

94. DeBevoise advertisement, *Vogue*, 1 October 1922, 117.

95. Advertisement, *Vogue*, 1 May 1928, 164.

96. U.S. patent 1,472,796, awarded to Lewis Fritz, 6 November 1923; U.S. patent 1,766,278 awarded to Mary A. Bollwine, 24 June 1930.

97. Strapless evening dresses appeared at least as early as 1914. "Paris Will Be Paris, Weather or Not," *Vogue*, 1 May 1914, 84. Two examples of strapless brassieres were U.S. patent 1,431,206 awarded to Blanche Yurka, 10 October 1922, and U.S. patent 1,420,248, awarded to Nellie L. Fay, 20 June 1922.

98. Teresina Maria Negri, U.S. patent 1,502,436, filed 25 January 1921, awarded 22 July 1924.

99. Laura Ethel Mailleue, U.S. patent 1,417,930, filed 14 May 1919, awarded 30 May 1922. *Trained Nurse* reported the innovation in its December 1919 issue seven months after the patent was filed. The three-year wait for the patent suggests the dramatic novelty of this concept, even though breast *augmentation* represented a very old quest.

100. Softness was an attribute of the invention, as reported in the patent text.

101. Lingerie features in *Vogue*, *Harper's Baza(a)r*, and *Delineator* often showed brassieres from such French firms as Cadolle. Evidently, wealthy American women were securing some of their underthings from French sources.

102. The Museum at Fashion Institute of Technology, Accession number 81.213.4. According to *Vogue*, 6 July 1929, 52–53, Elsa Schiaparelli designed a crocheted brassiere of silk thread, for wear under a bathing suit. It appears from the thumbnail sketch to have had conical cups, with straight bands between the cups and in back.

103. Laura I. Baldt, *Clothing for Women: Selection and Construction* (Philadelphia: Lippincott, 1929), 441.

104. Brown, *Setting a Course*, 213–18.

105. St. Germain, "The Flowering of Mass Society," 37.

106. Frank E. Fellman, *The Gossard Corsetiere and Merchandiser* 1916–1918. The exception was an advertisement by Maxwell & Klein for a "No-Bak Brassiere," which does state that it was "used and endorsed by many of Hollywood's leading screen stars" *Vogue*, 27 August 1929, 98. This firm, based in Hollywood, was destined to succeed as the Hollywood-Maxwell Company in the 1930 and to be bought by Munsingwear in 1957.

107. "Dressing on a War Income," *Vogue*, 1 August 1918, 80.

108. *CUR*, July 1925, 19.

Chapter 4. Brassieres Rise, Stocks Fall

1. Nathan M. Ohrbach, *Getting Ahead in Retailing* (New York: McGraw-Hill, 1935), 4. Ohrbach's was a well-known budget department store in the New York metro area.

2. *CUR*, March 1930, 76.

3. *Women's Wear Daily*, 20 July 1937, sec. 2, cited in Heidi L. Boehlke, "Ruth M. Kapinas, Munsingwear's Forgotten 'Foundettes' Designer," *Dress* 20 (1993): 46.

4. "Are We Going to Make Profits in 1933?" *CUR*, January 1933, 61.

5. "To Point or Not to Point," *CUR*, February 1933, 72. Dorothy Bickum news item *CUR*, February 1933, 99.

6. *Harper's Bazaar*, August 1935, 41. Slacks were occasionally worn to class, but less so than skirts. Sweater twin sets, often associated with the 1950s, actually came into fashion in the late 1930s.

7. *CUR*, October 1929, 76.

8. Gossard advertisement, *Harper's Bazaar*, April 1936, 160.

9. With a tip of the hat to the Limelighters and their song "Vicki Dugan."

10. Some women may have worn such dresses without brassieres, but we have no direct evidence of this practice.

11. Alix later took the name of Madame Grès and remained active until 1987 when she closed her house. Anne Stegemeyer, *Who's Who in Fashion*, 3d ed. (New York: Fairchild, 1996), 92–93.

12. "New Facts in Figures," *Vogue*, 15 June 1933, 53.

13. "From Us to You," *CUR*, March 1932, 59.

14. Boehlke, "Munsingwear's Forgotten Designer," 45.

15. This discussion of Lastex owes much to Heidi Lori Boehlke, "Ruth M. Kapinas, U.S. Patent No. 2,180,111 and Munsingwear Foundettes: A Study in Technological Change," M.A. thesis, University of Minnesota, 1987, 35–37, 41.

16. Edward F. Roberts, "What Is Its Future?" *CUR*, March 1932.

17. *Women's Wear Daily*, 11 November 1932, 7.

18. Frances R. Donovan, *The Saleslady* (Chicago: University of Chicago Press, 1929), 203.

19. For a discussion of the training and function of corset fitters in the 1920s, see Jill Fields, "'Fighting the Corsetless Evil': Shaping Corsets and Culture, 1900–1930," *Journal of Social History* 33 (1999): 369, 370, 372.

20. Job Analysis Information Section, Division of Standards and Research, *Job Descriptions for the Retail Trade* (Washington, D.C.: Government Printing Office, April 1938), 269–70.

21. *CUR*, March 1930, 115.

22. Cecil C. Hoge, *The First Hundred Years Are the Toughest* (Berkeley, Calif.: Ten Speed Press, 1988), unnumbered figure opposite 83.

23. E. B. Weiss, *How to Sell to and Through Department Stores* (New York: McGraw-Hill, 1936), 7. Weiss, Vice President of Gray Advertising, discussed the returns. We made the connection to fitters.

24. "To Have and to Hold," *CUR*, October 1932, 53.

25. "Milgrim's Corset Shop," *CUR*, October 1932, 56.

26. According to an article in *CUR*, February 1942, Fay-Miss had been established in February 1932 (18). Tiny advertisements in the back pages of the magazine showed a Brooklyn address in October and November 1932 and a Manhattan address by December 1932.

27. "Plain Talk," *CUR*, March 1933, 51. So far as we can determine, only men were appointed to merchandise manager positions.

28. Weiss, *How to Sell*, 19. Weiss interpreted the "M.M." in a more positive way, as the one who could coax more net profit from the merchandising operation and preserve the financial health of the store.

29. Leslie Weiner, *The Lovable Story: A History of the Lovable Brassiere Company*, in-house publication, ca. 1953, 77.

30. Albert Corrado, chairman of the board, Leading Lady, interview with authors, 30 July 2000. Corrado provided the authors with many insights into the brassiere industry, including this valuable link of Victor and Abraham Becker to Beautee-Fit brassieres. The Beckers received a total of eleven patents for bras, none of which mentioned or was assigned to the Western Corset Company/Beautee-Fit. Conversely, company advertising does not mention the Becker name. The Beckers will be profiled in Chapter 6.

31. Joseph R. Bowen, U.S. patent 1,997,995, filed 5 July 1933, awarded 16 April 1935.

32. David M. Kennedy, *Freedom from Fear: The American People in Depression and War, 1929–1945* (New York: Oxford University, 1999).

33. U.S. National Recovery Administration, *Code of Fair Competition for the Corset and Brassiere Industry* (Washington, D.C., 1933).

34. Some industries avoided major layoffs by shortening workers' hours, thereby cutting costs to meet reduced business.

35. Andrew J. Haire, "Favorable Factors That Will Help Manufacturers to Make More Profits." *CUR*, February 1933, 63.

36. *CUR*, January 1933, 61–62.

37. Haire, "Favorable Factors That Will Help Manufacturers to Make More Profits," February 1933, 63–64.

38. Weiss, *How to Sell*, 61–64.

39. Kennedy, *Freedom from Fear*, 350–51.

40. David L. Cohn, *The Good Old Days: A History of American Manners and Morals, as Seen Through the Sears, Roebuck Catalogs, 1905 to the Present* (New York: Simon and Schuster, 1940), 503.

41. Added appeal came from the fact that movie theaters were among the first buildings to be air-conditioned.

42. Advertisement, *Mademoiselle*, June 1939. 81.

43. Weiner, *The Lovable Story*. From the founding of the company, Lovable set an example of racial integration in workrooms and staff cafeterias. Tom Garson, interview with Colleen Gau, 20 April 2000.

44. African-American consumers of brassieres are almost impossible to trace before the emergence of *Ebony*, in which a handful of manufacturers advertised. Details will be provided in Chapter 7.

45. *CUR*, November 1932, 48.

46. *CUR*, January 1933, 69.

47. Venus introduced its College Girl line in the early 1940s, advertising regularly in *Mademoiselle*.

48. Carter's advertisement, *CUR*, March 1933, 82.

49. By the late 1930s and early 1940s, Poix's advertisements in high fashion magazines were minuscule parts of the "Fashion Discoveries of the Month" montage, where they were grouped with ads for swimsuits, jewelry, and dresses, e.g., *Vogue*, 15 May 1940, 101. Inclusion in occasional editorial articles testified to the existence of G. M. Poix, until at least 1948.

50. David Kennedy, *Freedom from Fear*, 165.

51. Lances, Merzon, and Gordon advertised in national magazines, and may have had national sales via mail order. They appear to have been based primarily in New York.

52. *Vogue*, 15 February 1935, 13.

53. *CUR*, October 1932, 65.

54. "College Girl," *Harper's Bazaar*, August 1934, 26–31, 106, 108. College women were reported as routinely wearing brassieres, panties, and slips as their set of underwear, for both day and evening, although a style designated as "shorts" rivaled panties in the West and South.

55. Boehlke, *"Munsingwear's Forgotten Designer,"* 23.

56. It was patented, however, by Mary Bollwine in 1928 and awarded in 1930.

57. *CUR*, November 1932, 42.

58. William S. Bainbridge, "Non-malignant Breast Conditions, Diagnosis and Treatment," *American Journal of Obstetrics and Gynecology* 19 (February 1930): 255–66. Paul S. Seabold, "The Well-fitted Brassiere and Its Use," *Pennsylvania Medical Journal* 39 (October 1935): 16–19.

59. Bainbridge, "Non-malignant Breast Conditions," 266.

60. Fred Lyman Adair, ed., *Maternal Care and Some Complications* (Chicago: University of Chicago Press, 1939), 24, 26; Adair, "Standards of Prenatal Care," *American Journal of Obstetrics and Gynecology* (1931): 464.

61. *CUR*, October 1931, 119.

62. In their 1940s ads in *Mademoiselle*, both Lances and Merzon listed lower prices, usually $1.50 to $2.50.

63. U.S. Bureau of the Census, *Sixteenth Census of the United States: 1940. Population* vol. 3, *The Labor Force*, part 1: United States Summary (Washington, D.C., 1943), table 71, p. 116.

64. Out of 13 million unemployed workers at the nadir of the Depression, 400,000 were women. In 1935, the four top job titles for women were office workers (1,964,000), servants (1,635,000), schoolteachers (854,000), and saleswomen and clerks (706,000). "Women of the U.S. Work," *Fortune*, July 1935, 50.

65. *CUR*, December 1931, 73; *Dry Goods Merchant Trade Journal*, February 1934, 62.

66. U.S. patent 1,681,119, filed 24 June 1927, awarded 14 August 1928. Kennedy also held a patent on a combination garment, U.S. patent 1,933,983, filed 29 July 1930, awarded 7 November 1933; and under Rosamond Klin a style to wear hitched to a girdle, U.S. patent 2,118,406, filed 9 January 1936, awarded 24 May 1938. She listed an address in Chicago on her American advertisements, but her residence continued to be shown as London in patent texts. Interestingly enough, Vivian Fitch Kemp received two U.S. patents that looked very much like the Kestos and were assigned to a British corporation, Kempat Ltd. These were U.S. patent 2,022,317, filed 23 April 1932, awarded 26 November 1935; and U.S. patent 2,156,478, filed 5 April 1935, awarded 2 May 1939.

67. So, amazingly, did a Kleinert brassiere-cum-dress shield, shown in the April 1933 *Dry Goods Merchant Trade Journal*.

68. Maureen Alden, "The Beguilement of Zeus—In All the Better Shops," *Costume* 33 (1999): 68–73. Alden quoted Elizabeth Ewing as identifying the patent holder of Kestos as Mrs. Rosalind Klin. See patent information in previous note.

69. Marcel Cadolle, U.S. patent 1,786,895, filed 7 October 1929, awarded 30 December 1930; U.S. patent 2,103,060, filed 23 November 1934, awarded 21 December 1937.

70. Kapinas moved to Minnesota, despite her own thriving business in New York, because she wished to secure a divorce, and Minnesota laws offered wider grounds than did New York for dissolution of marriage.

71. Boehlke, "Ruth M. Kapinas," 4.

72. Ibid., 50.

73. Ibid., 4, 6.

74. *The Story of Munsingwear*, 36; Munsingwear annual report, 1936, 2. Cited in Boehlke, "Munsingwear's Forgotten Designer," 46.

75. Boehlke, "Ruth M. Kapinas," 21, 23.

76. Ariel Le May, U.S. patent 1,904,644, filed 18 January 1932, awarded 18 April 1933.

77. "Model Brassiere Celebrate Tenth Anniversary," *CUR*, February 1946, 139.

78. Elvira Campa McKeefrey, U.S. patent 1,566,109, filed 6 July 1925, awarded 15 December 1925; U.S. patent 2,048,638 filed 2 March 1936, awarded 21 July 1936. The rapid approval of her patents testifies to their manifest originality.

79. "Fine Figger of a Woman," *Harper's Bazaar*, November 1934, 102.

Chapter 5. Dutiful Brassieres

1. David M. Kennedy, *Freedom from Fear: The American People in Depression and War, 1929–1945* (New York: Oxford University Press, 1999).

2. Judy Barrett Litoff and David C. Smith, *American Women in a World at War: Contemporary Accounts from World War II* (Wilmington, Del.: Scholarly Resources, 1997), 1.

3. Kennedy, *Freedom from Fear*, 510.

4. Litoff and Smith, *American Women in a World at War*, 35–36; Betty O'Connell, Personal Communication, 20 June 1999; Jenne M. Holm, *Encyclopedia of American Military History*, vol. 3, *Women in the Armed Forces*, (New York: Scribner, 1994), 1998.

5. Lee Kennett, *For the Duration: The United States Goes to War, Pearl Harbor 1942* (New York: Scribner, 1985), 43.

6. Margaret Vining, interview with author, 20 July 1999. Vining is museum specialist in military history, Smithsonian Institution, National Museum of American History, Washington, D.C. Interviews with several women veterans of World War II illustrated the variability in the undergarments issued by the different service groups. The WAC group based in Des Moines, Iowa, were issued khaki brassieres; however, one interviewee assured an author that she and her fellow enlistees found the regulation bras uncomfortable and so continued to wear their own. Debate in Congress also focused on giving individuals a cash allowance for undergarments. This argument continued for two years without resolution and in the meantime many women provided their own nonregulation garments.

7. Elizabeth Mooman Kramer O'Connell, 6 June 2000, interview with Colleen Gau. O'Connell served from November 1943 until November 1945 in England and France. She had to send home for underwear because the PX in England offered no women's clothing and there was a negligible black market. In France, O'Connell found that patriots kept the black market active, in defiance of the Nazis. Dressmakers used recycled parachute silk to make lingerie. Black lingerie was in particular demand by GI Joes as gifts for the women at home.

8. Dr. Putnam was one of the many black women who joined the women's armed services. She enlisted on 20 August 1942 and was issued "flesh colored lingerie," but by February 1943, everything was changed to drab olive green. Putnam reported that the brassieres fit fine, but the issued shirts were not cut properly for buxom women and were too tight to fit over the breasts. Female personnel cut the tails off their shirts to make underarm gussets to enlarge the shirts. This repair precluded women removing their jackets. Putnam later went to school on the GI bill, earned a Ph.D. in history,

and worked in the military history department at the Museum of American History at the Smithsonian Institution. Martha Putnam, telephone interview with Colleen Gau, 21 July 1999.

9. One interviewee stated that on certain navy bases girdles were absolutely required; however, that was not true at all installations but was based on the commanding officer's expectations.

10. Fort Des Moines was a major training center for WAACs. Mera Galloway, "I Am a WAAC," *Mademoiselle*, September 1942, 137, 199–201.

11. "WACS Prove a Good Market," *CUR*, August 1943, 61.

12. *CUR*, June 1946, 159. Reprinted from the *Saturday Evening Post*.

13. "Uniforms and You," *Vogue*, 15 March 1942, 41.

14. "WACS Prove," 61.

15. Kennedy, *Freedom from Fear*, 615–18. The goals were exceeded, and vastly greater productivity was achieved in 1944–45.

16. Albert Parry, ed., *What Women Can Do to Win the War* (Chicago: Consolidated Book, 1942), 12.

17. William Henry Chafe, *The American Woman: Her Changing Social, Economic, and Political Roles, 1920–1970* (New York: Oxford University Press, 1972), 195. Cited by Sandra Stansbery Buckland, "Fashion as a Tool of World War II: A Case Study Supporting the SI (Symbolic Interaction) Theory," *Clothing and Textiles Research Journal* 18, no. 3 (2000): 140–51.

18. Kennedy, *Freedom from Fear*, 776.

19. Litoff and Smith, *American Women in a World at War*, 201–2, 208. In fact, farmers were given an occupational exemption from the draft. Kennedy, *Freedom from Fear*, 633–34.

20. Litoff and Smith, *American Women in a World at War*, 167.

21. Parry, *What Women Can Do*, 5.

22. "Women War Workers," *CUR*, October 1943, 63–64.

23. "Women War Workers," *CUR*, January 1944, 74.

24. "Women War Workers," *CUR*, December 1943, 68. As if in support of this point, a comely and plump woman adorned the first page of the article. She was caught by the camera as she polished airplane crankshafts at the Ohio Crankshaft Company in Cleveland. The perception of young American girls as "quite figure conscious" is echoed by Reata Howard, a buyer at an Oregon department store. "Customer Education," *CUR*, 4 November 1941, 48, 99.

25. "Women War Workers," *CUR*, November 1943, 86.

26. Kennedy, *Freedom from Fear*, 748.

27. Lockheed also required women in certain types of jobs to wear breast protectors to prevent injury and guard health. Plants often ran two or three shifts to meet production goals, thus exceeding the forty-hour weeks that had begun to be adopted in the Depression.

28. "New Goods and Specialties," *The Rubber World*, September 1943, 305.

29. "Breast Protectors for War Workers," *CUR*, March 1943, 77.

30. "Consumer Corset Survey," *CUR*, November 1942, 53–55.

31. Parry, *What Women Can Do*, 12–18.

32. Kennedy, *Freedom from Fear*, 641.

33. Mark Jonathan Harris et al., *The Home Front: America During World War II* (New York: G. P. Putnam, 1984), cited by Kennedy, *Freedom from Fear*, 769.

34. Mildred Graves Ryan and Velma Phillips, *Clothes for You* (New York: D. Appleton-Century, 1947), 513.

35. Kennedy, *Freedom from Fear*, 641.

36. In order to promote the image of nylon as a luxury fiber, Du Pont pressured the Lovable Company to sell nylon brassieres at higher prices than their usual range. Telephone interview with Tom Garson, Lovable Company President to Colleen Gau, 20 April 2000. See also Leslie Weiner, *Lovable Story*, Lovable Company, 1953.

37. German U-boats attacked U.S. shipping in 1942–43, sometimes in direct view of East Coast inhabitants. Seeing a flaming oil tanker or merchant ship focused many American minds on the Nazi threat.

38. Rumors of atrocities seeped out of Europe, but the enormity of the Holocaust only reached the United States when Allied armies penetrated Germany in 1945.

39. According to the phrase used by Joseph R. Bowen, "No 'Heil Hysteria,'" *CUR*, May 1942, 61. A *CUR* feature on Sam Yaffe, head of Bien Jolie, credited him with preventing "some government boy wonder" from declaring the corset industry nonessential.

40. "Simplification of Lines to Conserve Labor and Materials," *CUR*, March 1943, 54.

41. Kennett, *For the Duration*, 115.

42. "WPB Announces Corset Restrictions," *CUR*, May 1942, 47.

43. Quantity was also insufficient: Only 5,000 tons of Buna S had been made in 1941. Kennett, *For the Duration*, 115.

44. "Vital Changes in Corsetry," *CUR*, September 1943, 73.

45. "Pocket-Eye Metalless Tape," *CUR*, March 1943, 80.

46. "Concern over the Cotton Situation," *CUR*, October 1944, 83.

47. Elinor Barnes, *A Wardrobe for the WAAC* (Philadelphia: Quartermaster Report History Project, 1953); Robert W. Burns, *Passing in Review: History of Nurses and WAC Uniforms in the European Theater, 1942–1945*; Erna Risch, "A Wardrobe for Women of the Army," Quartermaster Corps Historical Study, no. 12 (October 1945); Maidenform Archive, National Museum of American History, Smithsonian Institution.

48. Maiden Form Brassiere Company, Inc., "Application for a Declaration of Essentiality to the USA War Manpower Commission." National Museum of American History, Maidenform Archive, no. 585, box 52, fl. 5. Maiden Form produced its "Variation" model for women in the United States Armed Forces. This model was intended for the average figure.

49. "Supply Situation More Acute," *CUR*, January 1945, 148.

50. "Retrospect and Prospect," *CUR*, December 1943, 63.

51. *The Maiden Form Mirror*, July 1945, 3. The original khaki nylon and cotton webbing pigeon vest is in the National Museum of American History, Costume History Department, accession number 1997.0117.54. The blueprints are in the NMAH Maidenform Archive, no. 585.

52. *CUR*, October 1941, 43–44.

53. "To Simplify and Standardize Lines," *CUR*, October 1941, 80. According to advertisements in this trade journal, many companies specialized in producing components such as hook and eye tapes and shoulder straps, beginning in the 1930s.

54. Jane Russell, *An Autobiography: My Path and My Detours* (New York: Jove Books, 1986), 58.

55. *CUR*, December 1942, 62.

56. Kennett, *For the Duration*, 124.

57. Kennedy, *Freedom from Fear*, 637.

58. "Plan Now for Post-War," *CUR*, November 1942, 50.

59. "Washington Wants Institutional Advertising Copy," *CUR*, July 1943, 56.

60. The implication is that sewing machine operatives were now welding and running lathes, with the blessing of H & W executives. This was hardly likely; the women who switched to heavy industry may well have hoped to stay there and earn wages that apparel makers could never pay.

61. In effect, they were limited to output of at most 75 percent of their monthly average in the first three months of 1941.

62. Elsa Schiaparelli, "Needles and Guns," *Vogue*, 1 September 1940, 57, 104–5. "Schiap" wrote of the struggle to maintain workshops in Paris and then in Biarritz, as the Germans moved ever closer and work became increasingly difficult. Her couture house reopened in Paris and continued to produce designs in her absence. Germans wanted the luxury goods, and saw to it that cooperative couturiers had the necessary materials. Lou Taylor, "The Work and Function of the Paris Couture Industry During the German Occupation of 1940–44," *Dress* 22 (1995): 34–44. The Chambre Syndicale is the professional organization to which every couturier(e) belongs.

63. Sandra Stansbery Buckland, "The New York Dress Institute: A Collaboration Between Unions and Manufacturers" (abstract), *Proceedings: International Textile and Apparel Association, Inc.* (1999), 78–79.

64. "X-ray of American Fashion," *Vogue*, 1 August 1944, 78, 124, 133.

65. *CUR*, November 1941, 73.

66. "CBS Television Show Presents 'Pre-Order,' 'Post-Order' Fashions," *Women's Wear Daily* (10 April 1942): 7.

67. *CUR*, December 1944, 120.

68. *CUR*, December 1942, 63.

69. Tara Maginnis, "'She Saves Who Sews for Victory': Home Sewing on the American Home Front," *Costume* 26 (1992): 60–70.

70. The Spool Cotton Company, *Make and Mend* (1942), 1. Women were hired by the U.S. Office of Price Administration to monitor compliance with ceiling prices. Kennedy, *Freedom from Fear*, 776.

71. "Revival of the Fitter," *CUR*, December 1939, 47–48.

72. *CUR*, May 1944, 72–73.

73. "Your Sales Staff," *CUR*, March 1941, 43–44.

74. "Use This New Aid to Consumer Self-Service," *Maidenform Mirror*, February 1944, 3.

75. Du Pont had returned to production of nylon fiber for civilian goods in late August 1945. Susannah Handley, *Nylon: The Story of a Fashion Revolution* (Baltimore: Johns Hopkins University Press, 1999), 48.

76. Ibid., 43, 46, 49.

77. *CUR*, December 1942, 63.

78. For further discussion of the performance properties of nylon (and other textiles), see Sara J. Kadolph and Anna L. Langford *Textiles*, 8th ed. (New York: Merrill, 1998).

79. Advertisement, *CUR*, February 1942, 29.

80. U.S. patent 1,798,274, filed 5 July 1929, awarded 31 March 1931.

81. *Harper's Bazaar*, December 1934, 103.

82. According to a *CUR* article, wired brassieres had to be fitted to each customer, to minimize discomfort and secure ideal fit. "Wired Brassieres in the Limelight," July 1946, 125.

83. "The Wired Bra," *Life*, 22 July 1946, 67–68, 70.

84. Robert D. Friedel, *Zipper: An Exploration in Novelty* (New York: W. W. Norton, 1994).

85. Bernard Notes, M.D., U.S. patent 1,948,076 filed 9 August 1933, awarded 20 February 1934. Roy S. Neal produced an uncomfortable-looking nursing bra with the zippers over the nipples: U.S. patent 2,050,064, filed 12 August 1935, awarded 4 August 1936. Roxine Laffoon patented a nursing bra with a central zipper, U.S. patent 2,340,332, filed 2 December 1940, awarded 1 February 1944. Laffoon did produce her brassiere in the 1950s.

86. Charles E. Zimmerman and John F. Skold, U.S. patent 2,345,649, filed 4 December 1939, awarded 4 April 1944.

87. "Mrs. Gabrielle Poix Yerkes," obituary, *CUR*, September 1941, 57.

88. Kennedy, *Freedom from Fear*, 781. The birthrate, meaning the number of babies per thousand women of childbearing age, reached a level in 1943 not previously attained since prosperous 1927.

89. Albert Corrado, interview with authors, 31 July 2000.

90. Henry M. Plehn, U.S. patent 2,411,462, filed 14 July 1944, awarded 19 November 1946.

91. U.S. patent 2,305,051, filed 1 November 1940, awarded 15 December 1942; U.S. patent 2,421,448, filed 22 October 1945, awarded 3 June 1947.

92. Abraham S. Becker and Victor I. Becker, U.S. patent 2,317,664, filed 20 May 1942, awarded 27 April 1943; U.S. patent 2,327,488, filed 20 May 1942, awarded 24 August 1943.

93. The Depression forced many men who had worn custom-tailored suits to accept the ready-to-wear versions.

94. Frank Farino, U.S. patent 2,890,702, filed 10 May 1957, awarded 12 June 1959.

95. Albert Corrado, interview with authors, 31 July 2000. Mr. Corrado is the son of the late Mr. Farino and current chairman of the board of Leading Lady. The third generation of the family is now actively managing the business.

96. "At the Stork Club," *CUR*, June 1944, 111.

97. Harry Gluckin, U.S. patent 2,483,273, filed 29 April 1946, awarded 27 September 1949; Jack Glick, U.S. patent 2,480,643, filed 22 May 1946, awarded 30 August 1949.

98. Lillian Hunau, U.S. patent 2,421,561, filed 19 July 1946, awarded 3 June 1947.

99. Raymond Redares, U.S. patent 2,431,929, filed 16 April 1945, awarded 2 December 1947.

100. Actually, Renee's Bree-V-Bra plunged well below the lower margin of the breasts. Advertisement, *CUR*, October 1941, 38.

101. *CUR*, August 1946, 19; September 1946, passim.

102. *CUR*, February 1946, 16–17.

103. Josephine Moullet, "Dramatize Teen-Age Merchandise," *CUR*, June 1945, 89.

104. "Teen-Age Market: It's 'Terrif,'" *Business Week*, 8 June 1946, 72, 74–76.

105. *CUR*, September 1946, 180.

106. "Brand Names Will Keep Customers," *CUR*, December 1944, 86, 107.
107. "Plan Now for Post-War," *CUR*, November 1942, 69–70.

Chapter 6. Boom and Busts

1. Scottie Reston, *Mademoiselle*, August 1947, said in discussing the situation in America, "From the period of Casablanca through Potsdam we have seen a general and rapid deterioration in our relations to the Soviets." Senator Joseph McCarthy, Republican from Wisconsin, instigated a spurious search for Communist Party members who might be in positions in the government, and, went on to question people in many walks of life in his "un-American Activities" hearings in Congress in the 1950s.

2. When Gen. Dwight D. Eisenhower became president in 1952, the fear of fallout from atomic bombs was rampant. The population was encouraged to build and supply bomb shelters, schoolchildren were coached in "duck and cover" drills, and the military buildup was commenced in earnest.

3. David Halberstam, *The Fifties* (New York: Villard Books, 1993), 134–35. In 1946, Levitt created the largest housing project in American history, twenty miles from Manhattan.

4. Ruth Schwartz Cowan, *More Work for Mother* (New York: Basic Books, 1983).

5. David Halberstam, *The Fifties*, 178. Eisenhower pushed this legislation because he had experienced muddy U.S. "highways" during a cross-country trek with army personnel just after World War I. Geoffrey Perret, *Eisenhower* (New York: Random House, 1999).

6. "Researchlights," *CUR*, November 1958, 56–67. Population grew to 144 million by 1948, and 1947 saw the birth of 3.5 million babies. "News and Views," *CUR*, January 1948, 134.

7. Typical nursing bras were offered in pink and white cotton batiste but were bulky and awkward to use. *CUR*, January 1948, 97. Figure 32 represents the first patented design from Fancee Free; Dozier's later styles achieved a smarter, smoother look.

8. In her ad in CUR, March 1957, Herma Wiedle Dozier emphasized that Fancee Free was "the only maternity line designed by a Registered Nurse with years of obstetrical experience," and that this, "means sales and profit for you because it's known and prescribed by doctors from coast to coast." This company opened for business in St. Louis, Missouri, in 1947 with garter belts and added nursing brassieres in 1952. Dozier held three patents: 2,706,816, awarded 26 April 1955; 3,046,990, awarded 31 July 1962; 3,087,494, awarded 30 April 1963.

9. Nicola White, *Reconstructing Italian Fashion: America and the Development of the Italian Fashion Industry* (Oxford: Berg, 2000).

10. Pauline Gordon, "Elegante: The Paris Conception of Fashion," *CUR*, October 1950, 87; Pauline Gordon, "I Just Saw Paris," *CUR*, October 1948, 114.

11. "Fresh Problems: 22 Answers," *Vogue*, June 1948, 145–46. Recommendations were made for tennis, gardening, riding, sunbathing, and town and country fashions.

12. Anne Fogarty, *Wife-Dressing* (New York: Julian Messner, 1959), 66.

13. J. Walter Thompson advertising agency was one company who worked with several brassiere makers to promote their products.

14. Alfred Kinsey, Wardell B. Pomeroy, and Clyde E. Martin, *Sexual Behavior in the Human Male* (Philadelphia: W. B. Saunders, 1948).

15. Grace Metallious, *Peyton Place* (New York: Julian Messner, 1956).

16. *CUR*, January 1947, 181.

17. Several others preceded this design, notably Deala of Miami's X-Pert Separation brassiere, introduced in *Mademoiselle* in November 1953, described as an exclusive feature to ensure "outlift."

18. This was patented by Israel "Hi" Pilot on June 30, 1936, U.S. patent 2,045,871.

19. *Mademoiselle*, June 1954, 106.

20. *Harper's Bazaar*, January 1952, 148. The description noted that the tangent straps suspend the frame at six points rather than the cup sections, allowing greater freedom of arm and shoulder motion in greater comfort, without slipping."

21. S. W. Gunn, "Mastectomy," *World Journal of Surgery* 22, no. 5 (May 1998): 425–26.

22. *Mademoiselle*, January 1951, 39. The eiderdown pads were available in "regular and just accents" sizes, and were said to be "easy to wash, quick to dry."

23. *CUR*, January 1950, 176.

24. Secret Charm was made by Celebrity Bra, Inc. of New York and claimed to have originated the use of foam rubber in bras. Advertised in *Mademoiselle*, April 1952, 161, it had both strapless and bandeau styles featuring a "choose your own fullness" fitting. Celebrity brassieres sold from $1 in nonpadded styles, padded styles started at $2.

25. Presumably the individual could choose more or less bosom for different occasions. It was patented in the United States and several foreign countries, according to *CUR*, January 1952, 78. Directions illustrated three steps: adjust, insert tube to inflate, and press to seal. The marketing slogan stated, "It's Perfection Without Detection." Advertised in *Mademoiselle*, June 1955. An earlier preinflated version was shown in *Mademoiselle*, November 1954, 135.

26. *CUR*, October 15, 1948, 161. The attraction of the scent petal was ostensibly to prevent staining of outer clothing by the perfume or cologne. The brassiere sold for $2.50 in nylon or satin and $2 in cotton.

27. *CUR*, April 1950, 129.

28. *CUR*, November 1949, 93. Quotes an Associated Press report by a New York surgeon: "The day of the boyish figure, when women were afraid to show they had breasts and tried to plaster them down with tight-fitting brassieres, was a period that did much toward developing breast cancer. Fortunately, the present custom is one of support."

29. *CUR*, started emphasis on breast cancer almost as soon as World War II was ended. Articles and public awareness promotions were seen in almost every issue throughout the late 1940s and 1950s.

30. Identical Form was advertised in leading professional and health publications and featured photographs of a woman with postsurgical scars of radical mastectomy and three bra designs. Miriam Gates sold many types of breast pads, including a weighted surgical model of foam rubber covered with white acetate jersey, seen in *CUR*, November 1958, 43. Lov-é claimed more physicians recommended their brand in *CUR*, November 1958, 38.

31. Marjory L. Joseph, *Essentials of Textiles* (New York: Holt, Rinehart and Winston, 1998), 111, 104.

32. *CUR*, January 1947, 144–45

33. *CUR*, June 1959, 152.

34. Jeff Pirtle, letter to Colleen Gau, 27 June 2000.

35. *Mademoiselle*, November 1958, 228.

36. Fogarty, *Wife-Dressing*, 66.

37. *CUR*, September 1954, 19. This may have been based on an earlier version by Agnew Mfg. Company of Dallas, called the Bra-Dryer. *CUR*, October 1948, 160. This consisted of aluminum cups with rolled, grooved edges. The wet brassiere was fitted over each form and held in place by springs. It came in sizes small, medium, and large and was "attractively put up in an eye-appealing blue and white polka dot box." The cost was $1.50 to $1.75.

38. Bess V. Oerke, *Dress* (Peoria, Ill.: Charles A. Bennett, 1956), 256.

39. Three patents were held for this innovation, U.S. patent 2,485,570–72. The name is given as Sydne or Syd. The applications were filed at various times from 6 January, 1947 through 26 May 1948. Three addresses were listed as well.

40. *Vogue* (Incorporating *Vanity Fair*), November 1950, 56. The Avant Bra with front closure was available in white, pink, and black in prices ranging from $1.75 for broadcloth to $3.50 for embroidered nylon marquisette; it also came in a long-line model to size 44 for $3.50 and $5.

41. *Mademoiselle*, June 1959, 4. The MagiClose Bra advertised "no hooks, no eyes, yet inches of adjustment, perfect control and comfort." As far as we could discern, this was the only brassiere using the hook and loop fastener.

42. *CUR*, July 1958, 66

43. U.S. patent 2,428,572, awarded 7 October 1947. Centerfront shaping was accomplished with a draw-ribbon in a casing.

44. Hollywood-Maxwell broadcast over Radio 50 from New York with several word spots per day. An example is this about the Nu-Vu: "Nu-Vu bras by Hollywood-Maxwell for bountiful busts! Specially designed with dauntless uplift that reins in heavy, pendulous inches firms them lifts them into smart, young lines! Exquisite separation! Firm control! Inner cups prevent slipping Nu-Vu bras by Hollywood-Maxwell for bountiful busts . . . in lovely, long-wearing fabrics . . . just $__ at (store name) today!"

45. *CUR*, April 1949, 144. Entitled "Heavenly Freedom," the film dramatization of how a Wonder-Bra was made lasted eight minutes and was shown in store display windows.

46. Maiden Form would officially change its name to Maidenform in 1950. Smithsonian archival material, Maidenform Mirror, October 1950.

47. *CUR*, March 1957, 26. Maidenform announces the 30 millionth Chansonette bra will be sold in the coming months. It was heralded as "the world's most popular bra."

48. *CUR*, January 1954, 75.

49. Jeff Pirtle, telephone interview, 27 June, 2000.

50. *CUR*, March 1958, 6.

51. Halberstam, *The Fifties*, 473.

52. *CUR*, January 1949, 50–51.

53. Mary Suzuki, "The Fitting Room," *Mademoiselle*, October 1953, 56; January 1954, 52; Tracy Richard, "Please Be Fitted," *Farm Journal*, February 1953, 152–53.

54. A survey of Sears catalogs showed four full foundation garments offered for

each brassiere in the 1940s, with a gradual change to three to one proportion by the end of the 1950s.

55. Jeff Pirtle, interview with Colleen Gau, 27 June 2000. Penney's first catalog was produced in 1963. Prior to 1949, Penney's proprietary label Lady-Lyke was produced by its wholly owned subsidiary, the Crescent Corset Company. In 1949 it sold that unit and changed the private label to Adonna.

56. *CUR*, July 1954, 56. Melvin Marden was the editor and research Director for Haire Publishing Company.

57. Oerke, *Dress*, 85.

58. Tom Garson, grandson of the founder, 20 April 2000, told Colleen Gau in a telephone conversation that, "Grandpa (Frank Garson) remembered his sweat-shop days." His uncle Dan Garson had made a point of sitting with his integrated workforce in their Atlanta factory's cafeteria during the early years of the company.

59. *CUR*, September 1954, 74. In a 1954 survey of retail pricing by the Charles W. Hoyt advertising agency, the following conclusions were drawn: (1) for merchandise selling under $5, prices ending with 9 were most popular; (2) above $5, the most popular pricing ended with .95; above $25, prices that ended with .50 were the most popular. Prices ending with digits 1, 2, 4, and 6 were seldom used.

60. Mildred Graves Ryan and Velma Phillips, *Clothes for You*, 2d ed. (New York: D. Appleton, 1954), 301, 295.

61. Charma, Exquisite Form, Gossard, Leading Lady, Lovable, and Maidenform were examples of companies with licensing and/or production outside of the United States.

62. *CUR*, November 1956, 85.

63. The slogan "Behind every Olga, there really is an Olga" was used for more than a decade and frequently featured photographs of Olga montaged with an exotic or foreign locale, along with the ad copy about her intimate wear designs.

64. Candace A. Wedlan, "The Pillar of Panties," *Los Angeles Times*, 11 August 2000, E-1, E-4.

65. The first patented brassiere that exposed the nipples was U.S. patent 2,457,369, awarded to Bernice Harman in December 1948. Incredibly, the statement of intent mentions, "the conical or cupped breast pockets of the brassiere having central circular openings for accentuation of small busts and minimizing the large bust." The Peek-a-Boo brassiere sold by Frederick's was very similar in design, but we were not able to determine whether the company used Harman's design. Another bold style was shown by Deala of Miami in *CUR*, September 1948, 128, and featured satin undercups and diagonal straps with the breasts exposed from the nipple up.

66. The Bleumette was not the first patented stick-on brassiere (U.S. patent 2,728,079). Designed by Lea Williams in California, it was marketed nationally in drugstores and five-and-dime stores and by mail order; two pairs cost $2.98. Its claim was that uplift could be produced and held for hours when the need for a strapless and backless or bare look was desired. The half-moon-shaped, rubberized, flannel supports were adhered to the wearer's skin with glue. Anecdotal reports of allergic reactions could not be corroborated in the medical literature. Another stick-on brassiere, U.S. patent 2,869,553, Nici D'Or, awarded January 1959, and described as disposable. The breast cups were described as preferably made from paper with an inexpensive adhesive that was admitted to be ineffective after one use. The patent listed other references with

similar features: U.S. patent 1,971,113 by Mary Maier in 1934; and U.S. patent 2,615,164 by Fred Graf in 1952.

67. *Vogue* (incorporating *Vanity Fair*) 15 October, 1948, 148. Advertisement for Marja of Texas says that the "Half Hi-A" brassiere "is provocative, daring and different."

68. *Mademoiselle*, December 1948, 52. Mail-order company Blacton's of New York advertised the "half 'n half," "the ultimate in décolleté or daring described as "strapless, topless, boneless."

69. Its inventor Charles L. Langs was first noted by *Business Week*, 16 July 1949, 25. A follow-up mention came in *Business Week*, 12 June 1954, 110–12.

Chapter 7. Ban the Bra?

1. Attributed to Ida McNeil, advertising director at Bali. "Bra Makers Get a Lift from Fashion's Plunge," *Business Week*, 4 April 2001, 64–65.

2. "Industry Leaders Express Hope for Creative, Expanding New Decade," *CUR*, January 1960, 96–103.

3. David Halberstam, *The Fifties* (New York: Villard Books, 1993), 591–97.

4. Jane Stern and Michael Stern, *Sixties People* (New York: Alfred A. Knopf, 1990), 180.

5. This did not happen quickly: Friedan's work was initially turned down or edited beyond recognition by *McCall's*, *Ladies' Home Journal*, and even *Redbook*. Halberstam, *The Fifties*, 596.

6. "Candidate Taunted," *Detroit Free Press*, Tuesday, 3 May 1966, 20A. This was a clear case of life belatedly imitating art. See Figure 40 for the 1952 Maidenform ad.

7. Cynthia Taeuber, *Statistical Handbook on Women in America* (Phoenix: Oryx Press, 1991), tables D7–5 and D7–6.

8. "Planning Guide '69" *CUR* (November 1968): 97.

9. Hollywood Vassarette advertisement, *Harper's Bazaar*, November 1964.

10. Extensive inquiries to discover the number of mastectomies performed has yielded sparse information. More than a dozen medical library reference departments have attempted to assist without result, including searches on Medline and the Internet. The National Cancer Institute and the Cancer Society did not supply statistics when requested on numbers of mastectomies performed annually since 1900. Reference librarians at several public libraries were enlisted in this effort without avail. Insurance companies and professional insurance organizations did not provide these data. Medical professional organizations including American College of Surgeons, American College of Obstetricians and Gynecologists, and the American College of Plastic Surgeons were not able to supply these data. *American Journal of Surgery* published "Ohio Breast Cancer Survey, 1960–1969," which included fifty-one surgeons reporting on 7,267 patients in the ten-year period; *AJS*, 122 (December 1971): 765–69. Carl M. Mansfield, *Early Breast Cancer: Its History and Results of Treatment* (Basel, Switzerland: S. Karger, 1976), lists summaries of collective results reported in European and American literature from 1850 to 1963, but it is difficult to interpret.

11. Amy Sue Bix, "Diseases Chasing Money and Power: Breast Cancer and AIDS Activism Challenging Authority," *Journal of Policy History* 9, no. 1 (1997): 5–32. In 1990, $90 million was spent on breast cancer research; by 1995, $465 million.

12. Lindsy Van Gelder, reporter for the *New York Post*, used this opener in describing a protest of the Miss America competition on 7 September 1968: "Lighting a match to a draft card has become a standard gambit of protest groups in recent years, but something new is due to go up in flames this Saturday. Would you believe a bra burning?" Susan Brownmiller, *In Our Time: Memoir of a Revolution* (New York: Dial Press, 1999), 36–37.

13. Gossard interviewed homemakers to help design their number 3380 Flair brassiere in 1967; *CUR*, March 1967, 7.

14. "Retail Management Section," *CUR*, July 1968, 42–44.

15. Stern and Stern, *Sixties People*, 93.

16. Marjory L. Joseph, *Essentials of Textiles*, 4th ed. (New York: Holt, Rinehart, & Winston, 1998), 139.

17. Bali advertisement, *CUR*, October 1961, 15. It showed a model wearing the Vyrene Water Bali Bra. Seemingly this did not contain water but was a pun on "water ballet." The ad intimated that it was quoted directly from an in-house newsletter called *Bali Hoo*, vol. 1, no. 3.

18. Stern and Stern, *Sixties People*, 146–69.

19. Despite its long-lived fame, the miniskirt did not appear on the U.S. scene in any strength until the late 1960s. Even in 1965 hemlines in fashion periodicals bared only the knees.

20. To which one self-assured matron rejoined that *her* legs were *in* and *her* bosom was *out*—in a calf-length dress with deep décolletage.

21. Yves Saint Laurent, Diana Vreeland, et al., *Yves Saint Laurent* (New York: Metropolitan Museum of Art, 1983).

22. Nicola White, *Reconstructing Italian Fashion: America and the Development of the Italian Fashion Industry* (New York: Berg, 2000).

23. "Bra Makers Get a Lift," *Business Week*, 4 April 1964, 64–65.

24. Ann Gardiner, "How They Differ from Us," *CUR*, April 1960, 60.

25. "Women's Brassieres," *Consumer Bulletin*, March 1965, 24–27.

26. "A Sticky Situation with a Strapless Bra," *Consumer Reports*, August 1967, 411–12.

27. Rudi Gernreich, U.S. patent 3,338,242, filed 4 June 1965, awarded 29 August 1967. Gernreich was making something of a career of notoriety, having shown skimpier and skimpier bikinis in the early 1960s and a topless bathing suit in 1964. "Me? In That!" *Life*, 12 August 1964, 55–57.

28. "Vogue—and Vague," *Newsweek*, 22 March 1965, 90.

29. *Mademoiselle*, February 1950, 47.

30. *Woman's Day*, August 1965.

31. *Harper's Bazaar*, October 1965.

32. "Question . . ." Column, *CUR*, January 1965, 95–96.

33. Ibid., 96.

34. "The Young Image," *CUR*, July 1968, 26–27.

35. Advertisement, *Glamour*, November 1963, 169.

36. Even into the early 1960s, "sports bra" meant an outerwear garment, usually in novelty cotton prints. See e.g., *CUR*, July 1960, 57.

37. Advertisement, *Seventeen*, August 1968.

38. Emily James and Robert W. Henson, U.S. patent 3,430,632, filed 3 Febru-

ary 1967, awarded 4 March 1969. The patentees lived in Greenville, Texas, but Henson Kickernick was incorporated in Minnesota. This spandex and tricot design had front seams, but its back section and shoulders were cut in one piece for comfort and inconspicuousness. The completed bra stretched horizontally (stitched zigzag) but maintained vertical stability. It had step-in or slip-over-the-shoulders options.

39. Advertisement, *Mademoiselle*, April 1969. Also seen in *CUR*, May 1969, 51.

40. *CUR*, January 1967, 18–19.

41. "How Important Are Color and Design Coordination to Underfashions?" *CUR*, February 1963, 33. The information in this article came from a survey of store personnel conducted by the Formfit Institute.

42. Kathy Johnson, interview at her home in Minneapolis with Colleen Gau, April 1995.

43. Advertisements, *Mademoiselle*, December 1960, 7, and October, 1961, 104.

44. *New York Times Magazine*, 28 September 1969, 103. Cotton-Aire by Youthcraft, ironically consisting of Celanese Fortrel Polyester, spandex, and a small (undisclosed) percentage of cotton.

45. *New York Times Magazine*, 8 September 1968.

46. "Your Planning Guide for '62," *CUR*, October 1960, 57. Thirty-five percent married between the ages of 20 and 24 years.

47. In "Selling to the Maternity Customer," the columnist warned against "indiscriminate use of claims, such as 'medically approved' or 'designed under supervision of doctors' in promoting particular maternity bras" (*CUR*, March 1966, 86–87).

48. "Ten Ways to Improve Your Maternity Bra and Girdle Sales," *CUR*, October 1967, 72.

49. La Leche League was founded as a support group by seven women in Franklin Park, Illinois, in 1957. The organization became international in 1963. La Leche's success can be measured by the steady increase in rates of breast-feeding from a low of 20 percent in 1956 to between 31 percent and 79 percent among various demographic groups in the 1990s. "In-Hospital Breast Feeding Rates," published by Ross Products Division, Abbott Laboratories.

50. "Cultivate Teens: They Are Your Big Spenders of Tomorrow!" *CUR*, May 1961, 37.

51. Teencharm ad, *New York Times Magazine*, 26 February 1967. Teenform ad, *CUR*, April 1963, 50–51.

52. "Hop on the Pre-teen Gravy Train," *CUR*, May 1961, 48. In fairness, it must be noted that the columnist wrote that teens were adopting bras for modesty as well as for a status symbol.

53. Eugene Gilbert and Company did the survey. "Your Planning Guide for '65," *CUR*, October 1964, 31–33.

54. Eugene Gilbert and Company, for *Seventeen* magazine.

55. Exquisite Form was one of the leaders in packaging bras, beginning in the mid-1950s when only Playtex girdles had been packaged. "Irwin Roseman: Innovator at Exquisite Form," *CUR*, May 1964, 34. Manufacturers and suppliers argued about who should give the training sessions to sales clerks. Often *CUR* featured instructions on self-training in fitting.

56. "A Look at the Negro Market," *CUR*, April 1966, 86, 88.

57. Carol Hall, interview with Jane Farrell-Beck, 8 December 2000.

58. Color television images were shown as early as 1940, but this technology did

not capture a wide market until the 1960s. David E. Fisher and Marshall Jon Fisher, *Tube: The Invention of Television* (Washington, D.C.: Counterpoint, 1996), 364.

59. "Brigitte Bardot Signs Contract with Lovable," *CUR*, January 1960, 194.

60. "Planning Guide for '67," *CUR*, November 1966, 30.

61. Mercy Dobell, "Don't Get into a Tizzy or Panic over Scare Headlines," *CUR*, November 1968, 67.

62. *CUR*, January 1969, 19. The fad for coordinates sparked the Wayne-Gossard union, according to company news items.

63. Irving Kleiman, "Computer Key to Inventory Control," *CUR*, February 1968, 46–47, 88, 92, 94. Kleiman was the treasurer-secretary of Bali. He was describing a program run on the magnetic-tape-based Honeywell 200 computer, installed in 1965 to replace Bali's older RAMAC computer.

64. The number of times the average stock is sold in a given period of time. Grace I. Kunz, *Merchandising: Theory, Principles, and Practice* (New York: Fairchild, 1998), 395. An industry average stock turn was about 3.5; Bali claimed its customers realized 5 to 7 stock turns.

65. "Mike Stein, Bali's New Man for the '70s" *CUR*, November 1969, 36.

66. Sol Rubinstein, "Bras Are More Important than Shoes," *CUR*, April 1960, 46–47.

67. "The Hows and Whys of Exporting," reproduced from a pamphlet by the Department of Commerce, State of New York, *CUR*, April 1964, 36–39.

68. Stephen S. Putziger, "Foreign Licensing Is Big Business," *CUR*, April 1960, 48–49.

69. This company was founded in about 1950 by Koichi Tsukamata, who by 1964 was "bra king of Japan" with products in 98 percent of retail outlets. So entrenched a company could keep quality high; there was no need to put products on sale in the absence of competition.

Chapter 8. Wondering About Bras

1. "Bra Makers Get a Lift from Fashion's Plunge," *Business Week*, 4 April 1964, 65.

2. "Occupational Distribution of Women 1977 and 1970," *Ms.*, February 1979, 98. Comparison of the median weekly wage of workers sixteen years and older in 1970 showed white men earned $157, black men $133, white women $95, and black women $81. In 1978, the same groups earned $279, $218, $167, and $158, respectively.

3. "Occupational Distribution."

4. Gerrie Pinckney and Marge Swenson, *New Image for Women*, 2d ed. (Reston, Va., Reston Publishing Company, 1984); Barbara Coffey, *Glamour's Success Book* (New York: Simon and Schuster, 1979); Charlene Mitchell with Thomas Burdick, *The Extra Edge: Success Strategies for Women* (Washington, D.C.: Acropolis Books, 1983); Allison Kyle Leopold and Anne Marie Cloutier, *Short Chic* (New York: Rawson, Wade, 1981); Doris Pooser, *Always in Style with Color Me Beautiful* (Washington, D.C.: Acropolis Books, 1985); Emily Cho and Linda Grover, *Looking Terrific: Express Yourself Through the Language of Clothes* (New York: G. P. Putnam, 1978); Janet Wallach, *Looks That Work* (New York: Viking, 1986).

5. "How to Get Dressed and Still Be Yourself," *Ms.*, April 1979, 49–51, 75–76.

6. Al Corrado, interview, 9 August 2000.

7. Copyrighted ad from Maidenform's 1991 campaign seen in several publications, including *Mademoiselle, Vogue*, and *Ladies' Home Journal*. National Museum of American History, Smithsonian Institution, Maidenform Archive 585, box 46, folder 10. Another ad from the 1990 campaign showed four close-ups of women in corsets, farthingales, and bustled outfits. Its copy read, "Isn't it nice to live in a time when women aren't being pushed around so much anymore? Women have spent the last ten centuries conforming to their lingerie. Fortunately, lingerie has finally gotten around to conforming to women."

8. "Fairchild 100, Top 10 Intimate Apparel," *Women's Wear Daily*, 15 December 1999, 15–73.

9. *Encyclopedia Britannica* online, "ILGWU," states: "From the 1970s the ILGWU's membership shrank as firms in the United States shifted much of their apparel production to Asia and Latin America to take advantage of lower labor costs. In 1995 the ILGWU merged with Amalgamated Clothing and Textile Workers' Union to form the Union of Needletrades, Industrial and Textile Employees."

10. Natori survived a lawsuit charging them with fraudulent business practices and avoidance of import duty in 1999. Lori Leibovich wrote about Natori bras in her book *A Good Bra is Hard To Find* which can be found on the Mothers Who Think website: www.salon.com.

11. U.S. patent 818,104, Lora Blanche Lyon, filed 14 July 1905, awarded 17 April 1906.

12. Poirier's only Canadian patent, 877,604, was issued 10 August 1971, according to the Canadian patent online record. The text is not available and the file date is unlisted, although the design was said to have been made in 1964. Gossard held the licensing agreement until 1994.

13. "Bra Wars," *Economist*, 2 December 2000, 64. With its molded core of plastic, this is the hottest selling brassiere in Britain.

14. Rebecca Quick, "Mrs. Wachner's Effort to Build a Better Bra Has 'Secret' Motives," *Wall Street Journal*, 10 April 2000, A1, A19.

15. Ginger Noel, Victoria's Secret, public relations, telephone conversation with Colleen Gau, 7 October 2000.

16. Candace A. Wedlan, "The Pillar of Panties," *Los Angeles Times*, 11 August 2000, E1, E4.

17. Joan Kron, "Vacuum Stacked," *Allure*, July 1999, 104–5. In a telephone conversation, 30 August 1999, Baker informed us that the device would be commercially available and would be reported in an undetermined issue of the *Journal of the American Medical Association*.

18. Lisa Arbetter, "Bra-vo!" *In Style*, February 2000, 112, 114, 116, 118–20, 122, 124.

19. "The Best Bra Guide Ever," *Good Housekeeping*, August 2000, 43, 44, 45, 48.

20. Between 1863 and 1969, more brassiere patents were awarded to men than to women, primarily because men secured multiple patents, whereas women were likely to content themselves with one or two patents.

Selected Bibliography

"Active Women Need Support." *Woman's Home Companion*, May 1943, 65.

Agnell, J., ed. *Lingerie and Sleepwear: 21 Original Designs You Can Make Yourself*. New York: St. Martin's Press, 1981.

Albrecht, Juliana K. "Women's Riding Clothes in the Central United States: Ideal Fashion and Actual Practice." Master's thesis, Iowa State University, 1986.

"Analyzing the Spring Style Tendencies in Brassieres." *Corset and Underwear Review*, February 1917, 56.

Apple, Rima D. *Mothers and Medicine: A Social History of Infant Feeding, 1890–1950*. Madison: University of Wisconsin Press, 1987.

Arbetter, Lisa. "Bra-vo!" *In Style*, February 2000, 112, 114, 116, 118, 120.

"Are We Going to Make Profits in 1933?" *Corset and Underwear Review*, January 1933, 61.

"At the Stork Club." *Corset and Underwear Review*, June 1944, 111.

Auvenshine, Martha Ann, and Martha G. Enriquez. *Comprehensive Maternity Nursing: Perinatal and Women's Health*. Boston: Jones and Bartlett, 1990.

Ayalah, Daphna, and Isaac J. Weinstock. *Breasts: Women Speak About Their Breasts and Their Lives*. New York: Summit, 1979.

Babcock, Lucile. "What Should Business Women Wear?" *Delineator*, September 1930, 36, 48.

Baldt, Laura I. *Clothing for Women: Selection and Construction*. Philadelphia: J. B. Lippincott, 1929.

Banner, Lois W. *American Beauty: A Social History Through Two Centuries of the American Ideal, and Image of Beautiful Women*. Chicago: University of Chicago Press, 1983.

Barnes, Elinor S. *A Wardrobe for the WAAC*. Philadelphia: Quartermaster's Department of the Army, 1943.

Barr, Estelle D. *A Psychological Analysis of Fashion and Motivation*. New York: Columbia University, 1934.

Beney, M. Ada. *Cost of Living in the United States, 1914–1936*. New York: National Industrial Conference Board, 1936.

Binkin, Martin, and Shirley J. Bach. *Women and the Military*. Washington, D.C.: Brookings, 1977.

Birdwell, Russell. *Women in Battle Dress*. New York: Fine Editions, 1942.

Bishop, Hudson D. *The Obstetric Duties of Mother and Nurse*. Cleveland: J. H. Lamb, 1904.

Bix, Amy Sue. "Diseases Chasing Money and Power: Breast Cancer and AIDS Activism Challenging Authority." *Journal of Policy History* 9, no. 1 (1997): 5–32.

Blau, Herbert. *Nothing in Itself: Complexions of Fashions*. Indianapolis: Indiana University Press, 1999.

Bloodgood, Joseph Colt. "The Changing Clinical Picture of Lesions of the Breast." *American Journal of Medical Sciences* 179 (1898): 27.

Boehlke, Heidi L. "Ruth M. Kapinas, Munsingwear's Forgotten 'Foundettes' Designer." *Dress* 20 (1993): 45–52.

Boucher, François, and Yvonne Deslandres. *20,000 Years of Fashion: The History of Costume and Personal Adornment*. New York: Harry N. Abrams, 1987.

Bowen, Joseph R. "No 'Heil Hysteria'." *Corset and Underwear Review*, May 1942, 61.

"Bra Wars." *Economist*, 2 December 2000, 64.

Bradley, Frances Sage. "Which—A Well Baby or a Boyish Form?" *Hygeia*, June 1927, 298–99.

"Brand Names Will Keep Customers." *Corset and Underwear Review*, December 1944, 86, 107.

"Brassiere Merchandising." *Gossard Corsetiere and Merchandiser*, 15 August 1916, 2, 16.

"Breast Protectors for War Workers." *Corset and Underwear Review*, March 1943, 77.

Breckenridge, Sophonisba P. *Women in the Twentieth Century: A Study of Their Political, Social and Economic Activities*. McGraw-Hill, 1933.

Brooks, Agnes. "Recurring Cycles of Fashion." *Antiques* 33 (1938): 343.

Brown, Dorothy M. *Setting a Course: American Women in the 1920s*. Boston: Twayne, 1987.

Brownmiller, Susan. *In Our Time: Memoir of a Revolution*. New York: Dial Press, 1999.

Bruce, J. Mitchell. "On Supernumerary Nipples: Examination of Males and Females." *Boston Medical Journal* (1879): 68–70.

Brumberg, Joan J. *The Body Project: An Intimate History of American Girls*. New York: Random House, 1997.

Bruneau, Marguerite. *Histoire du costume populaire en Normandie, Tomes I et II*. France: Cercle d'action et d'etudes Normandes, 1938–86.

Buckland, Sandra Stansbery. *The New York Dress Institute: A Collaboration Between Unions and Manufacturers*. New York: International Textile and Apparel Association, 1999.

———. "Fashion as a Tool of World War II: A Case Study Supporting the SI (Symbolic Interaction) Theory." *Clothing and Textiles Research Journal* 18, no. 3 (2000): 140–51.

Calasibetta, Charlotte M. *Fairchild's Dictionary of Fashion*. New York: Fairchild, 1988.

Caldwell, Doreen. *And All Was Revealed*. New York: St. Martin's Press, 1981.

Camp, S. H. *Anatomical Studies for the Practitioner*. Jackson, Mich.: S. H. Camp & Company, 1933.

"Candidate Taunted." *Detroit Free Press*, 3 May 1966, 20A.

Carter, Ernestine. *The Changing World of Fashion: 1900 to the Present*. New York: Putnam, 1977.

Chafe, William H. *The American Woman: Her Changing Social, Economic, and Political Roles. Clothing Selection: Fashions, Figures, Fabrics, 1920–1970*. New York: Oxford University Press, 1972.

Chambers, H. G. and V. Moulton. *Chicago*. Philadelphia: J. B. Lippincott Company, 1961.
Coffey, Barbara, and the editors of *Glamour*. *Glamour's Success Book*. New York: Simon and Schuster, 1979.
Cohn, David L. *The Good Old Days: A History of American Morals and Manners, as Seen Through the Sears, Roebuck Catalogs 1905 to the Present*. New York: Simon and Schuster, 1940.
Colvin, Geoffrey. "CEOs: America's Worst Boards." *Fortune 500*, 17 April 2000, 141, no. 8, online.
Committee Report on Dress. Washington, D.C.: National Council of Women of the U.S., 1893.
"Concern over the Cotton Situation." *Corset and Underwear Review*, October 1944, 83.
"Consumer Corset Survey." *Corset and Underwear Review*, November 1942, 53–55.
Cooke, Joseph Brown. *Nurse's Handbook of Obstetrics*. Philadelphia: J. B. Lippincott, 1915.
Cooper, Sir Astley. *Illustrations of the Diseases of the Breast*, Part 1. London: S. McDowall, 1829.
Corbin, Hazel. "Suggestions for the Care of Breasts During Pregnancy." *American Journal of Nursing* 23 (April 1923): 545–47.
The Cost of Living in New York City, 1926. New York: National Industrial Conference Board, 1926.
Cover, John Higson. *Advertising: Its Problems and Methods*. New York: D. Appleton and Company, 1926.
Cowan, Ruth Schwatrz. *More Work for Mother*. New York: Basic Books, 1983.
Cremer-Van der Does, Eline C. *The Agony of Fashion*. Poole, Dorset: Blandford Press, 1980.
Crosby, Caresse [Mary Phelps Jacob]. *The Passionate Years*. London: Alvin Redman Limited, 1955.
Cunnington, C. Willett. *Feminine Attitudes in the Nineteenth Century*. London: Heinemann, 1935.
———. *English Women's Clothing in the Nineteenth Century*. London: Faber & Faber, 1937.
———. *The Perfect Lady*. London: Max Parrish & Company, 1948.
Cunnington, C. Willett, and Phillis Cunnington. *The History of Underclothes*. New York: Dover, 1992.
Current Listing and Topical Index to the Vital and Health Statistics Series, 1962–1977. Hyattsville, Md.: U.S. Department of Health, Education and Welfare, 1978.
Danforth, William C. "The Care of Pregnancy." *Boston Medical and Surgical Journal* 193 (20 August 1925): 331–38.
Davenport, M. *Book of Costume*. New York: Crown, 1948.
Deaver, John B. *The Breast: Its Anomalies, Its Diseases, and Their Treatment*. Philadelphia: P. Blakiston's Son, 1917.
DeBuys, L. R. "Observations upon the Breasts of Mothers of the Newly Born." *Annals of Clinical Medicine* 1 (1923): 204–10.
Denny, Grace. *Fabrics*. 4th ed. Chicago: Lippincott, 1936.
Devereaux, Laverne. *Sew Lovely Lingerie*. Minneapolis: Sew Lovely Publications, 1971.

"Diana Vreeland." *Ms*. August 1975, 31–32.

Dickinson, Robert L. "The Corset: Questions of Pressure and Displacement." *New York Medical Journal* (1887): 507–16.

———. *Textbook of Obstetrics for Practitioners and Students*. Philadelphia: W. B. Saunders, 1895.

———. "Simple and Practical Methods in Dress Reform; with Schedules of Instructions to Patients and Illustrations." *Transactions of the American Gynecological Society* 18 (1893): 411–33.

Dickinson, Robert L., and Lura Beam. *The Single Woman: A Medical Study in Sex Education*. Baltimore: Williams & Wilkins, 1934.

Dobell, Mercy. "Don't Get into a Tizzy or Panic over Scare Headlines." *Corset and Underwear Review*, November 1968, 67.

"Doing Justice to the Brassiere Department." *Corset and Underwear Review*, November 1916, 36.

Donegan, Jane B. *Hydropathic Highway to Health: Women and Water-cure in Antebellum America*. New York: Greenwood Press, 1986.

Donovan, Frances R. *The Saleslady*. Chicago: University of Chicago Press, 1929.

"Dressing on a War Income." *Vogue*, 1 August 1918, 80.

Duffey, Mrs. E. B. *What Women Should Know*. 1873; reprint, New York: Arno Press, 1974.

Ecob, Helen Gilbert. *The Well-Dressed Woman*. New York: Fowler & Wells, 1892.

Edwards, Rebecca. *Angels in the Machinery: Gender in American Party Politics from the Civil War to the Progressive Era*. New York: Oxford University Press, 1997.

Eichler, Lillian. *Book of Etiquette*. Vol. II. Garden City, N.Y.: Nelson Doubleday, 1923.

Elliott, Margaret, and Grace E. Manson. *Earnings of Women in Business and the Professions*. Michigan Business Studies, 3, no. 1 (September 1930): 178–79.

Ellison, Steven. "Robustier." *People* (12 June 2000): 126.

Emmet, Boris, and John E. Jeleck. *Catalogues and Counters: A History of Sears, Roebuck and Company*. Chicago: University of Chicago Press, 1950.

Enloe, C. *Does Khaki Become You? The Militarization of Women's Lives*. Boston: South End, 1983.

Evans, Sara M. *Born for Liberty: A History of Women in America*. New York: Free Press, 1989.

Evans, Wilmot H. *Diseases of the Breast*. London: University of London Press, 1895.

Ewing, Elizabeth. *Dress and Undress: A History of Women's Underwear*. New York, Drama Book Specialists, 1978.

———. *Underwear: A History*. New York: Theater Arts Books, 1972.

"The Fall Outlook for Brassieres." *Corset and Underwear Review*, July 1915, 50–51.

Fields, Jill. "'Fighting the Corsetless Evil': Shaping Corsets and Culture, 1900–1930." *Journal of Social History* 33 (1999): 355–84.

Finn, Holly. "Upholders of Firm Standards." *Financial Times*. London (2000): 13.

Fisher, David E., and Marshall Jon Fisher. *Tube: The Innvention of Television*. Washington, D.C.: Counterpoint, 1996.

Fletcher, M. A. *Illustrated Catalogue of Ladies' and Children's' Underwear, Constructed on Dress Reform and Hygienic Principles*. N.p., c. 1900.

Flower, B. O. "The Next Step Forward; or Thoughts on the Movement for Rational Dress." *The Arena* 6 (1892): 635–44.
Flynt, Olivia P. *Manual of Hygienic Modes of Underdressing for Women and Children*. Boston: C. M. A. Twitchell, 1882.
Fogarty, Anne. *Wife-Dressing*. New York: Julian Messner, 1959.
Fourt, Lyman. E. *Clothing: Comfort and Fashion*. New York: M. Dekker, 1970.
Friedel, R. *Zipper: An Exploration in Novelty*. New York: W. W. Norton, 1994.
"From Us to You." *Corset and Underwear Review*, March 1932, 59.
Galbraith, Anna. *Personal Hygiene and Physical Training for Women*. Philadelphia: W. B. Saunders, 1911.
Galloway, Mera. "I Am a WAAC." *Mademoiselle*, September 1942, 137, 199–201.
Gamber, Wendy. *The Female Economy: The Millinery and Dressmaking Trades, 1860–1930*. Urbana: University of Illinois Press, 1997.
Gardiner, Ann. "How They Differ from Us." *Corset and Underwear Review*, April 1960, 60.
Gau, Colleen R. "Historic Medical Perspectives of Corseting and Two Physiologic Studies with Reenactors." Ph.D. diss., Iowa State University, 1998.
Gernsheim, Alison. *Victorian and Edwardian Fashions*. New York: Dover, 1981.
Gevitz, Norman. *Other Healers: Unorthodox Medicine in America*. Baltimore: Johns Hopkins University Press, 1988.
Goldman, Jean G. (Mathes). *Profitable Corset and Brassiere Merchandising; A Guide for Retailers, Manufacturers and Fitters*. New York: Fairchild, 1963.
Gorham, D. *The Victorian and Feminine Ideal*. London: Croom Helm, 1972.
Gousse, Susanne, and Andre Gousse. *Costume in New France from 1740 to 1760: A Visual Dictionary*. Chambly, France: La Fleur de Lyse, 1997.
Gray, Cleo. "Clothing in Relation to Women's Health." Thesis, University of Wisconsin, 1926.
Gunn, S. W. "Mastectomy." *World Journal of Surgery* 22, no. 5 (1998): 425–26.
Halberstam, David. *The Fifties*. New York: Villard Books, 1993.
Hall, Carrie A. *From Hoopskirts to Nudity: A Review of the Follies and Foibles of Fashion, 1866–1936*. Caldwell, Idaho: Caxton Printers, 1938.
Halsted, W. S. "The Results of Operations for Cure of the Breast Performed at the Johns Hopkins Hospital." *Annals of Surgery* 20 (1894): 497.
Handley, Susannah. *Nylon: The Story of a Fashion Revolution*. Baltimore: Johns Hopkins University Press, 1999.
Harris, Leon. *Merchant Princes: An Intimate History of Jewish Families Who Built Great Department Stores*. New York: Kodansha International, 1994.
Harris, Mark Jonathan, Franklin D. Mitchell, and Steven J. Schecter. *The Home Front: Americans During World War II*. New York: Putnam's Sons, 1984.
Heide, Robert, and John Gilman. *Home Front America: Popular Culture of the WWII Era*. San Francisco: Chronicle Books, 1995.
Helvenston, Sally. "From Feathers to Fashions: How the Turkey Revolutionized Women's Clothing." *Michigan History Magazine*. September-October 1996, 28–35.
"Here and There in the Industry: A New and Added Season." *Corset and Underwear Review*, November 1929, 71.

Hoerle, Helen C., and Florence B. Saltzberg. *The Girl and The Job*. New York: Henry Holt and Company, 1919.

Hoge, Cecil C., Sr. *The First Hundred Years are the Toughest*. Berkeley, Calif.: Ten Speed Press, 1988.

Hollander, Anne. *Sex and Suits: The Evolution of Modern Dress*. New York: Alfred A. Knopf, 1994.

Holm, Jenne M. "Women in the Armed Forces." *Encyclopedia of American Military History*. Vol. 3 (New York: Scribner, 1998).

"Hop on the Pre-teen Gravy Train." *Corset and Underwear Review*, May 1961, 48.

"How Important Are Color and Design Coordination to Underfashions?" *Corset and Underwear Review*, February 1963, 33.

"The Hows and Whys of Exporting." *Corset and Underwear Review*, April 1964, 36–39.

"How to Get Dressed and Still Be Yourself." *Ms.*, April 1979, 49–51, 75–76.

Huenckens, E. J. "Breast Feeding." *American Journal of Nursing* 24(June 1924): 751–57.

Hungerford, Mrs. M. E. "What It Costs to Dress a Daughter." *Harper's Bazar*, 11 March 1893, 191.

Illustrating the Breast Before, During and After Lactation. Providence, R.I.: Davol Rubber Company, 1938.

"Irwin Roseman: Innovator at Exquisite Form." *Corset and Underwear Review*, May 1964, 34.

Jackson, Kenneth T., ed. *The Encyclopedia of New York*. New Haven: Yale University Press, 1995.

Janes, M. *The Oxford French Minidictionary*. New York: Oxford University Press, 1986.

Johns, Maxine. "Women's Functional Swimwear, 1860–1920." Ph.D. diss., Iowa State University, 1997.

Joseph, Marjory L. *Essentials of Textiles*. 4th ed. New York: Holt, Rinehart and Winston, 1998.

Kadolph, Sara J., and Anna Langford. *Textiles* 8th ed. Upper Saddle River, N.J.: Merrill, 1998.

Kennedy, David M. *Freedom from Fear: The American People in Depression and War*. New York: Oxford University Press, 1999.

Kennett, Lee. *For the Duration . . . : The United States Goes to War, Pearl Harbor-1942*. New York: Charles Scribner's Sons, 1985.

Kidwell, Claudia B., and Margaret C. Christman. *Suiting Everyone: The Democratization of Clothing in America*. Washington, D.C.: Smithsonian Institution Press, 1974.

King, James. "Woman and Her Clothes." *Dress*, March-April 1889, 190–92.

King, E. M. "The Human Dress." *The Arena* 6 (1892): 627–30.

Kinsey, Alfred C. *Sexual Behavior in the Human Female*. Reprint. Bloomington: Indiana University Press, 1998.

Kinsey, Alfred C., Wardell B. Pomeroy, and Clyde E. Martin. *Sexual Behavior in the Human Male*. Philadelphia: W. B. Saunders, 1948.

Kitchens, Matilda. *When Underwear Counted; Being the Evolution of Underclothes*. Talladega, Ala.: Brannon Printing Co., 1931.

Kleiman, Irving. "Computer Key to Inventory Control." *Corset and Underwear Review*, February 1968, 46–47, 88, 92, 94.

Köhler, Karl. *A History of Costume*. London: G. G. Harrup, 1928.

Kron, Joan. "Vacuum Stacked." *Allure*, July 1999, 104–5.
Laboissonniere, Wade. *Blueprints of Fashion*. Atglen, Pa.: Schiffer, 1997.
"Ladies in the Winter of 1929 and Ladies in the Winter of 1930." *Vogue*, 4 January, 1930, 50–52.
Lane-Claypon, Janet E. *Hygiene of Women and Children*. London: Henry Frowde & Hodder & Stoughton, 1921.
Langner, L. *The Importance of Wearing Clothes*. Toronto: S.J. Reginald Saunders, 1959.
Larkin, Charles R. "Drying Up the Lactating Breasts." *American Journal of Obstetrics* (20 April 1927): 527.
La Roe, Else K. *The Breast Beautiful*. New York: House of Field, 1940.
———. *Care of the Breast*. New York: Froben Press, 1947.
Larrimore, Karen Brown. "The Changing Line of the Corset, 1820–1915." Ph.D. diss., University of Wisconsin, 1984.
Laubner, Ellie. *Collectible Fashions of the Turbulent 30s*. Atglen, Pa.: Schiffer, 2000.
Levitt, Sarah. "From Mrs. Bloomer to the Bloomer: The Social Significance of the Nineteenth Century English Dress Reform Movement." *Textile History* 24, no. 1 (1993): 27–37.
Leibovich, Lori. "A Good Bra Is Hard to Find." *www.salon.com*, July 1997.
Lemisch, Jesse and Naomi Weisstein. "Bra-Burning: True and Definitive History." www.lists.village.virginia.edu, 1998.
Lent, Anna. "Braces for the Stout Woman." *Ladies' Home Journal*, 24 (February 1907): 71.
Leopold, A. Kyle, and A. M. Cloutier. *Short Chic*. New York: Rawson, Wade, 1981.
Lewis, Charles H. "An Outline of Prenatal Care." *Calfornia and Western Medicine*, 30 (February 1929): 108–11.
Litoff, Judy Barrett, and D. C. Smith. *American Women in a World at War: Contemporary Accounts from World War II*. Wilmington, Del.: Scholarly Resources, 1997.
Littlejohn, Robert M. "History of Nurses and WAC Uniforms in the European Theater, 1943–1945." *Passing in Review*. R. W. Burns, ed., Philadelphia: United States Quartermaster General (1955): 32.
Lobenstein, Ralph W. "The Development of Prenatal Care in the Borough of Manhattan, New York City." *American Journal of Obstetrics* 76 (September 1917): 381–92.
"A Look at the Negro Market." *Corset and Underwear Review*, April 1966, 86, 88.
Mahoney, Tom and Leonard Sloane. *The Great Merchants: America's Foremost Retail Institutions and the People Who Made Them Great*. New York: Harper & Row, 1966.
Mansfield, Carl M. *Early Breast Cancer: Its History and Results of Treatment*. Basel: S. Karger, 1976.
Marchant, June. *Rehabilitation of Mastectomy Patients: A Handbook*. London: Heinemann Medical Publishers, 1978.
Martensson, K. *Kwik Sew Method*. Golden Valley, Minn.: Sew-Knit-N-Stretch, 1970.
Matlack, Margaret. "Budgeting the Successful Business Woman's Clothes." *Ladies' Home Journal* (April 1926): 93, 97–98, 103.
Mayer, Joseph. *The Revolution in Merchandise*. New York: Greenberg, 1939.
McGinnis, Tara. "She Saves Who Sews for Victory: Home Sewing on the American Home Front." *Costume: Journal of the British Costume Society* 26 (1992): 60–70.
"Me? In That?" *Life* (1964): 55–57.

Meigs, Grace L. "Maternal Mortality from Childbirth in the United States and Its Relation to Prenatal Care." *American Journal of Obstetrics* 76 (September 1917): 392–401.

Metallious, Grace. *Peyton Place*. New York: Julian Messner, 1956.

Meyer, C. *Everything About Sewing Swimwear from Vogue Patterns*. New York: Vogue Patterns, 1972.

"Mike Stein, Bali's New Man for the '70s." *Corset and Underwear Review*, November 1969, 36.

Miller, Annie Jenness. "Artistic and Sensible Dress for Streetwear." *The Arena* 6 (1892): 495–98.

Miller, Elizabeth Smith. "Reflections on Woman's Dress, and the Record of Personal Experience." *The Arena* 6 (1892): 491–93.

Mitchell, C., and T. Burdick *The Extra Edge: Success Strategies for Women*. Washington, D.C.: Acropolis Books, 1983.

Mobil Travel Guide: Southwest and South Central. New York: Fodor's Travel Publications, 1995.

Morantz-Sanchez, Regina Markell. *Sympathy and Science: Women Physicians in American Medicine*. New York: Oxford University Press, 1985.

Murray, J. H., ed. *Rational Dress For Women: Strong-Minded Women and Other Lost Voices from the Nineteenth Century*. New York: Pantheon Books, 1982.

"Mrs. Gabrielle Poix Yerkes." *Corset and Underwear Review*, September 1941, 57.

"New Goods and Specialties." *The Rubber World*, September 1943, 305.

Newton, S. M. *Health, Art, and Reason: Dress Reformers of the Nineteenth Century*. London: John Murray, 1974.

Niemoeller, Adolph F. *Complete Guide to Bust Culture*. New York: Harvest House, 1939.

Norman, E. M. *Nurses in War: A Study of Female Military Nurses Who Served in Vietnam During the War Years, 1965–1973*. New York: New York University Press, 1986.

Noun, Louise. "Amelia Bloomer, Biography: Part 1, The Lily of Seneca Falls." *Annals of Iowa* 47 (Winter 1985): 575–617.

"Occupational Distribution of Women 1977 and 1970." *Ms.*, February 1979, 98.

Oerke, Bess V., and Elizabeth Jerner, *Dress: A Clothing Textbook*. Peoria, Ill.: Chas. A. Bennett Company, 1960.

"Ohio Breast Cancer Survey, 1960–1969." *American Journal of Surgery* 122 (December 1971): 765–69.

Ohrbach, Nathan M. *Getting Ahead in Retailing*. New York: McGraw-Hill, 1935.

Ormond, L. "Female Costume in the Aesthetic Movement of the 1870s and 1880s." *Costume: Journal of the British Costume Society* 2 (1968): 33–38.

"Paris Will Be Paris, Weather or Not." *Vogue*, 1 May 1914, 84.

Parker, William. *Cancer: A Study of 397 Cases of Breast Cancer*. London: n.p., 1885.

Parry, A., Ed. *What Women Can Do To Win the War*. Chicago: Consolidated Book Publishers, 1942.

Payne, Blanche, Geitel Winakor, and Jane Farrell-Beck. *The History of Costume: from Ancient Mesopotamia through the Twentieth Century*. 2nd ed. New York: Harper Collins, 1992.

Pearce, Arthur W. *The Future Out of the Past: An Illustrated History of the Warner Brothers Company on Its 90th Anniversary*. Bridgeport, Conn.: Warner Brothers Company, 1964.

Peck, Helen Chesley. "The Nurses' Part in a Breast Feeding Campaign." *Public Health Nurse* 16(June 1924): 293–98.
Pepin, Harriet. *Modern Pattern Design: The Complete Guide to the Creation of Patterns as a Means of Designing Smart Wearing Apparel*. New York: Funk & Wagnalls, 1942.
"A Perfect Bra: The Best Bra Guide Ever." *Good Housekeeping*, August 2000, 43–45, 48.
Perret, Geoffrey. *America in the Twenties: A History*. New York: Simon and Schuster, 1982.
———. *Eisenhower*. New York: Random House, 1999.
Peiss, Kathy. *Cheap Amusements: Working Women and Leisure in Turn-of-the-Century New York*. Philadelphia: Temple University Press, 1986.
Pinckney, Gerrie and Marge Swenson. *New Image for Women*. 2nd ed. Reston, Va.: Reston Publishing Company, 1984.
"Plan Now for Post-War." *Corset and Underwear Review*, November 1942, 69–70.
"Planning Guide for '67." *Corset and Underwear Review*, November 1966, 30.
"Planning Guide '69." *Corset and Underwear Review*, November 1968, 97.
"Pocket-Eye Metalless Tape." *Corset and Underwear Review*, March 1943, 80.
Pofeldt, E. "Outlaw Fashion." *WWD*, 3 (6 May 1996): 4.
Pomeroy, Frances W. (AKA Viscountess Harberton). "How Is It We Get On No Faster?" *The Arena* 6 (1892): 621–24.
Population 1920. Washington, D.C.: Department of Commerce, 1923.
Putziger, Stephen S. "Foreign Licensing Is Big Business." *Corset and Underwear Review*, April 1960, 48–49.
Quick, Rebecca. "Mrs. Wachner's Effort to Build a Better Bra Has 'Secret' Motives." *Wall Street Journal*, 4 October 2000, A1, A19.
"Recent Deaths, Mrs. Olivia P. Flynt" *Boston Evening Transcript*, 2 February 1897.
Renbourn, Edward T. *Materials and Clothing in Health and Disease: Medical and Psychological Aspects*. London: H. K. Lewis, 1972.
"Researchlights." *Corset and Underwear Review*, November 1958, 56–67.
Reston, Scott. "Post War America." *Mademoiselle* (1947): 60.
"Retail Management Section." *Corset and Underwear Review*, July 1968, 42–44.
"Retrospect and Prospect." *Corset and Underwear Review*, December 1943, 63.
Richards, Lynne. "The Rise and Fall of It All: The Hemlines and Hiplines of the 1920s." *Clothing and Textiles Research Journal* 2 (1983–84): 42–48.
Richardson, Frank H. "The Nursing Mother: A Study in Lactation." *New York State Journal of Medicine* 22 (April 1922): 161–65.
Rickertson, J. *Means of Preserving Health*. New York, 1806.
Risch, E. *A Wardrobe for the Women of the Army*. Washington, D.C.: Office of the Quartermaster General, Historical Section, 1945.
Robb, Isabel Hampton. *Educational Standards for Nurses*. 1907; reprint, Cleveland: Garland, 1984.
Rosenfeld, Isidor. *The Practical Designer for Women's and Misses Underwear*. New York: Leading Pattern Company, 1918.
Ross, N. W. *The WAVES: The Story of the Girls in Blue*. New York: Holt, 1944.
Rothacher, Nanette. *The Undies Book*. New York: Scribner, 1976.
Rothenberg, Robert E. *The Complete Book of Breast Care*. New York: Crown Publishers, 1975.

Rubenstein, Sol. "Bras Are More Important than Shoes." *Corset and Underwear Review*, April 1960, 46–47.

Russell, Frances E. "Woman's Dress." *The Arena* 3 (1891): 353–60.

———. "Lines of Beauty." *The Arena* 6 (1892): 499–503.

Russell, Jane. *Jane Russell: An Autobiography, My Path, My Detours*. New York; Jove Books, 1986.

Ryan, Mildred Graves, and V. Phillips. *Clothes for You*. New York: D. Appleton-Century-Crofts, 1947, 1954.

"Sahlin Awarded Patent." *Corset and Underwear Review*, September 1916, 37.

Saint Laurent, Yves, et al. *Yves Saint Laurent*. New York: Metropolitan Museum of Art, 1983.

Saywell, S. *Women in War*. New York: Viking, 1985.

Schiaparelli, Elsa. "Needles and Guns." *Vogue*, 1 September 1940, 57, 104–5.

Seabold, Paul. "The Well-Fitted Brassiere and Its Use." *Pennsylvania Medical Journal* 39 (October 1935): 16–19.

Seely, C. P. *American Women and the U.S. Armed Forces: A Guide to the Records of Military Agencies in the National Archives Relating to American Women*. Washington, D.C.: National Archives and Records Administration, 1992.

"Selling to the Maternity Customer." *Corset and Underwear Review*, March 1966, 86–87.

Sharp, M., and M. Smith. *Superior Surgical Elastic Stockings, Abdominal Supporters, etc.* Chicago: Sharp and Smith, 1891.

Shields, Arthur M. *Clinical Treatise on Diseases of the Breast*. London: Putnam, 1898.

Shoemaker, Sr. Mary Theophane. *History of Nurse Midwifery in the United States*. 1947; reprint, Washington, D.C.: Garland, 1984.

"Simplification of Lines to Conserve Labor and Materials." *Corset and Underwear Review*, March 1943, 54.

Sklar, Kathryn Kish. *All Hail to Pure Cold Water: Women and Health in America*. Madison: University of Wisconsin Press, 1976.

Smith, Fred B. "The Care of the Lactating Breasts." *American Journal of Obstetrics and Gynecology* 18 (November 1929): 784–89.

Solderbergh, P. *Women Marines: The World War II Era*. Westport, Conn.: Praeger, 1992.

Sparkes, M. W. "Some Factors in the Establishment and Continuation of Lactation." *Nursing Times* 24 (31 March 1928): 363.

Steele, F. M., and E. L. S. Adams. *Beauty of Form and Grace of Vesture*. New York; Dodd, Mead, 1892.

Steele, F. M. "Artistic Dress." *The Arena* 6 (1892): 503–7.

Steele, Valerie Fahnestock. *Fashion and Eroticism: Ideals of Feminine Beauty from the Victorian Era to the Jazz Age*. New York: Oxford University Press, 1985.

Stehlin, John S., Richard A. Evans, et al. "Treatment of Carcinoma of the Breast." *Surgery, Gynecology and Obstetrics* 149 (December 1979): 911, 913–14.

Stern, Jane, and Micheal Stern. *Sixties People*. New York: Alfred A. Knopf, 1990.

Stewart, Isabel M. *Education of Nurses*. New York: Saunders, 1943.

St. Germain, Amos. "The Flowering of Mass Society: An Overview of the 1920s." In *Dancing Fools and Weary Blues: The Great Escape of the Twenties*, ed. Lawrence R. Broer and John D. Walther. Bowling Green, Ohio: Bowling Green State University Popular Press, 1990.

"A Sticky Situation with a Strapless Bra." *Consumer Reports*, August 1967, 411–12.

Stokes, Terry. *Intimate Apparel*. Brooklyn, N.Y.: Release Press, 1980.

"Supply Situation More Acute." *Corset and Underwear Review*, January 1945, 148.

Taeuber, Cynthia. *Statistical Handbook on Women in America*. Phoenix, Ariz.: Oryx Press: 1991.

Talbot, Constance. *The Complete Book of Sewing: Dressmaking and Sewing for the Home Made Easy*. New York: Graystone Talbot, 1943.

Taylor, Lou. "The Work and Function of the Paris Couture Industry During the German Occupation of 1940–44." *Dress: Journal of the Costume Society of America* 22 (1995): 34–44.

Tebbel, John. *The Marshall Fields: A Study in Wealth*. New York: E. P. Dutton, 1947.

"Ten Ways to Improve Your Maternity Bra and Girdle Sales." *Corset and Underwear Review*, October 1967, 72.

Textile World, Comp Trademarks, Labels, Prints to the Textile Industry. 2nd ed. New York: Bragdon, Lord and Nagle, 1921.

Textile World Journal, A Directory of Textile Brands and Trademarks. New York: Bragdon, Lord and Nagle, 1918.

Thesander, Marianne. *The Feminine Ideal*. London: Reaktion Books, 1997.

"To Simplify and Standardize Lines." *Corset and Underwear Review*, October 1941, 80.

Treves, Frederick. *Dress of the Period and Its Relation to Health*. London: Hillman & Son, 1882.

"22 Problems . . . 22 Answers." *Vogue*. June 1948, 145–46.

"The Undercover Story." *Catalog of Museum Exhibition*. Kyoto, Japan: Kyoto Institute of Fashion, 1972.

"Uniforms and You." *Vogue*, 15 March 1942, 41.

U.S. Bureau of the Census. *Eleventh Census of the United States*. Washington, D.C., 1890.

———. *Fifteenth Census of the United States: Manufacturers 1929*. Vol. 2. *Reports to Industries*. Washington, D.C.: 1933.

———. *Fourteenth Census of the United States*. Washington, D.C., 1920.

———. *Historical Statistics of the United States, Colonial Times to 1970*. Washington, D.C.: Bureau of Commerce, U.S. Department of the Census, 1976.

U.S. Department of Health, Education and Welfare. *Current Listing and Topical Index to the Vital and Health Statistics Series, 1962–1977*. Hyattsville, Md.: Department of Health Education and Welfare, 1978.

U.S. National Recovery Administration. *Code of Fair Competition for the Corset and Brassiere Industry*. Washington, D.C., 1933.

U.S. Office of Price Administration. *Make and Mend for Victory*. Washington, D.C., 1942.

Van Blarcom, Carolyn Conant. *Getting Ready to Be a Mother*. New York: Macmillan, 1929.

———. *Obstetrical Nursing*. New York: Macmillan, 1923.

Velpeau, Alfred A. *A Treatise on the Diseases of the Breast*. London: Sydenham Society, 1856.

Verbrugge, M. H. *Able-Bodied Womanhood: Personal and Social Change in Nineteenth Century Boston*. Oxford: Oxford University Press, 1988.

Vicinus, M., Ed. *Suffer and Be Still: Women in the Victorian Age*. Bloomington: University of Indiana Press, 1973.

"Vital Changes in Corsetry." *Corset and Underwear Review*, September 1943, 73.
"Vogue—and Vague." *Newsweek*, 22 March 1965, 90.
"WACS Prove a Good Market." *Corset and Underwear Review*, August 1943, 161.
Walton, Frank. *The Thread of Victory*. New York: Fairchild, 1945.
Warman, Edward. *Health Influenced by Underwear*. New York: American Sports Publishing, 1910.
Warner, Deborah Jean. "Fashion, Emancipation, Reform, and the Rational Undergarment." *Dress: Journal of the Costume Society of America* 4 (1978): 24–29.
"Washington Wants Instituational Advertising Copy." *Corset and Underwear Review*, July 1943, 56.
Watson, Lillian Eichler. *Book of Etiquette*. Vol. 2. Garden City, N.Y.: Nelson Doubleday, 1923.
Wedlan, Candace A. "The Pillar of Panties." *Los Angeles Times*, 11 August 2000, E1, E4.
Weeks-Shaw, Clara S. *Textbook of Nursing for the Use of Training Schools, Families, and Private Students*. 1885; reprint, New York: Garland, 1984.
Weiner, Leslie. *The Lovable Story*. New York: Lovable Brassiere Company, 1953.
Weiss, E. B. *How to Sell to and Through Department Stores*. New York: McGraw-Hill, 1936.
"What Fashion Demands of the Brassiere." *Women's and Infants' Furnisher*, August 1917, 33–34.
White, Nicola. *Reconstructing Italian Fashion: America and the Development of the Italian Fashion Industry*. New York: Berg, 2000.
Wilberforce-Smith, William. "On the Alleged Differences Between Male and Female Respiratory Movements." *British Medical Journal* (11 October 1890): 843–44.
Wilson, Violet I. *Sewing Without Tears: A Complete and Fully Illustrated Handbook on Sewing for Both the Amateur and Professional Dressmaker*. New York: Charles Scribner's Sons, 1972.
Winterburn, Florence H. *Principles of Correct Dress*. New York: Harper Brothers, 1914.
Woman's Institute of Domestic Arts and Sciences. *Harmony in Dress*. Scranton, Pa., 1926.
"Women War Workers." *Corset and Underwear Review*, November 1943, 86.
"Women's Brassieres." *Consumer Bulletin*, March 1965, 24–27.
Woodburne, R. T. *Essentials of Human Anatomy*. New York: Oxford University Press, 1983.
Woolson, Anna G., and C. Hastings, eds. *Five Essays on Women's Health: Dress Reform*. 1874, reprint, Arno Press, 1984.
"WPB Announces Corset Restrictions." *Corset and Underwear Review*, May 1942, 47.
Yalom, Marilyn. *A History of the Breast*. New York: Alfred A. Knopf, 1997.
Yarwood, Doreen. *Encyclopedia of World Costume*. London: B. T. Batsford, 1978.
"Yes Virginia, Women Will Continue to Wear Bras." *Corset and Underwear Review*, October 1969, 27.
"The Young Image." *Corset and Underwear Review*, July 1965, 57.
"Your Planning Guide for '62." *Corset and Underwear Review*, October 1960, 57.
"Your Planning Guide for '65." *Corset and Underwear Review*, October 1964, 31–34.

Index

Acknowledgments

Over the six years it took to research and write this book, we have received generous help of other scholars, library professionals, and collectors. Some of them have become friends; others are known to us only as effective and gracious representatives of their institutions. We owe an enormous debt of appreciation to the staffs of

the Chicago Public Library, Herstory Project
the Cleveland Public Library, Special Collections and Nottingham Branch
the College of Physicians of Philadelphia
the Edmonton, Alberta Public Library
the Hennepin County, MN Public Library
the John W. Hartman Center for Sales, Advertising, and Marketing History, Special Collections Library, Duke University
La Leche League
the Library of Congress
the Military History Library, Carlisle Barracks, PA
the Milwaukee Public Library
the Minneapolis Public Library, Nicollet Mall
the Minnesota Historical Society Library, St. Paul
the National Archives
the National Institutes of Medicine
the New Jersey Historical Society Library
the New York City Public Library and Business Library
the New York Surgical Association Library
Platt Hall, Cunnington Costume Collection, at Manchester, England
the Rochester MN Public Library
the University of Iowa, Medical Library, Special Collections
the University of Minnesota, McGrath Library

the University of Rhode Island, Special Collections
the University of Wisconsin Health Sciences and Main Libraries

A special word of thanks goes to these stalwart helpers:

Iowa State University Library: Diana Shonrock, Rita Marinko, Jeff Kushkowski, Susan Congdon, Wayne Pedersen, Kristi Schaaf, Mary Jane Thune, Kathy Thorson, Becky Jordan, Bob Sickles, and Tanya Zanish-Belcher.

Center for the Study of the History of Nursing, University of Pennsylvania: Karen Buhler-Wilkerson, Joan Lynaugh, Neville Strumpf, Margo Szabunia, and Betsy Weiss. Nursing contacts: Rita Beatty, Helen Dopsovic, Nadine Landis, Kay Persek, Stephanie Stachniewicz, and Edna LaPorte Strumpf.

Cleveland Public Library: Francis Collins, Jeffry Martin, Ann Olszewski, Chris Albano, and Margaret Baughman

Mayo Medical Library, Rochester, Minnesota: Andy Lucas, Hilary Lane.

National Museum of American History, Smithsonian Institution: Costume Department: Shelley Foote, Priscilla Wood, and Claudia Brush Kidwell. Military History Section: Margaret Vining and Martha Putnam. Archives: Mimi Mimick

Philadelphia Museum of Art: Costume Curator, Kristina Haugland

College of Physicians of Philadelphia: Charles Greifenstein

Metropolitan Museum of Art, Costume Institute: Alexandra Kowalski

Fashion Institute of Technology: Bret Fowler and Valerie Steele

Hartman Center, Duke University: Ellen Gartrell

University of Alberta, Costume Collection: Shawna Lemiski

Goldstein Gallery, University of Minnesota: Nancy Cyr, Lindsey Shunt, Marilyn DeLong, and Becky Yust

Minnesota Historical Society: Adam Scher and Linda McShannock

New Jersey Historical Society: Grace-Ellen McCrann

University of Rhode Island: Joy Emery, Margaret and Alfred Ordonez, Linda Welters, Cressie Murphy-David, David Maslyn, and Sarina R. Wyant

Graduate students collected advertisements, recorded patent data, sent us tidbits of information, and even created replicas of early patented breast supporters. We wish to thank Mary Alice Casto, Carol Hall, Susan Herrold, Maxine (Micki) Johns, Eundeok Kim, Eunjeong Lee, Cassandra Moon, Jennifer Paff Ogle, Laura Poresky, and Alyson Rhodes-Murphy.

We benefited from the research expertise and encouragement of Maureen Alden, Carlos Benevides, Anne Bissonnette, Amy Sue Bix, Lois Brooks, Sandra Stansbery Buckland, Allison Engel, Norma Gau, Mela Hoyt-Heydon,

Kathy Johnson, Lisa Layman, Mary Lofton, Alan I. Marcus, Judy McGaw, Michael McKenna, Elizabeth Mooman Kramer O'Connell, Alexandra Palmer, Heather Prescott, Sally Queen, Cynthia Regnier, Nancy Rexford, Edith Sandford, and Geitel Winakor.

We gained many insights from Priscilla Wood's private library.

Company owners, family, and staff answered our questions at various stages in the development of the manuscript: Catherine Brawer, Al Corrado, John Cronce, Lily DeBevoise, Barbara Ettenger, Tom Garson, Doreen Brennan Langa, Steve Masket, Ginger Noel, and Jeff Pirtle.

For handling endless faxes and giving sympathetic ears we thank Shirley Bauge and LouAnn Doyle.

For hospitality, Phyllis and Vin Tortora and Priscilla Wood cannot be surpassed.

Supplementary financial support for travel came from John W. Hartman Center, Duke University; Center for the Study of the History of Nursing, University of Pennsylvania; College of Family and Consumer Sciences and Council for Scholarship in the Humanities, Iowa State University. A one-semester professional development assignment (sabbatical) from Iowa State University was also most beneficial.

Thanks to Barbie Zelizer for suggesting a perfect book title.

Finally, we extend heartfelt appreciation to our editors: Patricia Smith, who guided us in proposing this project and shaping the manuscript, and Robert Lockhart, Noreen O'Connor, and Cory Stephenson, who helped bring it to completion.